Rob Davies is an investigative ... 'he *Guardian*'s business desk. H' the gambling industry ar ' a British Journalism A book. @ByRobDavies

Further praise for *Jackpot*:

'The UK's addiction to gambli..g is a complex tale, but Rob Davies tells it with such clarity and through the personal experiences of those affected most. A shocking and important book.' Baroness Ruth Davidson

'Powerful and factually precise, this book will be with us forever to remind us all of why a public health approach is needed when gambling is concerned.' Professor Henrietta Bowden-Jones Obe

'Davies's eye-opening catalogue of facts and figures is humanised by interviews with gambling addicts and their loved ones.' *Telegraph*

'Methodical, sensitive and occasionally harrowing polemic about the gambling industry . . . a compelling case. The book has echoes of Patrick Radden Keefe's award-winning *Empire of Pain*.' *Sunday Times*

'A deeply researched and conscientious presentation of the ruinous impact of Britain's gambling culture on the lives of an unquantifiable number . . . a bleak and fascinating story.' *Irish Times*

'A serious attempt to grapple with the extent of Britain's problem.' *Spectator*

'A wide-ranging, deeply researched exposé of the gambling industry.' *Times Literary Supplement*

'Writing persuasively, and with a forensic eye for detail, Davies never forgets the human toll of gambling addiction and intersperses the cold, hard statistics with intensely personal stories of individuals who have had their lives, relationships and bank accounts wiped out by betting.' *Buzz Magazine*

# ROB DAVIES

# JACKP♦T

## How Gambling
## Conquered Britain

First published by Guardian Faber in 2022
Guardian Faber is an imprint of Faber & Faber Ltd
Bloomsbury House, 74–77 Great Russell Street
London WC1B 3DA

Guardian is a registered trademark of
Guardian News & Media Ltd
Kings Place, 90 York Way,
London N1 9GU

This paperback edition published in 2023

Typeset by Typo•glyphix, Burton-on-Trent, DE14 3HE
Printed and bound by CPI Group (UK) Ltd, Croydon, CR0 4YY

The right of Rob Davies to be identified as author of this work
has been asserted in accordance with Section 77 of the Copyright,
Designs and Patents Act 1988

A CIP record for this book
is available from the British Library

ISBN 978–1–7833–5225–8

Printed and bound in the UK on FSC paper in line with our continuing
commitment to ethical business practices, sustainability and the environment.
**For further information see faber.co.uk/environmental-policy**

2 4 6 8 10 9 7 5 3 1

*For Jack and for Sacha*

# CONTENTS

# INTRODUCTION

Amid the grandeur of the Palace of Westminster, Lord Browne of Belmont rose to his feet and spoke the names of the dead.

It was as if the former schoolteacher was taking a macabre roll call as he reeled off, for the benefit of his colleagues in the British parliament's upper chamber, a list of young people who had taken their own lives after suffering from a gambling addiction. Browne lamented the failure of regulators, politicians and gambling companies to keep them safe.

'We should be in no doubt about the devastating effects online gambling can have on people's lives,' the peer of the realm warned.[1]

He did not know it yet, but Lord Browne could have added one more name to his tragic list.

That late-November day in 2017 was unusually warm for the season. But a day earlier, more than five thousand miles away in the more tropical climate of Hanoi, Vietnam, twenty-four-year-old Jack Ritchie had become the latest victim of an illness that few British people knew much, if anything, about, and for which there was next to no help available.

Jack was not the casualty of some freak accident, some caprice of fate that simply could not be helped. Rather, he and those who suffered in the same way were inevitable collateral damage, the wreckage left behind by a beast that had slipped its leash and run out of control. Their deaths were part and parcel of immeasurable change in the British gambling industry, a sector transformed by technological progress, lax regulation and corporate greed.

In the space of a few short years, a business rooted in the time-honoured traditions of the turf-scented racetrack and the cinematic glitz of the casino table had metamorphosed into something much larger and more pervasive. It had become a relentless automaton programmed to separate punters from their money by any means, at any cost.

Gambling companies inveigled their way into our lives, addressing us in both our living rooms and our public spaces, becoming household names in the process. They did so despite the fact that many of their products present unusually pernicious dangers, most of which have, until very recently, flown under the radar of public consciousness.

As a society, it is in our interests to think about how we got here, who benefited and suffered from these changes, and where we might go next. We must give voice to the people who have been hurt, or even lost, along the way.

That's why I want to start with Jack.

## JACK'S STORY

Photographs of Jack Ritchie depict a handsome, fresh-faced young man whose smile showed up as much in his eyes as in his broad grin. Pictures, of course, can mask the truth. But in the context of a life apparently filled with promise, Jack's last hours seem to make little sense.

On the day he died, Jack had been gambling online. He'd found himself overwhelmed once more by a persistent addiction that had dogged him, on and off, since before he was of age to gamble legally. 'I'm past the point of controlling myself and I'm not coming back from this one,' he wrote in a suicide note emailed to his parents back home in Sheffield, Yorkshire. Within hours Jack was gone, dead as a result of injuries sustained falling from a ninth-floor restaurant called 6 Degrees, a trendy Hanoi spot where he had enjoyed seemingly carefree nights out with the friends he had made so far from home.

Like many university-educated young Britons, Jack had been teaching English abroad while figuring out what he wanted to do next. For him, it was a chance to get on with a journey into adulthood that had, so far, been disrupted by a recurring problem.

Jack had started gambling aged seventeen. During lunch breaks at school, Jack and a group of friends would visit a bookmaker's shop in the Broomhill area of Sheffield. They would feed their dinner money into the fixed-odds betting terminals (FOBTs), digital roulette machines akin to the one-armed bandits of Las Vegas – high-tech souped-up versions of the fruit machines common in British pubs. To the boys, it seemed like harmless fun.

In time, FOBTs (pronounced 'fob-tees') would become a byword for addiction, for the worst excesses of the gambling industry. But back then, few people outside the world of gambling had heard of them. They had attracted some public concern here and there, notably among some of my predecessors at the *Guardian*. One of the first journalists to write about them was Simon Bowers, an excellent and thoroughgoing investigator with a knack for prescience. As far back as 2005, Simon's reporting[2] raised red flags over whether FOBTs had led to dramatic changes in the behaviour of addicts, becoming a source of acute addiction as much as they were a symptom. *Guardian* colleague Randeep Ramesh followed him in later years, taking the FOBT subject and delving deep[3] into it with his characteristic tenacity.

But despite all their hard work, it was a long time before FOBTs would become mainstream headline news, at least to the extent that most ordinary people had heard of the machines. There was little reason for Jack, or those who knew him, to think that his life was in danger.

As is the case with most young people, Jack's parents did not and could not know everything about his life. In the years since his death, Charles and Liz Ritchie have pieced together the details of what happened to their son by speaking to his friends and meticulously tracing his bank details.

Jack had enjoyed a big win almost as soon as he started gambling, an experience commonly cited among those who develop an addiction.

'Pretty much the first time they went in, he was the one who won £1,000 in two successive spins,' Liz told me. 'He had to go back after school and collect the cash.'

Winning that much money would be a momentous day in the life of any seventeen-year-old. But those visits to the bookmaker had started as something else, a social thing, a bit of harmless fun, filling the odd bit of spare time in a life that was far from empty. Jack was known as gregarious, confident and likeable. A brighter-than-average teenager but with many of the same interests as any other young person approaching adulthood. He liked football and supported his local team, Sheffield United FC. He listened to The Strokes, world music and drum and bass. He also played guitar and sang – not all that well – in a band. The left-wing political movement that coalesced around Labour leader Jeremy Corbyn appealed to his sense of social justice. He did well at school and was popular, a focal point of his social group.

But while much of Jack's life was developing as his parents might have hoped, that first big win set him on a different track. Those lunchtime visits to the bookie's flipped a switch, activating something in his mind that he would never be able to shut down. As most of his friendship group lost interest in the FOBT visits and drifted away, Jack carried on. He would visit the bookie's on his own, sometimes showing up late for social occasions as a result. Friends knew that he gambled and noticed his absence sometimes but didn't consider what he was doing to be all that risky. Some even thought he had a talent for it.

Jack's parents became aware that he was gambling beyond his means when he confessed to having lost £5,000 given to him by his grandmother. Liz and Charles are both highly qualified professionals who earned enough to absorb their son's losses. They felt that, as long as he owned up to his teenage mistake and confronted it head-on, the family could put it behind them.

Charles took his contrite son around the bookmakers of Sheffield, signing him up to 'self-exclusion' schemes, whereby gamblers who want to close off the route to temptation can voluntarily add their name to a list of people barred from shops.

'At that stage you had to do it shop by shop, filling out a form, leaving a photograph of yourself, so members of staff would know you're self-excluded,' said Charles. 'That was a really humiliating experience. They were silent, desperate places with people sitting at the machines, monotonously punching the buttons. We'd come out of them and Jack would say: "That's not who I am."'

And it wasn't. Nothing could have been further removed from how Jack was when he wasn't gambling.

'He was a happy, cheerful person,' Liz recalled. 'This perception that somebody completely changes [when they have a gambling addiction] just isn't true. All of us bought into the idea it was somehow safe because it was only money.'

Rather than indicating a life-changing mental health problem, it seemed that Jack had made the sort of slip-up that people his age are expected to, even supposed to, as part of growing up. And so things returned to normal, or seemed to. Jack went on to university, where he combined his twin interests of music and politics in a dissertation about the role of music in the fall of South African apartheid.

Yet amid the stress of his studies and a new environment, Jack had increasingly turned to betting again. By now, online sports betting was a rapidly growing part of the gambling ecosystem and the young student was hooked. As it became clear later, Jack had started gambling online soon after self-excluding from local bookies, finding a new way to replace the buzz he'd got from FOBTs.

He gambled away his student loan within the first term at university and once more opened up to Liz and Charles when he came home for Christmas. They opted for pragmatic, logical steps, discussing the problem and its potential solutions with their son. They bought blocking software for his computer, a program that would simply lock him out of gambling websites. The software came with a twelve-month licence. It was only much later, trawling through his bank accounts after his death, that they discovered how Jack's addiction had lain dormant only to reawaken at the first opportunity. Their son had been bet-free for a year but had started gambling again soon after the software licence had expired.

'We were not aware of it because he wasn't losing such large amounts that he was having to borrow from us,' said Charles. 'It was a level that the industry would probably say counts as responsible gambling.'

It was after Jack left university and got a job, one he didn't much like, that things got worse. He had disposable income now, his own rented flat, the ability to get a bank loan and a credit card. But these trappings of adulthood, alongside an active social life, couldn't make up for the fact that he wasn't happy in his work. He began using his new-found financial resources to gamble in larger amounts. During one episode in 2015, he lost £8,000 over a couple of weeks, including £5,000 in just a few days. This was the only time he ever lost such a substantial amount of money so quickly, and he would always revert to much smaller sums – but that would ultimately make little difference.

On the weekend of Liz's sixtieth birthday, she and Charles went to London on a surprise trip that the family – Charles, their two daughters and Jack – had managed to keep a secret. But the celebrations stopped abruptly. The couple were in an art gallery when Jack phoned Liz from Sheffield and said he had lost a lot of money and felt suicidal. His gambling had actually been in profit over the previous two weeks but the loss of several hundred pounds in a day appeared to have triggered a sudden wave of despair. In the months that followed that call, a terrifying one for any parent, the Ritchies brought their son back into the family home and found him help via Gamblers Anonymous and an NHS programme called Improving Access to Psychological Therapies (IAPT). He had told GPs of his gambling before, but they had always lacked the expertise or the interest to refer him for proper treatment.

Jack's gambling was episodic. After every lapse he would snap out of it, focus on other things, stay away from temptation. His mood would improve and he'd start to feel that the problem wouldn't return. But it always did.

Unlike alcohol, tobacco or drugs, the effects of gambling addiction are rarely, if ever, written on the body for others to read. It does not cause physical changes or manifest intoxication. An inability to access it does not often result in withdrawal symptoms that are unpleasant, as with drugs, or potentially lethal, as with alcohol. The result is that the addiction can appear to come and go, disappearing for long periods before rearing its ugly head, often rapidly and without warning. In Jack's case, the addiction was hard to detect. He would have occasional mood swings but he largely gambled within his resources, meaning there was rarely any need to open up, even when he lost. All the while, he would seem to be his usual self, jovial and optimistic, albeit somewhat lacking in direction – nothing unusual for a lad in his early twenties. The incident on Liz's sixtieth birthday felt like a nadir, a turning point after which Jack resolved to seize new opportunities as a way of regaining control.

The opportunity to go abroad seemed like a chance for a fresh start. On a volunteering mission to Kenya in early 2017, Jack joined a group of young would-be entrepreneurs as part of a programme set up by former prime minister David Cameron. It sounded like just the thing for him. 'He asked me if I thought he should do it,' said Liz. 'I didn't think he was unsafe. I thought he was doing something that would enable him to find direction.'

Jack was safe, at least while he was in Kenya. Whether it was due to the difficulty of accessing gambling, or just that he was finding a sense of purpose, he didn't return to betting while there, or immediately after.

The relapse came during the next chapter of his life, one that had originally seemed like another positive step on the journey to fulfilment and maturity. After returning from Kenya, Jack had got in touch with friends in Vietnam, who had gone there to teach English. The idea of living abroad appealed to him and he prepared for the teaching role with a course in Spain, joining his friends in Vietnam in August 2017. His affable nature meant he would soon make even more friends and, exhausting as it could be, he enjoyed the teaching too.

'There was a lot of prep to do and it was quite a disciplined process but he was really knuckling down and you could tell from the conversations that he was getting better at it, enjoying it more and really loving it,' said Charles. 'He was living in a house with quite a large number of people, not all from the UK, having a great time and going on trips at the weekend.'

As far as his bank details show, Jack didn't gamble in the three months before packing for Hanoi. Charles thinks Jack believed at that point that he had slain the demon, that he was finally free. Perhaps the unfathomable depth of despair into which he would soon sink came from the eventual realisation that this wasn't true.

On Sunday, 19 November, Jack emailed his mum and dad saying

he was feeling a bit down and was thinking about coming back to the UK for a while. They called him immediately via Skype and he admitted during the conversation that he'd been gambling again.

'We spent a lot of the time cheering him up so that he didn't feel so bad about himself,' said Charles. 'We said if he wanted to come back we'd pay for his flight, we could clear his losses [of just over £1,000] and would he like to think about it for a day?'

'Are you alright?' Liz asked.

'Mum, I've got loads of friends here,' came the response.

It was true. For the most part things were going well in Vietnam, and Jack decided to stay. Again Liz and Charles bought him blocking software for his computer. He would never install it.

Liz was due to speak to him the next day, Monday, but he put her off because he was watching the TV show *Black Mirror* with a friend. They spoke on Tuesday, on a poor connection that made proper communication difficult. Things seemed to be fine and his bank accounts later showed that he hadn't gambled since that Sunday.

On Wednesday, 22 November, at lunchtime in the UK, 7 p.m. in Vietnam, Charles and Liz received the emailed suicide note. Moments earlier Jack had posted a series of pictures of himself on Facebook, left his drink sitting on the table, climbed over the 6 Degrees balcony and fallen to his death.

I don't want to intrude into the immediate aftermath, the shock and the suffering experienced by Jack's family and friends. I do, though, want to relate what Jack had been doing on that final day, a chain of events pieced together by his parents in the weeks that followed their darkest moment. Charles and Liz have no qualms about saying that gambling caused Jack's death and I know they vehemently challenge any suggestion that the causation isn't direct. However, it should also be said that the causes of suicide are sometimes extremely complex. There is help available for those who are struggling. Anyone reading this who feels that they might need it should consider contacting the Samaritans. You can reach them on any phone by dialling 116 123, or you can email jo@samaritans.org. Nothing I am about to relate should be seen as an explanation of, or justification for, what happened. But it is important context, the inescapable backdrop of a tragedy.

Liz and Charles have pored over what happened in those last hours, wondering if a slightly different confluence of events might have saved Jack's life.

'During that day, he'd started gambling in the morning,' said Charles. 'What had happened once again was that he'd gambled up to his overdraft limit. He'd won it all back and then lost it all again.'

Even so, Jack prepared his lessons as usual. He packed up his lesson plan, his pens and pencils. His moped was broken so he asked a friend to give him a lift to the language school, but the friend was running an errand elsewhere. Instead, he took a *xe ôm*, one of the motorbike taxis that are a common sight on the streets of Vietnam.

A road diversion took him past 6 Degrees, when usually he'd have gone a different way. At some point, as the moped weaved its way through the Hanoi traffic, he decided to get off and end his life.

The Ritchies believe that the impulse to get off the bike and cut short his life may be illustrative of the sudden onset of a dangerous mental state that can arise in the immediate aftermath of a gambling addict's loss of control. This mindset, they fear, was influenced by the language used around gambling addiction at that time, which said that 'problem gamblers', rather than addictive products, were at fault – the notion, inherent in the oft-used phrase 'responsible gambling', that the onus of responsibility lay primarily, even only, with the gambler.

'It feels like Jack didn't wake up that morning knowing and thinking he'd take his own life that night,' said Charles.

'The responsible-gambling model, which is straight out of the tobacco playbook, is a way of calling people who have been addicted the "problem" in order to avoid linking the products to the health harm they cause,' said Liz. 'People can't understand why these high-speed gambling games cause suicidal thoughts but they increase your impulsivity, increase your risk-taking and the responsible-gambling model says you're a worthless person. You crash out because you've run out of money but you're still totally physically capable of doing anything, unlike drugs or alcohol.'

## FROM GRIEF TO STRENGTH

One of the many things that has amazed me about Liz and Charles is their remarkable strength in channelling profound grief into a laser-like determination to bring about change. They wanted to understand how and why Jack had become a victim of gambling addiction and use that knowledge to prevent the same hellish nightmare being visited upon others.

We first met in early 2018, less than three months after Jack had died. They were visibly ravaged by grief, red-eyed and emotionally fragile. As they told me about Jack, I could not help but think of my own son, then just six months old, and the dangers he would have to navigate as he grew older.

I was profoundly moved but also inspired. These two bereaved parents would not let their son's death be logged as just another inexplicable mental health tragedy. It was not sheer bad luck, not something that simply couldn't have been helped. It was, they felt, the gut-wrenching real-life impact of predatory practices by the gambling industry, aided by the British state's abdication of its responsibility to protect citizens from harm.

The Ritchies have been pulling up trees ever since. Through their campaign group Gambling With Lives, they offer badly needed support to parents who have lost children to gambling-related suicide. They have used their formidable powers of debate and research – not to mention their genuine charm – to make their cause heard in the corridors of power. They have put the fear of God into Whitehall officials, often confronting political apparatchiks face to face with stern words when they feel their message is not being heard or understood. They have become an influential force in the campaign for reforms that would hit the gambling industry in the pocket, making their arguments articulately and with hard evidence. They also continue a legal bid, via Jack's inquest, to hold the state to account for failing to regulate the gambling industry properly.

'We never set out to be campaigners,' said Liz. 'We were just trying to understand what happened to him.'

## THE PREMISE: WHAT CONQUEST?

Charles and Liz have made their feelings abundantly clear: gambling killed their son. They blame the industry for designing and marketing the products that lured him in and they blame the government for creating the conditions in which high-octane gambling products could flourish unchecked, to the extent that it became a normal activity for seventeen-year-old boys with only a few pounds of lunch money.

But there's an elephant in the room. The subtitle of this book – *How Gambling Conquered Britain* – establishes a premise. It suggests that something changed, that Britain found itself in thrall to gambling, where it once was not. This is a notion that sets eyes rolling in some corners of the industry. It will provoke snorts of derision among a small but vocal cohort of libertarian ideologues who see, in any chronicling of gambling-related misery, the dread fist of the nanny state, impatient to crush anything that looks like fun. At time of writing, the government is in the midst of a landmark gambling review that looks likely to result in significant curbs on some of the practices that I will document in this book.

Some of the lobbyists, bloggers and think-tank pundits who oppose such reforms will argue, as they have done many times, that gambling hasn't conquered Britain at all but rather that British people have always loved to gamble, that participation has not increased and nor has addiction. The implication is that the only thing that has really changed is the appetite among alarmists and agitators to generate headlines, blowing minor dangers out of all proportion. Campaigners for reform have been denounced as 'prohibitionists'[4] – a word that has been carelessly, and sometimes cruelly, adopted and recycled ad nauseam by industry lobbyists, such as the Betting and Gaming Council (BGC), to describe honest and well-informed people advocating, in many cases, quite mild change.

This position relies on precisely the kind of selective interpretation that opponents of regulatory reform discern in those calling for it. What we have seen in the UK, and what we may soon see in other parts of the world, is complex, characterised by shifting trends in an industry that is heterogeneous and ever-changing.

We can certainly say that the gambling industry has, in recent years, been making more money than ever before. Irritatingly, we don't have the luxury of consistent samples that have measured both spending and participation since before the 2005 Gambling Act, the piece of legislation that transformed British gambling regulation and which we'll explore in greater depth. What we do know is that Britons' losses on land-based gambling – such as high-street bookmakers, racecourses or casinos – have remained pretty consistent since 2008. But since the internet came into every home, online operators have grown rapidly, to the point where they pocket the majority of the industry's winnings, more than £5 billion, every year.

We know also that one type of gambling is not the same as another.

A good starting point is that there are two broad categories. One is betting, wagering on real-world events like sport, where a degree of knowledge can be brought to bear to improve one's predictive ability in a world affected greatly by chance. The other is gaming, staking cash on games in which sensible styles of play may limit one's losses but where the odds are ultimately certain, in favour of the house, of course. Yet within these two baskets sit a dizzying array of products, all on offer at the touch of a button.

We lack robust evidence to tell us how much harm these different and evolving products are causing and whether the industry as a whole is doing more damage than it used to. Nor are we able to trace definitive causative links between gambling industry behaviour, government policy and gambling-related harm. But we do know that products that have been linked to higher rates of addiction – such as online slot machines and casino games, or virtual sports – are among the fastest-growing products in the business. Likewise rapid-fire 'in-play' sports betting, about which we have no reliable data to distinguish its addictiveness from that of a vanilla bet on the outcome of a match.

It's possible, I believe, to draw at least some conclusions from what we see in front of our eyes every day. We can document with some certainty how the UK has witnessed a shift in the prominence of gambling in the public consciousness, to the point that it is a staple in the media diet of British life, a ubiquitous presence in the advertising we see both inside the home and elsewhere. Unshackled by a political class in thrall to big business and high on the endless possibilities of new technology, the industry has forced its way into our minds to an unprecedented degree. The consequences are yet to be understood.

Betting and gaming companies now rank alongside any other consumer-goods or leisure brand, in terms of their access to the public sphere. With many of them now listed on the stock market, their directors are legally beholden primarily to shareholders, creating an incentive to leverage the industry's new-found mainstream status to maximise investment returns. Deploying an armoury of weapons including souped-up advertising, psychological sleight of hand and outright bribes, those companies have gravitated towards whatever smells most like profit.

The internet has triggered an epochal migration in the way that companies seek this profit, in the way they market to us, where they spend their money and how we are invited to spend ours. Where once devotees of casino games may have stood at the roulette or baccarat table, they now play the same games on a laptop or mobile phone. They may even dispense with such games altogether and simply resort to spin after spin on online slot machines. Once, the thrill of horse racing brought the romance of the turf into high-street betting shops. Now, the Sport of Kings has become subordinate to rapid-fire bets on trivial, chance outcomes, such as who will win the most corners or concede the most fouls in any random football match. The invention of so-called 'virtual' sports means some punters will stand in a bookie's watching an animated horse gallop round a track towards an outcome determined not by trainers, owners and jockeys, but by a random number generator.

This is a sector that was once soundtracked by the call of the croupier, or the drumbeat of hooves on turf, yet which now echoes with the jangling sound of online slot machine sound effects.

Many of those who used to enjoy sporadic participation in relatively benign activities such as the National Lottery weekly draw or an annual bet on the Grand National are now invited to dip their toes into ever-deeper waters. Responding to marketing, special offers and psychological prods, many consumers drifted towards compulsive, high-octane products such as FOBTs and online slot machines. As these proved to be reliable revenue-raisers, the migration became a self-fulfilling prophecy.

Innovation comes to all sectors, of course, and gambling addiction is not a new phenomenon. Yet the industry's metamorphosis has undoubtedly caused harm to many people. Moreover, the legacy of these changes is something we are some distance from comprehending. In some respects the immediate effects are abundantly clear, evident in the ceaseless, pervasive presence of gambling adverts in our media and around football, the national game.

We cannot grasp what changes are being wrought on the minds of young people. People turning eighteen in the early 2020s belong to the first generation to have grown up in a world where smartphones are part of life and in which gambling is essentially inescapable. They are the first generation to see gambling afforded the same status in our lives as products that do not put their consumers – not to mention their consumers' friends and families – at risk of financial ruin or psychological breakdown. We are voyaging into the unknown.

In trying to ascertain what dangers we face, and the ones that may lie ahead, I will explore how little we know and why we remain so ignorant, as well as how the measures we use to assess the scale of gambling addiction – and to treat those who suffer from it – are deeply inadequate, depriving us of the understanding we need to help those in difficulty.

This failure, I will argue, is not entirely an accident but is instead the result of persistent and obvious structural issues that politicians and regulators have lacked the understanding or the incentive to address swiftly enough, if at all. The absence of knowledge has worked to the benefit of the industry, whose fallback position is to point to a vacuum of information about the harm it is really causing as a reason to err on the side of caution when it comes to regulatory reform.

Towards the end of the book, we will learn who has benefited from all of this and how some of them have – over the course of a few short years – amassed almost unimaginable fortunes, siphoning cash out of the pockets of millions of ordinary folk, including those stalked by addiction, family breakdown and suicide. We will also explore how much is set to change as a result of the government's gambling review, which is likely to result in the industry's wings being clipped.

## WHY I'M WRITING THIS BOOK

This sort of talk makes me sound like I harbour a visceral dislike of gambling. I know there are some in the industry who believe that to be the case, that I'm a 'bookie-basher' bent on spoiling harmless fun, a typical *Guardian* metropolitan elitist sanctimoniously taking swipes at a legitimate industry out of sheer puritanism, snobbery or a mixture of the two.

I'm certainly no moral puritan and I don't have an inherent dislike of gambling. I have no problem accepting that it is a leisure pursuit that has its place in our culture. I'll make a confession, though, which is that I don't get it. What I mean by that is, while I've fallen victim to other addictive habits over the years, like smoking and alcohol overindulgence, gambling has never held much appeal. Perhaps the primary reason to gamble is the opportunity to win money, to outsmart the house. If it were possible to do that on a consistent basis, profitable gambling companies would not exist. The other attraction of gambling, the rush, the buzz, the dopamine hit that some people experience by putting their money on the line in a game of chance, simply doesn't happen to me.

As a cub reporter at the *Daily Mail*, long before I started covering the industry in earnest, I was invited to Royal Ascot by Ladbrokes. The *Mail* took a pretty relaxed approach to the acceptance of hospitality and I was curious to see what it would be like. My partner and I were entertained in the Royal Enclosure – top hat and tails for the men, hats or a 'substantial fascinator' for the women.

In between the courses of a lavish meal in the hospitality suite, Ladbrokes asked all the men in the room to put £20 into a 'Ladies' Pot'. One of the bookmaker's racing-form experts was roped in to stick the money down on some wiser-than-average bets, with any winnings to be distributed among said 'ladies'. The expert knew his stuff. If I remember correctly, my partner walked away with more than £100. We enjoyed the pageantry and the spectacle, seeing the horses at full gallop. We even saw the Queen. The wagering part, though, left me cold.

My more recent interest in the sector came about by chance. I was on a short-term contract at the *Guardian* when the paper advertised for a new energy correspondent, an attractive full-time position. I didn't get the job. Business editor Julia Finch sat me down and, seeing the disappointment writ large on my face, said, with characteristic delicacy: 'On a scale of one to ten, how pissed off are you?'

The consolation prize Julia offered was the 'sins' patch – taking in the tobacco, gambling, alcohol and cannabis industries. Sins proved to be fertile ground, particularly when it came to gambling. No preconception, no simmering anti-bookie resentment, was required. With even a modicum of graft, the stories seemed to flood in almost of their own volition, in astonishing volumes, often jaw-dropping tales. I sat down with self-confessed con man Tony Parente, who told me how he had been treated like a king by Ladbrokes[5] even as he poured the proceeds of an elaborate theft into their coffers, stealing ever more to fund his high-roller existence. At the other end of the spectrum, I spoke to destitute addicts desperately trying to stay away from gambling, even as their phone and email inboxes pinged every few minutes with bonus offers from gambling companies. I went undercover at an annual industry conference[6] and witnessed the outdated casual misogyny of pole-dancing displays aimed at convincing sweaty middle-aged executive men to buy one company's slot machines rather than another's. You don't see pole-dancing on most business-desk shifts.

I have also got to know people within the industry, most of whom have been likeable, moral, good people. Some disagreed with me on certain fundamentals but many didn't, feeling that the more rapacious parts of the sector were letting the side down for everyone else. Once, I was exchanging emails with a shop-worker at a high-street bookmaker's that was cutting staff. She faced the prospect of losing her job, depending on how success-fully she could convince people to sign up for online accounts. I asked her if she felt any resentment towards people like me for writing negative stories about FOBTs? After all, bookies closed some of their shops after the machines were eventually restricted. She wrote back: 'Why? It was all true.'

I have leaned heavily on everyone, from psychology professors to gambling executives and old-school bookmakers, interviewed media moguls, football players and politicians, read academic tracts, trawled bookmakers' shops and played online slot machines late at night during Covid-19 lockdowns.

Most importantly, I have relied on the patience and goodwill of a group of people who will never again be able to see gambling as the harmless leisure activity that it genuinely can be for many people. They are the gambling addicts who have snuck out of their child's birthday party to check the result of a Venezuelan under-twenty-threes football game, alienated their friends one by one until they had nobody left, or stolen from their employer and been sent to prison. They are also the children, siblings, friends and parents who have picked up the pieces of an addict's life or – in the worst cases – watched those lives snuffed out.

I listened to the grief of people like Liz and Charles Ritchie and resolved to work harder to hold the industry to account when its worst excesses needed to be exposed. I thank all of them and hope to do their kind collaborative efforts no disservice.

# 1. A BRIEF HISTORY OF GAMBLING

It hath this ill property above all other Vices, that it renders a man incapable of prosecuting any serious action, and makes him always unsatisfied with his own condition; he is either lifted up to the top of mad joy with success, or plung'd to the bottom of despair by misfortune, always in extreams, always in a storm.

CHARLES COTTON, *THE COMPLEAT GAMESTER* (1674)

## THE ORIGIN STORY

Prostitution may be the world's oldest profession but gambling matches its cousin in vice as one of the most enduring leisure pursuits. Archaeologists have brushed the dust off early forms of dice first thrown, perhaps while muttering some eldritch incantation, by civilisations that thrived as long ago as 6000 BC.[1] Games that hinged on chance – or perhaps the favour of the gods – entertained the subjects of Chinese dynasties and the ancient Egyptians, featuring through Grecian civilisation and the rise and fall of the Roman Empire. References in religious texts and mythology, as well as in accounts left to us by historians, indicate not only that gambling existed, but that it occupied a significant place in the cultural firmament, working in tandem with ineluctable concepts such as luck, hope and destiny.

In that sense at least, there is nothing new under the sun. Take, for instance, the habit of chasing losses – the tendency among losing gamblers to keep playing over and over again, in the hope of reversing their fortunes and winning everything back. Loss-chasing features in the *Mahabharata*, the Hindu epic poem written in Sanskrit, whose oldest passages date back to around 400 BC. Yudhishthira, eldest of the Pandava brothers, fritters away his wealth at pachisi, a dice game similar to ludo. In trying to win everything back, he eventually loses his kingdom, his fellow brothers, his wife and himself. That's one hell of a losing streak.

Gambling is embedded in Western culture too, a leitmotif that crops up in the metaphor deployed at one of the pivotal moments of European history. When Julius Caesar crossed the Rubicon River with his armies in 49 BC – the point of no return on the path to civil war in Rome – the historian Suetonius tells us of his momentous words to mark the gambit. '*Alea iacta est*,' the military strategist and soon-to-be dictator of the Roman Republic was said to have exclaimed: 'The die is cast.' His adoptive son and Rome's first emperor, Augustus, referenced dice play in rather less momentous terms. In letters to his stepson Tiberius, he frequently related his fortune – or lack of it – in dice games played over lavish dinners. It's easy to imagine him carelessly tossing dice, in between bites of that mouthwatering Roman delicacy, roast dormouse dipped in honey.

Gamblers of the ancient world will likely have interpreted their success or failure not as luck but as the will of one or more gods. In his book *Gambling*, the former England cricket captain Mike Atherton points to those who drew lots in the Old Testament to divide the lands of Canaan, or, in the New Testament, to distribute the garments of Christ. 'They were casting lots to divine the will of God: the casting of a lot was a direct appeal to God and the drawing of it was interpreted as His will,' writes Atherton. 'In that sense, the concept of pure chance could not exist at all.'[2]

The echoes of ancient ritual live on in the way we gamble too. In multiple ancient societies that thrived before recorded history, gamblers played with astragali, the tali, or knucklebones, of dead cattle, whose irregular shape meant they landed one of four ways when tossed into the air. This apparently crude but actually rather ingenious method of letting fate decide gives us the slang term for dice-throwing, 'rolling the bones'. Thus, the practices of millennia-old civilisations reverberate through the ages and find new voice in the mouths of Las Vegas casino patrons, blowing on their hands and appealing to Lady Luck. The thrill and trepidation experienced by the modern-day gambler is no different from the adrenaline coursing through the veins of our ancestors.

## KINGS AND VAGABONDS

Physical artefacts and written accounts tell us about the existence of gambling in some ancient civilisations and offer clues as to its cultural significance. Much less evidence survives to explain how successive rulers and governments dealt with a concern that occupies today's leaders – how to regulate it. This book will unpick the modern approach to gambling regulation, particularly in the UK, by any measure one of the major global centres of the industry. But to understand how we got to where we are, I want to rewind more than eight hundred years.

In England, perhaps the earliest recorded attempt to regulate gambling came during the twelfth-century reign of Richard the Lionheart, a king renowned as much for his militaristic displays of Christian fervour as for his fearlessness on the battlefield. Richard Cœur de Lion is probably best known in modern popular culture for playing *deus ex machina* at the end of the Robin Hood fable. In the film *Robin Hood: Prince of Thieves*, he appears – played by the late Sean Connery – to bless the eponymous hero and oversee his marriage to Maid Marian. Bryan Adams starts crooning, the credits roll, a damp-eyed audience goes home happy.

But in real life, the warrior king also boasts an important cameo in the history of gambling regulation. During the Third Crusade, the religious war waged by Christian armies against Muslim forces led by the sultan Saladin, Richard and his ally of convenience, Philip II of France, occupied Sicily in 1190 ahead of a planned assault on Jerusalem. Perspiring under the sweltering Sicilian sun, with homesickness, boredom and the torpid climate taking their toll, the troops frequently resorted to gambling. The habit began to cause ructions among the soldiers, particularly when unlucky losers proved unable to honour their debts. Mindful of the need for his Crusaders to be in good spirits and on their mettle for the upcoming holy war, Richard issued a decree: no soldiers or sailors were allowed to play any game for money, unless in the presence of officers, who could presumably intercede before disputes boiled over. Those who broke the rules were liable to be whipped naked through the camp for three days.[3] Sailors could expect one of the few punishments that was even worse: keelhauling. This especially grim sanction involves tying the unfortunate recipient to a rope looped underneath the ship. They are then dragged under the waves, below the hull, until they emerge, half-drowned, at the other side of the ship. Sometimes they would have to make more than one pass: rinse and repeat. Sean Connery's avuncular smile doesn't seem quite so benevolent now, does it? Knights and clergymen were afforded the privilege of gambling without risking either flogging or keelhauling, but they had to stop if they lost any more than twenty shillings in a day. Should they exceed these boundaries, they had to pay a further one hundred shillings, to be shared between the archbishops in the army.[4]

In the nearly eight and a half centuries that have elapsed since then, laws governing gambling have been constructed piecemeal and patchwork, written and rewritten according to expediency. Like Richard, successive monarchs and governments have mostly had little interest in constructing a lasting regulatory architecture to oversee gambling. Rather, they have been fundamentally reactive, responding to events and trends that posed a threat to social harmony or were deemed inherently immoral or in some other way deleterious to the public good.

This book is not a comprehensive history of gambling and I don't propose to catalogue the development of regulation exhaustively, but we do need to blow the dust off some ancient texts to inform our understanding of where we are today. Perhaps my favourite piece of gambling legislation is the Unlawful Games Act of 1541, passed towards the end of the reign of Henry VIII, when the gluttonous old beast was already five wives deep and his waistline was expanding at a rate of knots. Henry banned a range of leisure pursuits, some of them unfamiliar to modern ears, including 'bowling, coytes, cloysh-cayls, half-bowl, tennis, dicing and carding'. Officers of the law were required 'to make search weekly, or at the farthest once a month, in all places where houses, alleys, plays, or places of dicing, carding, or gaming shall be suspected to be had, kept, and maintained'.[5]

The successor of earlier laws, passed under Richard II in 1388 and Henry IV in 1409, the Act did not take aim at the morality of gambling, or the wider social implications of people losing more than they could afford. Indeed, many of the activities it targeted were not games of pure luck but rather of skill. There were more pragmatic reasons for Henry and his court to be concerned; this was a time characterised by constant tension with continental Europe, following England's rancorous separation from the Catholic Church.

Henry's tough stance on such games stemmed from the fear that activities pursued solely for sport and wagering would distract Englishmen from the practice of archery, the skill that had proved the linchpin of military success at Agincourt, the decisive battle in the Hundred Years War with France. The spreading popularity of such games meant that the nation's archery prowess was 'sore decayed, and dayly is lyke to be more mynished', the Act said. Parts of the legislation would endure untouched for more than four hundred years, although hopefully not out of lingering animosity towards the French.

By the reign of Charles II, though, attention had shifted to concerns that feel more familiar to a contemporary audience. With the Gaming Act of 1664, the government sought to legislate against gaming that was 'deceitfull, disorderly and excessive'.[6] This unholy trinity of adjectives rings bells. As we shall see, the tenets of today's gambling regulation have similar goals. The 1664 Act addressed cheating: it provided that anyone caught swindling their fellow gambler could be forced to repay three times the value of their winnings, half to the Crown and half to the victim of their misdeeds.

But it also dealt with the ogre of debt, prefiguring some of the regulation now thought of as promoting safer gambling. It was an early example of a provision specifically aimed at the prevention of harm, particularly among young noblemen who were liable to bet to the 'ruine of their Estates and Fortunes'. This part of the Act ruled that any gambling debt above £100 (over £10,000 in today's money) was unenforceable. Not only that but, if discovered, the winner should forfeit treble the value of any amount above the £100 threshold, again to the Crown and to the person on the wrong end of the wager. Any security given as collateral on the debts, such as ancestral estates, was also declared void. In their book *The Law of Gambling*, Stephen Monkcom and Colin Smith write that 'This latter provision reflected a growing concern that the social order was being subverted by the grant by losing gamblers of securities such as mortgages and conveyances for their indebtedness, with the consequence that their estates were being lost to their heirs and successors.'[7] In short, it was not so much personal misery that the Act sought to avoid but any threat to the seventeenth-century aristocratic order, the very glue that held the ruling classes together.

Attempts to build on the 1664 Gaming Act followed but these early campaigns to address harmful gambling proved futile, according to one observer. In 1722, an anonymous pamphleteer said of the 1710 Gaming Act that it had been 'entirely ineffectual'. 'Thousands of families since that time have been ruined in gaming only, and it daily increases.'[8]

Successive parliaments continued to take a reactive approach, playing a fairground game of whack-a-mole, hammering particular activities back down when they provoked concern, only for others to pop up elsewhere. The result was a mishmash of obsolete laws that nonetheless remained on the statute books for many years. The legendary parliamentarian and journalist Bill Deedes highlighted the absurdities this created during a speech in the House of Commons in 1956. Deedes reminded the House that there was 'still on the Statute Book an Act of 1738 which declares ace of hearts, pharaoh, basset and hazard to be lotteries and, therefore, illegal. In addition, an Act of 1739 declares passage and any game with dice or a device of like nature – with the honourable exception of backgammon – to be illegal; and an Act of 1744 brings "roulet otherwise roly-poly" within the scope of those earlier Acts. I think these facts require no embellishment.'[9]

## THE MODERN ERA

All the while, gambling remained a source of enjoyment, particularly among the wealthy, whose exploits sometimes became the stuff of legend. One well-known tale involves White's, a gentlemen's club founded in 1693 in London's salubrious St James's area. It would go on to become a haven for gambling, famed for the entries in the White's Betting Book, and it was there, in 1816, that Lord Alvanley supposedly bet £3,000 (nearly £300,000 in today's money) that one raindrop would reach the bottom of a window before another. The club remains a favourite of royals and aristocrats.

Yet it wasn't until 1845 that British parliamentarians made a concerted effort to wipe the slate clean and concoct what they hoped would be comprehensive legislation regulating gambling. This was a time in which perceived social ills, particularly the ravages wrought on those suffering in poverty, were rising up the agenda. Charles Dickens, whose own father had been imprisoned for non-payment of debts, was drawing attention to injustice and the grinding poverty endured by many working people in Victorian Britain, via novels drip-fed in newspaper serialisations to an eager public. Ideas of social justice were taking hold everywhere, forged in the crucible of increasing industrialisation that was, in many cases, victimising the poor and exploiting workers. *The Communist Manifesto* was three years away from being published.

It was amid this atmosphere that a select committee appointed by the House of Commons concluded that existing laws had not only proved ineffective in preventing the spread of gambling dens but that, crucially, they were aimed largely at protecting the wealthy. While the richest were afforded at least some degree of protection from losing their fortunes, the poor had little to prevent them squandering much smaller sums, money that might be the only thing standing between their families and starvation.

The result of these deliberations was the Gaming Act of 1845. Its first provision was to repeal parts of the aforementioned Unlawful Games Act of 1541 (to the delight, no doubt, of any remaining devotees of cloysh-cayls and half-bowl). But the most important and enduring element of the Act was that it deemed a wager unenforceable as a legal contract. This made it unattractive to bookmakers to take bets on credit unless they could be 100% sure that the punter would be willing or able to pay up if they lost.[10]

With credit out of the picture, cash became king. Betting houses popped up where punters could place wagers with ready money. These were outlawed in 1853, so gambling moved onto the street, only for that practice to be forbidden in 1906. A pattern was starting to emerge: successive pieces of legislation were proving to be blunt instruments, capable only of shifting perceived social ills around but never of actually preventing them. It was whack-a-mole again. If punters bet in gaming houses, the government criminalised those. If they gathered to place bets in the street, that was outlawed too. It was a legislative strategy that achieved very little except making felons of people who might otherwise have been law-abiding citizens.

Moreover, legal loopholes emerged that meant those with the means to do so could still gamble on credit, as long as they placed their bets by telephone. This meant one law for the wealthy, who could bet with relative ease, and another for ordinary working-class folk, who relied upon precarious street operations where book-makers employed 'runners' to collect debts, deploying various degrees of persuasiveness, including physical violence. Many of today's best-known bookmakers trace their legacy back to this era. William Hill founded his betting company in 1934, as a telephone or postal service, when the practice was still illegal.

This rather chaotic state of affairs persisted in much the same vein until 1961, when a system rooted in Victorian moralism gave way to an approach more suited to the libertine Swinging Sixties. The new approach was still a largely pragmatic one. It was not that gambling had been accepted by the ruling classes as a legitimate leisure pursuit; rather, politicians had recognised by now that too many people enjoyed the occasional flutter for gambling to be erased from British life altogether. It should, they concluded, at least be closely monitored, not to mention harnessed to provide much-needed revenues for the Exchequer as Britain continued its post-war reconstruction and tied in place the safety net of the welfare state.

'Gambling was thought to be fundamentally undesirable and only rather sleazy people do it,' Peter Collins, an advisor to several governments on gambling policy and author of *Gambling and the Public Interest*, told me. 'But like other vices it was better to be legalised and regulated, than to have an illegal industry.'

The result of this approach, started under the administration of Conservative prime minister Harold 'Supermac' Macmillan, was the Betting and Gaming Act of 1960, which fathered the modern-day betting shop. In the years that followed, soundtracked by Beatlemania against a backdrop of world-changing events such as the assassination of JFK, British high streets witnessed an explosion of bookies, with about 16,000 licences granted by 1965.

In 1968, with expansion deemed to have gone too far, the government of Labour prime minister Harold Wilson modified the law, bringing in a 'demand test' that prevented the award of a gambling-premises licence unless it could be shown that there was significant unstimulated clamour for one.[11]

By now, though, Britain's relationship with gambling had changed forever. Something of an equilibrium had been reached between civil liberties and the prevention of crime, disorder and exploitation. The high-street bookmaker became a regular fixture, and gambling, by extension, a semi-legitimate activity rather than a grubby underground vice. William Hill himself, who had according to some accounts described betting shops as a 'cancer on society',[12] had opened his first in 1966. Despite their new-found legitimacy, though, bookies retained some degree of mystique, still clad in the trappings of vice. Their windows had to be blacked out, for instance. Their doorways, like shops that sold pornographic magazines and videos, were veiled by beaded curtains.

Bookmakers remained cloaked in this garb well into the 1990s, yet by then they ranked alongside some of the stalwarts of British industry, in financial terms at least. When Japanese bank Nomura bought William Hill in 1997, it paid £700 million for the company, nearly £1.3 billion in today's money. The following year Ladbrokes agreed to pay £363 million for bookmaker Coral, although that deal was eventually unpicked by the competition regulator. This was a bona fide reputable industry, with its own regulatory framework, its own handsomely remunerated lobbyists and lawyers, City of London grandees in the boardroom and pin-striped, blue-blooded financial backers. Names such as William Hill, Ladbrokes and Coral thrived and expanded, securing a foothold in town centres alongside banks, chemists and grocery stores.

Gambling was making its way to the top table at long last.

## THE TURN OF THE MILLENNIUM

The way our antecedents dealt with gambling offers a telling glimpse into the collective psyche of the age, be it the anxiety of an ageing Henry VIII at his subjects' faltering archery prowess, or seventeenth-century concerns about foolhardy young aristocrats squandering the ancestral pile.

But we find ourselves today in the era of the Gambling Act of 2005, a piece of legislation that terraformed the modern gambling landscape. Its introduction under Tony Blair, the most electorally successful left-of-centre prime minister in British history, was fostered by the essentially free-market, socially liberal instincts of his New Labour project.

'It was part of that idea that we don't care how rich people get as long as we can fund the public services we want,' said Ruth Davidson, who would go on to become leader of the Scottish Conservative party but was, during the later Blair years, a BBC reporter.

Labour MP Richard Caborn's political career was already in full swing by then. He recalls the casual chumminess with which Blair allocated him the responsibility for gambling policy in 2001.

Caborn had been summoned to the prime minister's office to discuss his new brief as minister for sport. Gambling was thrown into the mix, almost as an afterthought, at the end of a conversation.

'As I stood up to walk away, he said: "Oh, by the way, would you take gambling? We've brought it from the Home Office into DCMS [the Department for Culture, Media & Sport]",' Caborn told me. '"Will you look into that?" And I walked out, not knowing anything about gambling.'

The process that followed, as Blair's ideological vision became reality, would turbocharge a multibillion-pound industry that has generated vast profits but, at times, displayed scant regard for the collateral damage visited on some of its customers.

Before we come to the Act itself, it's worth looking at the circumstances that set the scene for it. By the late 1990s, the National Lottery had established at least one form of gambling as a mainstream activity. Millions of people had started playing the weekly draw, with its highly quotable adverts that deployed the slogan 'It could be you', illustrated by a giant finger descending from the sky to point at the lucky winner. As one gambling consultant told Rebecca Cassidy, author of *Vicious Games*: 'The lottery was a Trojan horse for us.'[13]

Around the same time, online poker began growing in popularity, particularly among young men with a good grasp of the game, who used it as a way to fund their student lifestyle or supplement their early-career earnings. I was at university in the first four years of the twenty-first century and I remember friends telling me how much they were making online from 'fish', a poker term for suckers who play badly and lose money. It felt uncomfortably exploitative but at the same time I could see the thrill of it for young men (they were all men), using their smarts to make quick money.

Meanwhile, more traditional forms of betting were changing fast. Seasoned gamblers who enjoyed sports wagers now had the option of placing bets with offshore operators via the telephone or, increasingly, online, an activity that was essentially an unregulated free-for-all.

What spurred the government into legislative action, at least at first, was not so much the potential danger to gamblers but the impact on the country's finances. In the decades leading up to 2001, tax was levied on each bet itself, at a rate of 9p in the pound at high-street bookmakers. Gamblers could choose whether it was applied to their bet or their winnings. This made betting with UK operators less attractive than telephone operations based in low-tax jurisdictions such as Malta or Gibraltar, which could offer the same bets without the tax. Indeed, as the internet took off, betting companies who saw the opportunity it presented had been given little option but to go offshore. Online gambling was not yet legal in the UK and thus they flocked to overseas jurisdictions, which offered generous corporation and income tax regimes, not to mention light-touch regulation. Victor Chandler, the scion of a dynasty of bookmakers steeped in the history of the racecourse and greyhound track, led the rush to move offshore in 1998, with big names such as Ladbrokes following soon after. The result was dwindling receipts for the taxman, as punters' pounds flowed out of Britain.

'We thought, goodness me, they're all going to go,' said Stephen Timms, then financial secretary to the Treasury. The solution, he told me, was to 'do a deal'.

The handshake with the industry involved replacing the betting duty with a 15% tax on bookies' revenues, which came into effect in 2002.[14] This would make the prices offered by traditional UK bookmakers more competitive, helping them win back customers, boosting profit and reducing their incentive to rush offshore. For a time this worked, and the long-term decline in tax receipts was arrested.

In 2005 the *Guardian* wrote a glowing news piece hailing a 'brilliant' move by Gordon Brown, then chancellor of the Exchequer, working alongside Tony Blair.[15] The tax change had given the Treasury more money to spend, lending credence to that Blairite thesis that bumper corporate profit was to be applauded as long as it could fund schools and hospitals.

But the underlying fundamentals were unchanged. The move had benefited bookies who took most of their bets in shops, but the fast-growing online industry still had no legal status in the UK and, as the internet expanded, so did its utility as a platform for betting. Even after 2007, when online firms could set up shop in the UK, there remained relatively little incentive to move closer to the taxman and closer to the scrutiny of regulators, politicians and anti-gambling campaign groups.

It would not be until 2014 that the government overhauled the system effectively, this time taxing betting income at the point of consumption (where the gambler places the bet).[16] With the location of the consumer now determining where the tax was collected, there was no way of avoiding UK duty. Tax receipts soared. In the space of a year, overall betting and gaming duty increased from £2.1 billion to £2.7 billion. By then, the UK taxman had missed out on much-needed revenue, £1 billion between 2009 and 2013 alone, according to some estimates.[17]

There was another major consequence of New Labour's approach to gambling taxation: the explosion of fixed-odds betting terminals. These machines allowed punters to stake £100 every twenty seconds on casino-style games, chiefly roulette. We'll learn much more about FOBTs later in this book but they owed a great deal to Brown's 2002 tax change. They ran on very low margins, with an average of 97p in every £1 returned to the player. A tax on individual bets effectively eliminated much of the bookies' edge, rendering the machines unattractive. Brown's tax measure, taxing overall company profits rather than individual bets, changed the calculations. Almost overnight, they became an irresistible cash cow that the gambling industry would milk for nearly two more decades.

Within two years, FOBTs had become a bone of contention between the government and the industry. High-street bookmakers were installing the machines at a rate of knots, using the predictable income offered by a fixed-odds product to supplement more volatile income from sports wagering. They were cheap to maintain, occupied minimal shop floor space and guaranteed a steady stream of revenue. But their rapid proliferation was already stoking fears about gambling addiction. They hadn't hit the newspaper front pages yet, but anecdotal evidence was beginning to emerge about their addictive qualities.

There was uncertainty about their legal status too. The industry and the regulator – then called the Gaming Board for Great Britain – litigated a test case. The regulator, which oversaw casinos but not betting shops, argued that FOBTs were machines designed primarily for casino-style gaming and should therefore be limited to casinos. The Association of British Bookmakers, the industry's trade body, claimed that the machines could be used for betting and that their members, who did not fall under the Gaming Board's purview, should also be permitted to benefit. Knowing that a new Gambling Act was on the way, the two sides reached a deal out of court, a gift-wrapped solution for the politicians who would write the Act:

- Bookmakers would be allowed to install no more than four FOBTs per shop;
- They would have a maximum stake of £100 and a maximum prize of £500;
- Roulette would be the only casino game permitted;
- Speed of play – the permitted interval between bets – would be restricted.

For the government, it was a classic political solution. Costly legal fees for fighting what the public might perceive to be a niche battle had been averted, while a profit-hungry industry's appetites had, ostensibly, been curbed. For the ABB, it was a genuine coup that spared its members the loss of their most highly lucrative new product in years.

The future of gambling in Britain was already beginning to take shape, forged in the twin crucibles of the Treasury and the law courts. Now the Blair government was ready to press ahead with its more ambitious project – a comprehensive reform of gambling legislation, fit for the twenty-first century.

## THE ACT

In 2000 Blair's government had commissioned a panel of experts, headed by the distinguished economist Sir Alan Budd, to review gambling laws. A founding member of the Bank of England's Monetary Policy Committee, which set interest rates, Budd was a free-market economist tasked with reforms that might strike a balance between protecting the vulnerable while also placing trust in market forces to drive wealth and motivate companies to do the right thing.

Peter Collins describes the plan as typical of Blair's economic modernisation project. 'It basically said we should try to integrate gambling into the general leisure sector instead of treating it as a pariah activity. That was part of Blair's new Britain. It was the same sort of thing with twenty-four-hour alcohol licensing and there was a lot of public outcry over that too.'

In Budd's own words, the plan was 'a classic example of Britain's approach to policy-making in those days. The government would ask a group of generally middle-class men and women to consider issues with which they had little expertise or interest.'[18]

The commission's members might not have boasted much in the way of relevant expertise either, but they did not lack input from those who did. 'We put out a questionnaire with about fourteen questions on it,' Budd committee member Professor Jonathan Wolff told me. Wolff was chosen for his credentials as a noted philosopher and academic. Soon after he and his fellow committee members sought them, submissions came flooding in, from anyone and every-one with an interest in the future of gambling. 'Huddersfield Town Football Club sent us one page with yes or no answers. At the other end of the scale were the big companies and the trade bodies. They got consultants in to write very polished responses and you could see they'd spent thousands getting this stuff done. We had a stack of evidence that came up to my waist.'

More than two hundred submissions arrived, many of them from gambling firms and their lobbyists, while the panel gathered evidence in the field too. 'We went to a greyhound meeting, horse racing, and we also considered casinos so we went to Las Vegas and Blackpool, which was trying to use gambling to revive itself,' said Mihir Bose, the award-winning sports journalist, another member of the committee.

The resulting proposals would, in the report's own words, 'gener-ally increase the gambling opportunities for adults' while seeking to protect vulnerable people such as children and addicts.[19]

'Our driving force was that if people want to gamble, we won't take a moralising view and say you can't,' said Bose. 'We've been accused of opening the door but the door was opening already. It was better for it to be done in a regulated fashion.'

Under the Budd model, each liberalising measure would, in theory, come with a counterweight of some kind, arbitrating between civil liberties and player protection. The committee members believed that increased choice and competition would generally work to the benefit of the consumer. One way they sought to achieve this was by doing away with restrictions that limited the number of towns and cities permitted to license casinos. They also recommended abol-ishing the twenty-four-hour cooling-off period required between a customer signing up to join a casino and actually being allowed to play. This would make it easier to open dedicated gambling venues and sign up customers.

The countermeasure was a ban on 'ambient' gambling, such as fruit machines located in non-specialist venues like chip shops and taxi offices. The ideological intent was clear: adults who made a concerted choice to gamble should not be prevented from doing so by a busybody state. Nor should people going about their daily lives be constantly exposed to opportunities to squander their money.

The same philosophy applied to advertising it. Where previously only lotteries and bingo had been allowed over the airwaves, now the entire industry would be permitted to enter British homes via the television. This was the other end of the spectrum from the demand test of the 1960s, the one that said bookies could only open in areas where there was a public clamour for them. Instead, bookies would be able to pitch for new customers via the most powerful marketing tool known to mankind. By way of mitigation, the industry would agree not to show adverts before the informal 9 p.m. watershed, save during live sporting events.

The Budd committee was high-powered, its members were intelligent, well-informed people, and they were aware of developing trends, including the proliferation of FOBTs and the rise of internet gambling. They reckoned, quite reasonably, that it was better for gambling to be regulated and closely monitored for fairness and criminality, rather than being the preserve of offshore operators or criminal enterprises.

But they could not predict the future and nor were they in charge of writing the legislation. That was up to politicians.


## THE ACT ITSELF

The government accepted Budd's recommendations, in a written response published in 2002, under the slightly hubristic title: 'A Safe Bet For Success'.

Three years later, the Gambling Act of 2005 came into being. Like most pieces of primary legislation written in the modern era, the Act is lengthy, running to a mind-numbing 362 clauses, with eighteen accompanying schedules that clarify how the legislation is to work in practice. Its main aims were threefold:

- To reduce crime and disorder associated with gambling;
- To ensure that the activity was carried out fairly;
- To shield young and vulnerable people from harm.

Of the proposals that survived the knotty period of horse-trading that typically precedes bills passing into law, the most eye-catching were:

- It permitted television advertising of sports betting, online casinos and poker. Previously only bingo, the football pools and the National Lottery had been allowed;
- It established the Gambling Commission as the new regulator for the industry, responsible for granting licences to operate and controlling problem gambling;
- It did away with the demand test that had stipulated gambling premises could only be placed where there was demonstrable demand for them.

But the Act is perhaps more notable for what it did not include than for what it did.

The omission that garnered the most attention at the time was the disappearance of the so-called 'supercasinos'. These were to be massive resort-style destinations purpose-built for gambling that could, it was hoped, boost city-centre economies and fuel tourism, breathing new life into some of Britain's dilapidated seaside towns, sprinkling some of the moneyed glitz of Las Vegas and

Atlantic City over Manchester and Blackpool. The Budd report had recommended a significant easing of curbs on casinos and the government embraced the recommendation wholeheartedly, ultimately to its own cost.

Of all the proposals contained in the bill, nothing captured the public and political imagination quite like supercasinos. The *Daily Mail*, for decades the deafening loudspeaker of the moralistic right in the UK, was dead against them. Its legendarily fearsome editor, Paul Dacre, was given to waging furious crusades that he would personally orchestrate, stalking the newsroom floor like a Tyrannosaurus rex with a sore head and flinging out expletives at anything or anyone that displeased him. The antagonist that displeased him most was Tony Blair and he gleefully took up his cudgels against what he saw – with his fundamentally puritanical instincts – as one of the Blair government's more horrifying inventions. Sermonising to more than a million loyal readers, the *Mail* waged a long-running Kill the Bill campaign on its front page, against a policy it warned might become a 'magnet for mafia gangs, drug dealers and prostitutes'.[20]

The late Tessa Jowell, the Blairite MP – Richard Caborn's superior in her role as secretary of state for culture, media and sport – bore ultimate responsibility for pioneering the Gambling Act, and was having none of it. 'There's a whiff of snobbery in some of the opposition to new casinos,' she told the *Sunday Telegraph* in 2004,[21] drawing on a theme that remains common in critics of gambling reform to this day – the idea that those who favour tighter regulation are elitists who find working-class pursuits distasteful. 'People who think they should remain the preserve of the rich; others who find them gaudy and in poor taste; others who don't want the big investment that will come from the United States. They are entitled to those views, but they are not entitled to force them on others,' said Jowell.

Conservative leader Michael Howard, for the most part a rather ineffectual adversary to Blair, had spotted the chance to score a rare victory over the government, capitalising on the media frenzy. During the 'wash-up' process, the frenetic last few days before each parliament is dissolved, his party demanded that the eight supercasinos be reduced to one, or they would oppose the bill altogether, putting it at risk of failing to pass in time for the end of that session of parliament. The opposition leader's gambit won the day.

In the end, not even one was built. When Gordon Brown succeeded Tony Blair in 2007, resolving one of the tensest psychodramas in British political history, he scrapped plans for the only supercasino that was still in the works, in Manchester. Like Blair, Brown's instincts were pro-business. But he was also the son of a Presbyterian minister, with little appetite for recreating the excesses of Las Vegas in British cities and seaside towns.

All the while, as supercasinos gobbled up countless column inches and hours of political wrangling, something else that would ultimately prove far more important was slipping quietly under the radar: the internet.

It is difficult to understand with hindsight how something so central to our lives today garnered hardly a mention in the public discourse around gambling in 2005.

'Everybody had been so obsessed with supercasinos that I don't think that they had necessarily thought about other aspects of the legislation, or indeed how the industry was going to go,' recalled Tracey Crouch, then chief of staff to shadow home secretary David Davis but who went on to play a starring role in the story of gambling legislation, as the sports minister under a future Conservative government. 'It was all about supercasinos, I don't remember any other conversations.'

Yet the internet had certainly formed a big part of the backdrop to the Gambling Act. Budd and his fellow committee members had recognised the importance of getting online regulation right.

The committee was sufficiently up to speed with technology to realise that it must pay heed to 'on-line' gambling, although that hyphen gives some indication of how fresh a concept the web still was in the minds of the British establishment. The review body sought to strike a balance that recognised that, while the genie could not be put back in the bottle, it could be nudged in the right direction.

For betting on sports, little should change. The internet, Budd reasoned, was just another way of laying a wager on an event. For online gaming, operators should be subject to rules mirroring those governing casinos that offered land-based versions of the table games and slot machines that were now widely available online.

But somehow the part of Budd's vision that involved subjecting online gambling to the same curbs as its real-life cousin never materialised. Instead, a government that would later be lambasted for its light-touch regulation of the banking system adopted a similar approach to digital wagering.

Dan Waugh, of gambling consultancy Regulus Partners, is one of the most well-informed and fair-minded commentators within the industry. Of the legislation governing online gambling, he writes that 'the contrast with land-based regulation is striking – all forms of gambling may be made available within a single site; there are no caps on licence issuance; betting on credit is permitted [at time of writing, it no longer is]; and traditional stake, prize and speed of play specifications do not apply.'[22]

Tom Watson, the former Labour MP who was, until recently, one of the most prominent advocates of gambling reform, recalled his own involvement in the passing of the Act, as a relatively inexperienced Labour whip convincing unruly backbenchers to support the bill: Speaking in June 2019, during a speech at the think tank Demos, he said: 'We attempted to update laws and the framework was right. But what it couldn't do was predict the explosion in creativity in the design of new digital products. I've described it as a piece of analogue legislation that was not weatherproofed for the digital age.'

That description, an analogue law in a digital age, has become common parlance when referring to the Act. So what went wrong? It seems a reasonable assumption that neither the Budd committee members, nor the government, had any inkling of how profoundly the internet would develop, nor how it would transform our lives so rapidly and profoundly. While some businesses were slow to harness new technology, those that did were able to roll out new types of casino games – and new ways to bet on sport – that had never been imagined.

Indeed, one of the fundamental flaws of the 2005 Gambling Act was unavoidable: bad timing. The first iPhone was not released until 2007, the same year the Act came into force. The government had attempted to regulate internet gambling without knowing that, within the space of a few years, access to an online casino would be in every pocket. Lawmakers did not, or could not, envisage how good the industry would be, once unleashed, at harnessing this new-found power to drum up business. Nor did they give themselves an insurance policy to prepare for the unknown.

As I've mentioned before, online operators would not be required to hold a British gambling licence until 2014, meaning that vast swathes of the industry were developing, marketing and selling new products out of the sight of a British regulator. This ran contrary to what Budd had suggested. He'd reckoned that it would make sense to require an online operator to have a domestic presence in order to be licensed, both in terms of the location of its servers and as a registered company. Somewhere between the government largely accepting his report and the Act passing into law, this proposal had vanished.

The ever-changing tax regime only made matters worse. In 2001

Brown had attempted to bring firms back onshore, with some success, by tweaking the tax regime. In 2007 he altered it again, this time introducing a 15% flat tax on the income of online gambling companies regulated by the Gambling Commission. The solution, for gambling firms, was not to be regulated by the Commission but to move overseas, or, if they were there already, to stay offshore, in locations that operators with an online business had already learned to call home in the days when it wasn't legal for them to operate in their domestic market. Now, these firms were allowed to take bets in the UK, as long as they were based in a so-called 'white-listed' jurisdiction, including the likes of Malta and Gibraltar. If customers had a grievance over responsible-gambling measures or something as simple as whether a bet should pay out, they had to go not to the UK Gambling Commission but to an overseas regulator in a much smaller country, where the betting industry wielded enormous clout. One of the few not to do this was bet365, which stuck to its roots in Stoke.

As we have already seen, offshoring deprived the Treasury of tax but it also created a physical distance that greatly increased the temptation to push the boundaries of legislation. If no UK licence was required – and could not therefore be lost – what incentive was there for companies based overseas to go the extra mile to protect customers?

British operators rode two horses, owning land-based bookmaking networks in the UK and online divisions situated offshore. They grew rapidly, fuelled by technological development, aggressive advertising and the benefits of operating from a base overseas. Many of the most shocking cases of gambling companies failing to protect vulnerable people in recent years, stories that I'll document in the coming chapters, have involved phenomena that stem from that potent combination.

Take, for instance, the so-called VIP schemes, a system of perks and rewards offered to people who lose money, often orchestrated via a personal VIP manager tasked with befriending the customer and keeping them happy. Consider also direct marketing, the use of emails and text messages to nudge gamblers into cutting short any period during which they don't bet. Both rely on immediacy of communication, the ability to bet rapidly online and a lack of interventionist regulation.

Given that very few people in the public arena predicted these trends, there was no supercasino-style newspaper campaign against them and no political ambition to prepare for them. No curbs were placed on aggressive online salesmanship, and as a result it flourished pretty much unfettered until the present day, something I shall examine in greater depth later in Chapter 4.

There is another respect in which the Gambling Act failed almost entirely. It did very little to erect any effective ongoing mechanism to measure what impact gambling was already having, nor what the result of a more liberal regime would be. To this day, we understand relatively little about how much harm gambling is doing in wider society, whether the problem is getting worse or better and how we might go about tackling it. Anecdotal evidence tells us that many people suffer significant harm as a result of gambling and that, all too often, the firms that take their money do far too little to protect consumers. Regular NHS surveys give us a limited insight into which products are associated with higher levels of addiction. Beyond that we are – to some extent – flying blind.

Budd and his fellow review body members had identified the knowledge gap early on. In their report they admitted being 'struck by how little is known about either normal or problem gambling'. Much greater research into addiction was a must, they said, as well as ongoing work to assess the effect that any new regulation was having on problem gambling. The report went on to recommend that the NHS receive increased funding to tackle problem gambling, with gambling addiction properly recognised as a health issue.

Ideally, research would be funded by a statutory levy of at least £3 million a year. The report noted that the last major government-backed review of gambling, the Rothschild Commission of 1978, had also identified the need for much more research, but that this had not taken place.[23]

Most of Budd's recommendations in this area had disappeared into the ether by the time the Act was finalised. While regular surveys have been conducted into the prevalence of problem gambling, very little has been done to measure the effect that unfettered marketing or technological innovation have had on gamblers' mental health or addiction.

The regular NHS surveys tell us what percentage of the British population are problem gamblers but they are deeply flawed, as we shall examine in Chapter 6. We have no reliable means of gauging the harm being done to society by gambling. We know that certain products have higher rates of addiction but precious little about why, beyond what occurs to us as common sense, or what has been claimed in studies whose reliability is often questionable. It is only in recent years that any robust studies have emerged about the link between problem gambling and suicide, for instance. We have effectively been taking stabs in the dark for more than a decade.

## THE DIE IS CAST

When the Gambling Act eventually came into force in 2007, it was to relatively little fanfare. But there were already major question marks over whether the government had got it right.

The Conservatives' spokesman on gambling, Tobias Ellwood, questioned whether the Act was capable of managing new variants, such as internet gambling and games that could be sent through the airwaves to British children's mobile phones by overseas operators. 'Many online gambling companies will be advertising on our

TVs, probably from 9 p.m. tonight, but will already have moved to Gibraltar,' he told BBC Radio 4's *Today* programme.

Looking back with the benefit of hindsight, Matthew Hill, regulatory risk and analysis director at the Gambling Commission between 2008 and 2015, described as 'monumental hubris' the idea that the 2005 Act would lead to an era of agile response to regulatory challenge: 'There was this notion that the legislation had been in some way future-proofed – yet the system started creaking pretty much from the start.'[24]

Or, as Peter Collins put it to me: 'Government, as it usually does, failed to control the whole business of regulation, which is now fantastically expensive and delivers very little.'

Meanwhile, the industry developed at a rate of knots, developing new revenue-boosting products. Notable innovations include betting exchanges such as Betfair, which allowed punters to bet in new ways, betting against one another in a manner that mimics the stock market, buying some outcomes (backing them) and selling others (known as laying). Another was in-play sports betting, pioneered by bet365, which allowed rapid-fire wagers on events trivial to the game itself, such as the number of throw-ins during a football match. These developments were underpinned by the wildfire spread of the internet and the invention of the smartphone as a conduit allowing gambling at any location, at any time.

The UK had made probably the most ambitious attempt to formalise the law around gambling anywhere in the world – and this was the brave new world that had been dreamed into reality.

So what happened next?

There are two answers to that question.

The first is that Britain fulfilled Tessa Jowell's ambition, becoming, in her words, a 'world leader in the field of online gambling'. The 2005 Gambling Act established a thriving, regulated industry that sat at the heart of the leisure sector, providing – for the most part – legitimate and harmless enjoyment to millions of people. The industry contributed billions of pounds in tax revenue, sustained employment for hundreds of thousands of people and spurred both creative and technological innovation.

This answer isn't entirely wrong but it is incomplete, for, as we shall see, the starting gun had been fired on a fiercely competitive race for space, in an increasingly lucrative market. As firms battled for a slice of the British gambling spend, they unleashed a tidal wave of aggressive advertising and marketing that brought gambling into every living room and put a casino in every pocket.

Some members of the industry lost sight of their roots and lost interest in the products they were selling, motivated instead by whatever proved profitable. This created a massive and unavoidable incentive to push the boundaries of decency ever further in the pursuit of growth and market share.

Stewart Kenny, the co-founder and former chairman of Irish bookmaker Paddy Power, believes that the industry he started out in and the one that exists now are 'chalk and cheese'. 'I was pretty relaxed about the idea of my kids opening an online betting account eighteen or twenty years ago,' he told me. 'But now I wouldn't be so keen for my grandchildren to open an account when they reach eighteen and be bombarded with enticements to gamble on the online casino and the online slot machines. I unfortunately am being wise after the event. As a long-standing board director, I must take responsibility for some of these problems.'

While some veterans such as Kenny recognised that parts of the industry had got out of control, any objections they raised fell on deaf ears, as companies did what companies do, chasing profit to line the pockets of shareholders and a handful of industry barons who became fabulously wealthy.

At the other end of the chain, vulnerable people were driven down the thorny path of addiction. Let down by lax government regulation, those victims – and their families – were left with woefully inadequate resources to protect themselves from harm and pick up the pieces. It was a state of affairs that signed the death warrants of dozens, if not hundreds, who saw no other way out but suicide.

When I say that gambling conquered Britain, that's what I mean.

# 2. ADVERTISING: HOOK, LINE AND SINKER

Have a bang on that!
RAY WINSTONE, BET365 ADVERTS

Ninety-nine per cent of our customers will lose.
KENNY ALEXANDER, CEO OF GVC
(TO A HOUSE OF LORDS SELECT COMMITTEE, 2020)

For the best part of the last decade, it's been more or less impossible to watch a televised football match without the tuberous, disembodied head of Ray Winstone looming out of the ether at you.

'Bet in-play now,' he urges in his trademark cockney burr, while an animated version of bet365's logo bounces around in the background. One of the UK's most celebrated actors, Winstone got his big break in the gritty 1979 film *Scum*, playing a troubled young man who draws on his natural flair for brutality in order to dominate rival inmates at one of Britain's 'borstal' children's detention centres. Raised on a council estate in Enfield, North London, Winstone won the role thanks in part to a swaggering physical confidence honed during a successful stint as an amateur boxer. His affable, roguish schtick appeals in particular to young men, thanks to convincing cinematic portrayals of various jocular but physically imposing characters. The same qualities that made him so suited for such roles also make him an ideal choice to front a gambling campaign: self-assured, cool and in control. It's a persona that has turned him into the face of gambling ads in Britain. As one bet365 employee told an undercover *Daily Mail* reporter in 2019: 'You can't watch TV any more without bet365 popping up everywhere.'[1] Winstone owes his televisual ubiquity – not to mention the healthy fees that come with it – to the liberalisation of gambling laws outlined in the previous chapter.

Until 2007, the only gambling adverts allowed on television were for the National Lottery or bingo, which were granted exceptions to the prohibition covering the rest of the industry. The Act that came into force that year abolished these restrictions, amid a broader cultural shift towards permitting the industry to market itself to potential consumers rather than having to wait for them to show up. The change also applied in other areas, including licensing. Previously, bricks-and-mortar betting premises, such as casinos or bookmakers, were only allowed to open in locations where they could prove there was unmet demand for their services. Now they were allowed to set up shop wherever they liked, seeking out custom rather than waiting for it to come to them.

Just so with advertising. Where once a bookmaker or online casino relied primarily on word of mouth or repeat custom, it could now tout for business on the small screen. The result was an explosion of gambling adverts on broadcast television, at that time still the key conduit for brands to reach customers' eyeballs and, by extension, their wallets. As one senior advertising executive told me: 'It was just the culmination of TV channels, executives and the government being really greedy, just wanting their share of the gambling pound.' A brave new world of possibility opened up at the feet of the gambling companies, offering them the chance to jockey for airtime with established mainstream brands selling toothpaste, holidays and chocolate bars. It was an opportunity they grabbed with both hands.

A report by the UK broadcasting regulator Ofcom, published in 2013,[2] charts a seismic shift that has catapulted gambling into the consciousness of nearly everyone in the UK. In the six years after the Gambling Act took effect, the number of television advertising spots, not just for gambling but for products of any kind, doubled. Over the same period, the growth in gambling ads – coming from a standing start, of course – outstripped the broader market by a country mile.

During 2005, there were just 90,000 television 'spots' promoting some form of gambling. According to Ofcom, by 2011 that figure had increased more than tenfold to 955,000, going on to reach 1.4 million just a year later. Stripping out lotteries, which were already permitted to advertise before deregulation, the volume of gambling ads increased by a factor of about thirty-seven. The outcome was that gambling secured itself huge acreage on the advertising landscape. The industry had claimed slightly more than 4% of all commercial airtime by 2013.

For the creative agencies in the advertising world, the arrival of these entrants to the marketplace meant a new breed of client with money to spend. I spoke to Matt Edwards, an advertising guru who spent fourteen years with London-based group Engine, eight of them as chief executive of its ad agency WCRS. He was the architect of some of the industry's most successful campaigns. If you remember the Betfair table-tennis-playing octopus that featured during the company's 2014 World Cup campaign, that was one of his. Horses driving rally cars to promote the Cheltenham Festival? His too.

Edwards likens the emergence of gambling advertising to some of the other giant shifts in his industry, such as the dot-com boom or the emergence of mobile phone companies. 'We didn't set up a special betting division or anything but we definitely noticed the regulations being lifted,' he tells me. 'Agencies are pretty used to seeing these opportunities and getting their heads around it.' But gambling is unusual, says Edwards, in that most customers have accounts with multiple companies: 'Imagine if you were a whisky brand and not only are you trying to get people to buy your whisky but you have to get them to put it alongside five other brands in the cabinet and then drink yours more often. It's an unusual challenge.'

That constant jostling against competitors fuelled a certain culture that was reflected in the way gambling firms approached advertising, initially at least. 'It tended to attract quite unsophisticated market-eers, and the culture, for a lot of businesses in the early days, was incredibly laddish,' recalls Edwards. 'The clients would use phrases like "Let's get the greens in the jeans", meaning stuffing your pockets with pound notes. There was a lot of short-termism, very different to working with a Unilever, or a Coca-Cola, who are trying to build long-term equity within the brand. The problem is that every time they [gambling firms] do anything, it's just a land grab for the latest new customers.'

This combination of deep-rooted cultural machismo with the need for quick customer acquisition – 'greens in the jeans' – has sometimes resulted in some of the industry's edgier efforts falling foul of strict advertising rules.

For example, the 'Ladbrokes Life' campaign – launched, like Betfair's octopus, during the World Cup year of 2014 – featured a group of five male friends with nicknames tailored to their personal betting characteristics, such as The Gut-Truster, The Professor and The Believer. Set to a thumping soundtrack, it bore all the hallmarks of a Guy Ritchie film, with the same crudely drawn stereotype char-acters designed to help viewers identify with one or more of their on-screen counterparts.

The campaign survived the hundred-odd complaints sent to the

Advertising Standards Authority, although two posters associated with it – one of them captioned 'Once is lucky – twice is talent' – were banned.[3] Other efforts were deemed to have overstepped the mark entirely. Paddy Power's adverts have typically relied on near-the-knuckle humour. One from 2019, featuring Rhodri Giggs, the brother of footballer Ryan, riffed on the concept of loyalty, a nod to the tabloid scandal that ensued over the former Manchester United star's affair with his sister-in-law, Rhodri's wife. The spot featured the wronged brother consoling himself with Champagne and a sports car, imagery the ASA felt linked gambling to financial reward.[4] Another commercial had to be pulled in 2017 because it showed a security guard apparently placing bets while at work, another no-no in the advertising code.[5]

Such regulatory knuckle-raps weren't necessarily the accidental result of misguided marketing but rather of increasingly sophisticated strategies, as gambling firms learned more about advertising. Ads like these garnered nearly as much attention by being banned as they did by appearing on the airwaves in the first place. This air of devil-may-care flirtation with transgression of the rules helped fuel a perception of gambling as the preserve of life's daring risk-takers, the sort of chancers you might find in that Ladbrokes Life gang. Primarily targeted at men, they appealed directly to viewers' appetite for risk and placed it within a social context, making gambling just another part of friendship. This was a world away from the relatively recent image of the bookies behind the beaded curtain.

There have been more cautious strategies too, albeit equally smart in terms of their targeting. Some firms have taken the same approach you might expect from household products, by roping in popular primetime TV celebrities. Online casino firm 32Red spent big in 2017, bringing in the best-known TV presenting duo in Britain, Ant and Dec, to flog an online slot machine game linked to the pair's *Saturday Night Takeaway* show. It's an approach that brings gambling into the mainstream in a different way, by making it a normal feature not just of young men's social occasions but of family life too.

In recent years, as competition for male punters has become fiercer, firms have increasingly turned to women, who are under-represented in the gambling world, to build their customer base. The late and much-loved actor Barbara Windsor, known for her role in the bawdy *Carry On* film franchise – and later the soap opera *EastEnders* – racked up ten years as the 'Queen of Bingo' for the Jackpotjoy brand. The same company sponsors daytime TV show *Loose Women*, which has been known to pull in audiences of more than a million. Pink Casino's commercials declare the company as being for 'ladies who like to have fun', which they can do by playing online slot machine games such as Cleopatra and Pixies of the Forest.

Gambling firms may have started out as relatively unsophisticated advertisers but they've proved to be fast learners, understanding how to promote themselves with as much precision as more seasoned brands. The most obvious means of doing so has been to latch on to the increasingly global popularity of football. Globalisation, coupled with an increase in the number of games being broadcast by satellite broadcaster Sky (and, later, other channels), has turned football into fertile ground. It's become impossible to look at the industry's advertising strategy without seeing how deeply enmeshed it has become with the game.

During the 2018 World Cup, I worked with my brilliant colleagues Pamela Duncan and Rachel Obordo, data journalists who specialise in crunching large volumes of information to unearth stories. Between them they analysed the betting adverts broadcast during the championship on ITV, the only commercial broadcaster with the rights to show the matches. What we found was that, over the course of the World Cup, viewers were exposed to betting adverts for nearly ninety minutes, almost like an extra match tacked on to the tournament.[6] From the beginning of the contest, right through to England's heartbreaking semi-final loss to Croatia, which was watched by about 30 million people, ITV carried more than eight and a half hours of advertisements, of which just under an hour and a half were advertising betting. That is equivalent to 17% of World Cup ad breaks, or roughly one minute in every six. Bookmakers and online casino companies enjoyed one and a half times as much screen time as alcohol firms and almost four times that of fast-food outlets.

Tom Watson, then the deputy leader of the opposition Labour party, described the findings as 'one of the only downsides to this brilliant World Cup'. He would later go on to work as a consultant for Paddy Power after leaving politics, a subject we'll return to. But back then, as he built his political career, he was tapping in to a growing level of concern among the wider public about the number of gambling ads now on television.

Perhaps surprisingly, just a month after the World Cup drew to a close, many figures in the industry seemed to agree with Watson's concerns. 'Some sort of change is needed,' admitted Philip Bowcock, chief executive of William Hill. 'But that has to be led by government. It's incumbent on them to step up to the plate and have a serious discussion about it.'

That same week, despite its characteristically punchy TV advertising strategy, the now-merged gambling behemoth Paddy Power Betfair had declared itself 'supportive of further regulation . . . to reduce the volume of pre-watershed TV advertising to protect young children'.[7] The firm's chief executive, Peter Jackson, said he was open to tougher limits on the volume of ads but warned that it was 'difficult for the industry to do this on its own'. 'Even if progressive operators agree to restrict ads, unless there's legislation passed, less responsible operators step in and continue advertising,' he said. It was a reasonable position. Why should Paddy Power pull its adverts from the television, only to see rival firms swoop in to grab its customers? Yet according to people involved in discussions at the highest level of the industry, there was a growing recognition that something had to be done.

As chief executive of the Remote Gambling Association, the trade body for online operators, Clive Hawkswood watched the internal industry debate unfold. 'The concern was always: "If we take our ads down, someone else will take the slot. There won't be a benefit and we'll suffer."' In other words, many gambling firms advertised simply because everyone else was doing it and they couldn't afford to be left out. 'But it just didn't feel right,' he went on. 'Viewers were sick of the sound of Ray Winstone or whoever it might be and a lot of people in the industry felt the same way. They've got families, the same concerns as everyone else, and they didn't like sitting there watching the football with their kids and seeing it.'

For the firms supporting change, the job was to secure broad-based industry support through shuttle diplomacy, running back and forth between executives who supported the ban and those who did not – often the small, fast-growing firms who needed to advertise to build brand awareness. The biggest obstacle was the wrath of TV broadcasters faced with the loss of important advertising revenue.

'Sky went apeshit,' recalled another senior industry figure who witnessed some of the wrangling. But eventually even the broadcasters saw the potential long-term upside in defusing growing public distaste for the advertising frenzy. In late 2018 the Big Five gambling firms – bet365, GVC, William Hill, Paddy Power Betfair and Sky Bet – agreed to introduce the so-called 'whistle-to-whistle' ban on advertising.[8] Previously, they had been guided by a voluntary code that meant no advertising before 9 p.m., unless attached to live sports. This had been agreed shortly after the Gambling Act and, as the volume of live sport increased, meant practically unfettered access to the airwaves, particularly on sport-heavy weekends. The new code dictated that, from five minutes before a sports event started until five minutes after it finished, when viewing numbers were at their highest, the commercials would not air at all. The following summer's Ashes cricket series became the first major sporting event to be subject to the ban. Suddenly, if you wanted to find Ray Winstone's head, you had to go looking for it.

It would be churlish to suggest that there was no element of altruism at the heart of the measure. But the whistle-to-whistle ban has also been a PR success and, to the cynical mind, the apparent sacrifice bears some of the hallmarks of self-interest.

Chess players sometimes deploy a sacrificial gambit, deliberately allowing their opponent to take a piece and claim an apparent victory, when in fact the player is happy to lose the piece because it helps them develop a stronger strategic position in the long term. Similarly, lawyers in the midst of long and complex negotiations will sometimes give the false impression that a particular point is extremely important to them, only to yield on it further down the line. Their opposite number thinks a concession has been made and becomes more pliable. This has been called the 'high perceived value, low-cost concession' strategy.

The voluntary advertising ban was an eye-catching display of good faith that won widespread praise. Here was an industry apparently willing to listen to its critics and forfeit a prized freedom for the greater good. But exactly what were they giving up and why?

Any notion that the industry was playing the long game here relies on the idea that the loss of TV advertising during live sports is, in fact, a low-cost concession. That might seem, on the face of it, unlikely. Bookmakers would surely not have been spending money on prime commercial airtime unless such spots were a valuable tool in their marketing armoury.

In reality, the major gambling companies – the ones who actually pioneered the voluntary ban – had very little to lose. The likes of William Hill, Ladbrokes and even relative newcomer bet365 had established recognisable brand names. In the case of the former two and Paddy Power, they also had a high-street presence serving as a constant reminder to the general public of their existence. TV advertising was hugely costly and the gains were limited. As one seasoned gambling advertising executive told me: 'I believe this decision was probably made on commercial grounds, nothing to do with responsibility. They thought "We're all fishing in the same pond, we should stop doing it. If we all stop then no one's losing out." If you were made boss of Ladbrokes Coral and you're paid £40 million a year, you'd think the best way for us to cut our budgets is for everyone to stop spending in that space. You're talking about marketing budgets of tens of millions.'

Not only could major gambling companies reduce outgoings, they could also hamstring some of their up-and-coming challengers too. Less established so-called 'tier two' gambling firms (the likes of 32Red and 888 Casino) had been able to use TV exposure to play catch-up with legacy brands such as William Hill and Ladbrokes. Now they could not do so without being portrayed as irresponsible outliers breaching the voluntary whistle-to-whistle ban.

It is also debatable how much commercial airtime the industry really forfeited. Representatives of the Betting and Gaming Council have repeatedly made the claim that the ban resulted in a 97% reduction in children seeing gambling ads during live sports broadcasts.[9] That simply isn't the case. It may be true for the period beginning and ending five minutes either side of the game. That has resulted in a significant decrease during major tournaments such as the Euro 2020 championship. But outside the whistle-to-whistle period it's a free-for-all. Betting firms are still effectively promoting gambling products to any child who watches the build-up to a game, the post-match analysis, or any coverage after 9 p.m.

Not only that, but the industry has found ways to make up for lost ground.

The 2019–20 football season saw, for the first time, the introduction of a new, slightly later kick-off time for some games, at 8.15. It seemed an odd time to choose but it made perfect sense for broadcasters and their gambling advertisers, since the whistle-to-whistle ban only applied to any portion of a game shown before 9 p.m. An 8 p.m. kick-off meant that the half-time commercial break would arrive shortly after 8.45, within the period of the ban. Delaying kick-offs by a quarter of an hour allowed broadcasters to claw back some of their forfeited revenue by shunting that half-time ad break to the post-watershed period. For those games, some of that gambling money could be reclaimed.

But that wasn't the only way of limiting the damage. Later in this chapter I'll outline how some tools are more powerful for advertisers than televisions, largely because of the ability the internet affords them to target people individually, rather than relying on the scattergun approach of paying big money to advertise to lots of people at once and never knowing if they ignore you.

TV isn't always such a blunt instrument, though. Sky, which shows more televised sport than any other broadcaster in the UK, uses technology called AdSmart. It's a clever bit of kit that allows advertisers to influence the commercials you see in your home, targeting individual households based on what they're likely to be interested in. The bespoke combination of ads is downloaded to your Sky box and plays during commercial breaks. You and your neighbour might both be watching the game but you're seeing gambling ads and she's seeing package holidays. But how does Sky know what commercials will stop you from changing the channel? The answer lies in the company's privacy policy, which most people never bother reading.

The broadcaster learns about you by purchasing information from 'data brokers who supply us with contact information and modelled (i.e. predicted) household profile information such as affluence and household composition'.

It buys this data, it says, from credit rating agencies such as Experian. A video posted by Sky in 2017 said that Experian alone gave the company access to 21 billion bits of info about the UK population, more than 450 'data points' per household. It also buys data from specialist data firms including Dunnhumby, CACI, TwentyCi, TransUnion, Mastercard, Emma's Diary and Game.

And it works. In a 2017 'introduction to AdSmart' video posted on YouTube, a Sky executive explains that the 'tuneaway' rate – the number of people who turn over when the ads come on – fell by half where AdSmart was used. This proved, he said, that 'our audience is subconsciously giving their emotional consent to be advertised to'.

In December 2018, just after the whistle-to-whistle ban that had sent Sky 'apeshit' came into effect, Sky CEO Stephen van Rooyen explained that it was also possible for customers to withdraw that emotional consent should they choose to. He wrote an opinion piece for *The Times* newspaper,[10] explaining (quite reasonably) that criticism of gambling ads on television alone was unfair, because the vast majority of gambling ads were online. True enough. Sky was so passionate about keeping vulnerable people safe from a surfeit of gambling advertising that it was introducing a tool that would allow people to block gambling ads on their TVs. It was a laudable voluntary measure that van Rooyen described as 'the right thing to do'. The option would be available to customers from June 2020, he promised.

Helen Undy, director of the Money and Mental Health Policy Institute, praised Sky's decision, saying analysis from the institute had highlighted that those who are vulnerable to problem gambling are more likely to be influenced by its advertisement.

Except it never happened. With the whistle-to-whistle ban already crimping revenues from gambling advertisers, Sky quietly ditched the plan. In a chat forum on Sky's online help page, an employee explained to customers who enquired that the company had 'decided not to pursue the measures originally outlined'. The reason, I am reliably told, is that Sky felt the gambling industry had done enough, with the whistle-to-whistle ban, to regulate itself.

As far as I'm aware, Sky never announced its change of heart. In fact, a page on the Sky website that duplicated van Rooyen's article for *The Times* was deleted, although it has resurfaced since I asked Sky where it went.

But there is another, more important reason why the whistle-to-whistle ban was more PR win than genuine sacrifice. As van Rooyen pointed out in his defence of broadcasters, the reality is that TV ads are fast becoming less powerful and less relevant, a hangover from a time when the sole route into the national consciousness was via a single, immobile screen in the living room.

## THE INTERNET

By 2016 the amount of money wagered online had overtaken the value of bets placed in person, at casinos, bingo halls and bookmakers.[11] At last count, web-based play was soaring ahead, raking in £5.2 billion from punters compared to £4.3 billion at bricks-and-mortar venues. Meanwhile, the audiences and customers of the future are increasingly shunning television in favour of online entertainment. In 2017 children and teenagers watched one-third less television than they had in 2010.[12]

If most wagers are made via the internet, and future gamblers are increasingly spending their time online too, it makes perfect sense to throw your marketing dollars in that direction. Ofcom hasn't repeated its survey of advertising volumes since 2013 but there is some more recent data that quantifies this mass migration. A study by the consultancy Regulus Partners, on behalf of the UK's leading gambling charity, GambleAware, found that betting companies increased their marketing spend by 56% to £1.5 billion between 2014 and 2018.[13] The more granular detail reveals that the landscape had altered significantly by then: 80p of every pound that the industry spent on advertising was devoted not to those eye-catching TV spots that grabbed the headlines but rather to the internet. Television accounted for £234 million of the industry's outlay, having grown by 15% in three years. Web-based advertising accounted for more than treble that figure, at £747 million, having grown at a faster rate of 23%. Social media ads made up £149 million and were the fastest-growing segment of all, up by 53%. Just over £300 million was spent on affiliates: third-party websites or individuals who promote gambling companies in exchange for a commission when punters open an account or place a bet.

We'll explore some of these categories in greater depth, but it's worth considering how online marketing is something of a Wild West when compared to television. Both television and the internet are, in the UK, subject to separate codes, each regulated by the Advertising Standards Authority. Gambling companies have volunteered for tighter restrictions on television, which attracts the glare of public scrutiny from a population with a median age of forty that still thinks of TV as the main media conduit.

But the companies have been less forthcoming regarding the internet.

The whistle-to-whistle sports ban covers TV ads but no such measures apply online, where the vast majority of advertising spend goes. Similarly, a voluntary moratorium on TV and radio ads during the first Covid-19 lockdown of spring 2020 – in apparent recognition that lockdowns made potential addicts more vulnerable – was not extended to online.[14] Via online channels, casino operators continued to tout for the custom of people who were stuck at home and bored, restricted to the confines of four walls.

Not only that, but they continued to deploy a sales technique that has largely gone unnoticed in the debate around gambling advertising but which has potentially dangerous consequences: cross-selling. Operators have much to gain from directing customers from one product to another. Cross-selling, the act of convincing a buyer of one of your products to purchase something else, is a no-brainer.

Paddy Power founder Stewart Kenny explained to me how it works. 'Say a young person opens a betting account to have a bet on their favourite soccer team,' he told me. 'Within days they are being bombarded with ads for the casino and inducements to bet on the online slot machines, which are highly addictive.' He has consistently argued for an end to the practice. 'It isn't safe territory for young people,' he told me.

I've heard it said that gambling firms prefer you to play casino games and slots because people can win at horse racing or football but not, in the long-run, at gaming. That's only half the truth. Sure, you *can* win by betting on sport but vanishingly few people actually do. Not only is the house's edge built into the odds but if you show any real talent for picking winners, the amount you're allowed to bet will be dialled down, via a practice known as "stake factoring". Indeed, sports betting is typically a higher-margin business for the operators.

But Kenny's reference to addictive casino products is the salient point here. Casino games and virtual slots are associated with significantly higher rates of addiction than sports betting. Gambling firms will say that they don't want to profit from addicts – and in many cases this may be true. But what they see on the screen when the money starts flowing in isn't necessarily addiction. It's a customer who plays for longer and plays more regularly, at any time of the day or night, not just when the football is on. Casino and slots are a guaranteed stream of revenue and there's nothing that gets company finance executives salivating more than predictable income.

Yet online still does not attract nearly as much scrutiny as TV, despite being far tougher to police. As we shall see, the way the industry has marketed itself online does not so much test the limits of socially responsible behaviour as ignore them completely. This is partly due to the dizzying breadth of the online experience. The internet is a phenomenon so vast and varied as to be almost pointless as a category. It is a world in its own right, capturing a host of very different activities, from bog-standard websites to social media, video streaming, apps and podcasts. Nobody, not even the ASA, can hope to keep an eye on all of it. The sheer diversity of commercial outlets presents endless opportunity, not just for efficient marketing but for some of the most shameful behaviour seen in the modern gambling industry.

## SOCIAL MEDIA

The deregulation of gambling advertising that began in 2007 happened almost in tandem with the rise of the smartphone and social media. Facebook had launched in 2004, followed by Twitter in 2006. The iPhone hit the market in 2007 and changed the way we consume media irrevocably. The legislation that liberalised gambling in the UK was written before any of those inventions – and they turned the advertising world on its head. For advertisers, social media is like a precision-guided missile compared to the blunderbuss of television.

Bill Esdaile understands the gambling marketing landscape better than most. His marketing and communications agency, Square in the Air, boasts a client roster from across the sector. Bill is also a keen gambler and the horse-racing editor of London free paper *City A.M.* 'It [social media] is just another platform on which to recruit a younger, fresher audience,' he said. 'If you look at things like Twitter, betting firms have become more and more vocal on social media because it's a relatively cheap, active way [to advertise]. It's cost-effective, it's good reach and the client opts in to it, you choose who you want to follow. You don't choose what ads you want to watch on TV.'

Of course, you can buy TV airtime you think is likely to be popular with your potential customers, the most obvious example being bookmakers attaching promotions to football. As we've seen, some broadcasters are able to use tools such as AdSmart to narrow down the field that advertisers are trying to reach. But the likes of Facebook, YouTube and Twitter are able to provide, with crystal clarity, an insight into the interests and proclivities of their users. Probably the most notable example of this is the scandal generated by the company Cambridge Analytica, which, for a brief period, became the one-stop shop for all of your electioneering needs. It worked on Donald Trump's bid for the US presidency as well as on the Brexit campaign, harvesting data from Facebook users to improve the targeting of political campaign adverts.[15]

How do you harness this sort of power if you're a gambling company? Well, let's say I've set up my own online casino, Rob's Roulette. One of my first moves would be to target millions of people on social media by using the data that those platforms have about their members to make sure I'm not wasting my time. On Facebook, I would use the social network's Ad Manager tool. Ad Manager offers me the opportunity to define the target audience for Rob's Roulette using keywords. One of the stock phrases I'd have the option to choose is 'high-stakes gambling'. Facebook knows who is interested in betting large sums, and now so do I. On Twitter I could do much the same. I'd simply tell its advertising tools that I'm looking for people who follow the accounts of casinos, slot machine games or bookmakers. I can even pay for my account to appear in Twitter's suggestions of 'Who to follow', alongside influencer celebrities and media blowhards.

When those adverts reach their target, they don't always simply flash up in front of the user in the hope that they'll pay attention. Nowadays adverts can use more sophisticated calls to action that don't even look like betting adverts at first. For instance, a tweet from the Sky Sports Premier League account in December, on the eve of the fierce North London derby between Tottenham and Arsenal, contained a video of highlights from a previous high-scoring game between the two. Anyone who clicked on it wanting to relive some of those thrills and spills from yesteryear would have been taken to a page on bet365 with live betting odds for that day's game. Television doesn't offer anything close to that level of precision targeting, nor the ability to trigger an immediate spend. None of this has proven particularly controversial to date, perhaps because social media advertising is not particularly well under-stood by those of an age to be influential in politics or the upper echelons of the media.

But it is strange that, in a world where social media platforms have been singled out for criticism for the way they influence us, more hasn't been made of what they could be doing to protect those they sell to. In March 2020, polling firm Ipsos MORI published the results of in-depth analysis of Twitter by multiple teams of univers-ity researchers and the think tank Demos.[16] They had sifted through 888,745 tweets sent from 417 gambling-related accounts over a nine-month period, analysing details of the 825,000 followers of these accounts and 1.6 million tweets that mentioned one of the betting-themed Twitter accounts by name.

What they found was that children were still more likely to see gambling content on television – but that they were significantly more likely to engage actively with it on social media. Indeed, they found clear evidence of children doing so with concerning regu-larity. Approximately 41,000 UK followers of gambling accounts were likely to be under sixteen, while 6% of followers of 'traditional' gambling accounts were found to be children, a proportion that increased to 17% when looking specifically at accounts related to eSports – competitive video gaming. The researchers went so far as to create eleven 'avatars', fake internet user profiles with identities such as 'problem gambler' or 'child under 13', based on browsing history.

Gambling advertising was smartly targeted when it came to making money but less so when it came to protecting children. An avatar simulating someone aged between eighteen and twenty-four who liked to gamble was shown by far the most adverts – 692 over the course of a year. Most came from Gala Bingo, which appeared particularly keen to reach more people in that category, as none of the other avatars saw adverts from Gala Bingo at all.

The technology was not quite so effective at screening out the vulnerable. The avatar that saw the second-largest number of adverts was 'child under 13', at 289. The 'adult with a gambling problem' avatar was third, with 235. The report said that there was 'no evidence' that advertisers had taken significant steps to screen out children and gambling addicts, for instance by analysing their browsing history. Researchers also said there was 'little evidence' of responsible-gambling messages being promoted online, particularly on Twitter. Of the tweets analysed, fewer than one in ten was accompanied by any message about the potential pitfalls of gambling.

For this study, researchers had also interviewed young people and problem gamblers about their exposure to adverts, both online and on television. One person, in the sixteen and seventeen age bracket, told researchers: 'You are always going to know the Ladbrokes. It's like McDonald's, it is always there.' The research also shed light on the way that social media allows for precise targeting of specific audiences. It is a fairly well-known fact by now that an internet user's browsing history affects the ads they see. The more gambling websites you use, the more gambling you will see. It's called personalised advertising, as opposed to contextual advertising, which is based on the content to which it is attached (such as a sports car ad during a Formula One race). One problem gambler interviewed for the study put it like this: 'Well, with Facebook and Twitter, when I was opening accounts and had accounts, I was just flooded by it [gambling ads]. If I'd go on my Twitter page and my Facebook page, there'd be a new offer to open an account with a new company, so that'd be constant.'

Another interviewee, a seventeen-year-old, explained how he had become interested in gambling thanks to a William Hill advert that appealed to his fascination with the dragon-heavy TV series *Game of Thrones*. The advert offered the chance to bet on the central question at the heart of the show – who would end up ruling the fictional kingdom of Westeros. 'I was in bed scrolling through Facebook and saw this ad. It appeals [because I like] *Game of Thrones* and provides an interesting take on gambling I've never seen before – betting on the outcome of a TV show,' said the child. 'I also like how unique it is and how interested I am in this particular bet since it's predicting something I'm interested in. The odds advertised could be better. Also what is being betted on could be a bit ambiguous depending on how the show ends when you consider how *Game of Thrones* might end but I will consider maybe putting down a small bet, just for fun. I almost never bet so this is pretty impressive.'

The report pointed to the lack of any conclusive study to show that such exposure to advertising leads children and young people to gamble more. But its authors were confident enough to express a belief that 'there is a clear link between gambling advertising and the attitudes, current and likely future behaviours of children, young people and vulnerable adults.'

Yet neither Twitter nor Facebook are where it's really at among younger people. Far more influential is the video streaming website

YouTube. In May 2020, while writing this chapter, I spotted a Twitter post by a concerned parent whose eleven-year-old child had been researching the Second World War for a history project. The diligent student had clicked on a YouTube link about the Blitz, only for an ad for the bookmaker Coral to pop up.

It proved staggeringly easy to replicate the process. Imitating what a child might have done when seeking help with their homework, I typed 'The Blitz' into YouTube's search bar. The result offered an insight into how YouTube had honed its ability to target me with promotions. I didn't receive the same advert as the concerned parent's son but what I did see was a request for my help from You-Tube. It wanted to know how best to advertise to me. I was offered a list of bookmakers and online casinos and invited to tick a box indicating which I'd be most interested in hearing from again. Twitter runs similar surveys, via promoted posts that appear prominently in the timeline.

It was not until 2020 that YouTube's owner, Google, introduced greater functionality allowing internet users to block the majority of gambling and alcohol ads.[17] It remains to be seen how many gambling addicts or children will go to the effort to opt out. So what's the result of all of this? What does it really mean?

According to the Ipsos MORI report detailed above, two-thirds of people aged between eleven and twenty-four saw gambling ads on social media, compared to just 38% for billboards in the street. That's quite striking. Adverts consumed via social media reach targets via a device held in the palm of their hand that simultaneously transmits data about their browsing habits. In essence, it means that gambling firms are having private conversations with the majority of young people. They are doing so via tried-and-tested marketing methods. What's more, we have no real clue as to what effect this is having. After all, someone reaching adulthood in the early 2020s is among the first adults to have grown up in a world in which all this is considered normal. So normal, in fact, that in 2019 Ladbrokes thought nothing of tweeting an advert offering cheap online slots play if customers logged in on Christmas Day.

The authors of the Budd review and the politicians who passed the Gambling Act did not – and probably could not – have imagined this state of affairs.

## APPS

Like social media, apps come from a world that did not exist when modern gambling legislation was written. I have, as I write, the apps of six gambling companies installed on my smartphone. While I have them for research and journalistic purposes, it is not unusual for people much like me – youngish (or at least clinging on to the pretence of youth) and into sport – to have this many conduits to gambling installed on their phone. As recently as the noughties, newspapers and politicians were voicing grave concern about the prospect of supercasinos opening up in a handful of British towns, venues that customers would have had to travel to reach. Now, the modern punter has a supercasino, even several of them, in their pocket. The William Hill sports betting app alone has been downloaded at least a million times.

Apps are more than just a means to gamble. They are also an emerging way for advertisers to reach the eyeballs of smartphone users. The market for in-app advertising is projected to hit more than $220 billion by 2025, according to some estimates.[18] It makes sense. As with social media, an app user has already defined their interests. They have also offered insight into their spending habits by making a purchasing decision.

Much like social media, apps have become a Petri dish for practices that pose a risk to the vulnerable and the young. Take, for instance, a mobile phone game featuring characters from Nintendo's

Mario Kart franchise. Any of them playing the game might well have seen an advert for William Hill Vegas – offering a £200 bonus, a common form of inducement. Now, some of my friends might argue that Mario Kart is not the preserve only of children and I respect that position. But it's clear that under-eighteens feature prominently among its fans.

This incident, revealed in a ruling by the ASA,[19] was most likely an accident. But it was one that is symptomatic of how easy it is to be careless, some might argue negligent, in a fast-changing environment with so few controls. William Hill bought an advertising product from Google, which then served the ad to phones that had likely already viewed adult content. It was not possible, said William Hill, to avoid children seeing ads where devices were shared between family members. Google pointed out that its in-app advertising tool, Universal App Campaign, gave advertisers the option to exclude certain types of apps – cartoonish video games, for instance. It said William Hill had not used these tools. The ASA, after an investigation, agreed, and banned the advert.

There are other wince-worthy examples. *I'm A Celebrity . . . Get Me Out of Here!* is one of the most popular television shows in the UK, with more than 1 million viewers under the age of eighteen. Yet in order to cast votes on who should be ejected from the programme, viewers are required to download an app in which they immediately see adverts from online bingo, casino and slots firm Tombola, offering the 'chance to win a share of £250,000 for free'. There was no way to vote without viewing the ad for Tombola, the show's official sponsor over several years. After an outcry, the ASA banned that one too.[20]

Of course, apps aren't used only by children; some are dedicated to explicitly adult pursuits. Grindr is an app for, mostly, gay and bisexual men looking to meet for dates or hook-ups. It is a playground not just for horny blokes but also for online casino and slot machines, which are some of its frequent advertisers. In Grindr they have an audience of men often in something of an impulsive mood and literally seeking pleasure. It's a no-brainer for companies that make products such as virtual slot machines to place their ads there – and they do.

By far the most egregious example of in-app advertising gone wrong came to light in spring 2020. Escaping a gambling addiction is arduous, often painful and fraught with potential recurrences of the problem, not least because temptation is so visible in the world around us. Thankfully, some effective tools exist these days to help people prevent themselves from gambling online. One of them is blocking software that can be installed on a smartphone. The software prevents the owner of the device from ever accessing the websites of online casinos and bookmakers. I have heard recovering addicts say that such tools are the only thing standing between them and a new episode of their addiction.

But say someone looking for one of these apps had typed 'block gambling' into the App Store on their Apple iPhone. Before receiving any results they wanted, they would first have seen small adverts for Ladbrokes, Virgin Games and 888 Casino.[21] An advertising algorithm, designed to flag up products that might suit the user's existing interests, ended up putting temptation in the way of people trying to quit. It took addicts flagging the problem for it to be fixed.

## GOOGLE

Something similar goes on via Google, which – in part due to its sheer size – on occasion struggles to live up to its famous credo: *Don't be evil.*

The search engine giant banned gambling ads in 2004 but in 2008 overturned this decision for users in Great Britain, after the Gambling Act demonstrated the British government's tolerant attitude.

Search agency Greenlight estimated in 2008 that Google could make a minimum of £100 million a year in additional revenue.[22]

The change meant that gambling firms could pay to appear at the top of Google results, via the search engine's AdWords service. The way it works is complex but can be boiled down to this: companies bid to appear above the organic search results when users type in certain keywords. As with the social media ad platforms mentioned above, advertisers can target this based on a user's location and other metrics such as their interests, using data that Google possesses on, let's face it, pretty much all of us.

If I were selling garden equipment, I might bid to appear at the top of the page when you search 'gardening tips'. The bid price is set per click, meaning I would pay a few dollars every time someone clicks on my link. Most likely, this price will go up when more people are bidding on those keywords. As summer approaches in the northern hemisphere, for instance, I'd have to pay more to stave off competition from other garden equipment suppliers in Europe and North America.

This is a sure-fire way of targeting an audience because not only are you looking for them; if your targeting is accurate, they are also looking for you. According to data provided by data analytics business Kantar Media, gambling companies' demand for pay-per-click ads tends to soar around the time of sporting events, much like with any other form of advertising. 'Estimated industry spend on paid search rose from £20.1m in April to £39.2m in June as businesses aimed to cash in on an upsurge in interest around sporting events, including the FIFA World Cup,' Kantar wrote in 2018.[23] But sometimes, as sophisticated as the algorithms orchestrating paid search are, the system can break down, with dangerous consequences.

In 2019 the online casino Casumo had to retract an advert offering free spins and bonuses that popped up when people googled ways to bar themselves from gambling. The complainant had searched 'How to unsubscribe from all gambling', only for an advert for a Casumo app to pop up instead of the advice they were looking for.[24] The advert, in the paid-for listings that appear above organically generated search results, was headed 'Welcome bonus to new players Casumo 100% and 20 free spins', and also invited people to 'create an account & play now!'

In early 2020, at the same time as the App Store was advertising gambling to addicts, it emerged that people who searched Google for GamStop – an industry-wide scheme that allows people with a gambling problem to exclude themselves from all forms of gambling – were getting results designed to do just the opposite. The top result from a Google search by the *Independent* for 'GamStop UK' was an advert for a website recommending black market casinos, entitled: 'Not on GamStop Popular sites – Get 300 per cent Bonus.'[25] In other words, a search by someone seeking to stop gambling instead yielded an enticement to keep doing so, to the commercial benefit of both Google and the unscrupulous illicit website. One such site, which I will not name, even features articles from someone claiming to be a journalist called Rob Davies. He professes his interest in gambling addiction while also making lists of casinos you can use even if you have signed up to self-exclude from gambling, which is something of a contradiction. I wrote to him and was surprised that his English was remarkably broken for someone claiming to be a British journalist.

I've seen versions of misdirected search results pop up again and again over the years. For the most part they are, let's be charitable, horrific but honest mistakes that Google and the gambling firms themselves would rather did not occur. But they're the accidental result of a very intentional system.

## AFFILIATES, TIPSTERS AND STREAMERS

Advertising doesn't always look like advertising these days. We live in a world in which our brains are learning to filter out noise online, to the extent that we ignore many of the ads that pop up when we're browsing. Increasingly, brands are having to invent new ways to bypass the protective force field of cynicism that audiences have learned to erect when they recognise that someone is trying to sell them something.

One of the most tried-and-tested methods that has emerged over the past decade or so is the affiliate. The simplest definition of an affiliate is someone who directs other people towards gambling websites and takes a cut of the money the new customer goes on to spend. In the context of gambling, this means a percentage of whatever money you spend on betting goes to the person who recommended the site to you.

There are lots of ways this set-up can work but one common example is the 'tipster'. A person, let's call her Martha, has a website or a social media account. It might be called something like www.footballtips4u.com or, if it were a Twitter account, @PremierLeagueOdds. Martha writes articles or composes tweets about football matches, often humorous and apparently unrelated to betting. She creates a persona over time. She might also claim to be adept at analysing football data and to be able to predict, at least more accurately than the average punter, what will happen in a particular football match, from something simple such as who will win and by what score, to how many corners there are likely to be and who might receive a yellow card. She'll also tell you how much she has made this year from her own tips, information that is impossible to verify but which might make you want a piece of the action. This is typically done in a conversational style. 'I fancy Liverpool to stick four past Watford today, that defence has more holes in it than a Swiss cheese.'

Then, after that icebreaker, comes the real point of the tweet: 'Get 15–1 with Ladbrokes for Liverpool to score four v Watford.' The customer clicks, opens an account or places a bet, the affiliate gets paid.

There are dozens, if not hundreds, of active tipsters on Twitter alone; @AndyRobsonTips and @FootySuperTips each have around 400,000 followers at time of writing.

There are a number of different ways in which the tipster affiliate model typically works. One ex-affiliate – speaking on condition of anonymity – explained some of them to me. 'Probably the most appealing is cost per acquisition, or CPA,' he said. 'You get a fixed upfront fee for every player who makes a new deposit. At one time the online casino Casumo was paying 200 euros for a new player who deposited £10.'

Think about that for a second. The affiliate gets 200 euros when a customer deposits just £10. That tells you something pretty interesting about what that company expects to make from its new-found customer in the coming weeks, months and years.

'Revenue share is a model a lot of people have taken, which is a percentage of the customer's net losses, typically between 20% and 60%. They can be for the lifetime of the player's account but some big operators have been putting two- or three-year caps in recently.'

In some cases, the former affiliate explained, sophisticated or particularly skilled affiliates will negotiate more favourable terms, or bespoke deals that combine revenue sharing and up-front fees.

My colleague Mattha Busby cast a bright spotlight on the murky world of affiliates in 2017 in a series of articles for the *Guardian*. In one,[26] Peter Ling, who runs a betting advice business called the Secret Betting Club, pointed to the clear incentive that tipster affiliates have to recommend bets that look good on the face of it but are actually anything but.

Remember, they get paid a percentage of whatever you lose.

'This incentivises such tipsters to only put up losers, yet no self-respecting punter would knowingly follow the advice of a losing tipster,' he said. 'It has created a situation where losing tipsters are masquerading as being successful by using a variety of tactics, be it through social media where they create new accounts and delete posts to fit a narrative, or simpler things, such as quoting odds that don't exist.'

In recent years, a new breed of affiliate has emerged: the streamers. These are, for the most part, the preserve of the online casino world and slot machines in particular. A slots streamer will sit at their desk, playing online slot machines or roulette in front of an online audience that watches and comments. The key platforms are YouTube and Twitch, a website built for streaming, often of non-gambling video games. They command sizeable audiences. As I write this, popular streamer Chipmonkz has 43,000 subscribers to his YouTube channel and has put up four videos in the past twenty-four hours, racking up nearly 8,000 views. Rival slots streamer The Bandit has around 80,000 subscribers. He posts less often but regularly attracts more than 150,000 views for a single video.

Recovering gambling addict George Cooper, a thirty-six-year-old digital content editor for a newspaper, told me that streamers fuelled his addiction. 'At first it's like getting the buzz without actually gambling yourself. But then gambling is just in your head. You're either doing it yourself or watching someone else do it. That's what I was doing for a good couple of years.' He was drawn in partly by the light-hearted tone of the videos: 'My addiction was fuelled by stress and it felt like a fairly harmless bit of entertainment,' he said. 'These guys are quite chatty and have a nice presence, so it becomes an escape.' They would, on occasion, pay lip service to responsible gambling too. 'One guy lost £50,000 and was saying, "Don't do this, folks." Then he'd do an hour's video carrying on.'

There are big question marks over how much streamers ever actually lose. Many post links to the casinos they play on, acting as affiliate advertisers taking a cut of any business generated via their subscription channel. Increasingly, some online slot machine fans believe that many aren't even playing with real money, or at least not their own.

Although it has never been proven conclusively, there is good reason to believe that some online casinos are either funding streamers' bets or allowing them to play using a dummy account, where no real cash changes hands. It's a win–win deal. If the streamer is good at what they do, they are advertising their casino partner's slot machines to, potentially, hundreds of thousands of viewers. They take a cut of the profits.

And what of those watching? Well, age controls are virtually non-existent. Anyone can access casino streamers' YouTube videos. Twitch is available to anyone over the age of thirteen, although minors supposedly have to obtain the consent of a parent, which is easy enough to get for the purposes of, say, watching gamers playing a popular game such as Fortnite. Once you're on Twitch, though, there is absolutely nothing to stop a thirteen-year-old spending their day watching a casino streamer playing spin after spin of Eye of Horus, or any other popular slot machine game. Links to casino websites appear in the comments section to the right of the screen, making it as simple as possible for spectators to become players in just a few clicks.

## PODCASTS AND RADIO

Twitch streams are still a relatively niche form of entertainment but the same can no longer be said for podcasts, which are at the forefront of an audio renaissance. According to Ofcom, as of September 2019 more than 7 million people in the UK listened to a podcast every week[27], double the number who'd done so just five years previously. The beauty of podcasts, if you're an advertiser, is that they tend to be about niche subjects. Whether you're interested in murder mysteries, food, football or politics, there are dozens of options at your fingertips. It doesn't take a genius to figure out that if you're trying to promote gambling your money would be well spent on a podcast about sport.

The best podcasts, the ones that attract the highest audiences, are also time-consuming and arduous to make. They require research, a degree of editing dexterity and a good deal of patience, especially if it takes a while to build up your audience. All of this is much easier to commit to if you're getting paid. And therein lies an advertising match made in heaven: people who need cash and have a platform, coupled with an audience that has a particular passion.

One of my favourite podcasts is *The Fighting Cock*, a laddish, chaotic but intelligently put-together show aimed at the long-suffering fans of Tottenham Hotspur Football Club. Each week a rotating cast of regulars – always led by the show's irreverent and charismatic host, 'Flav' Bateman – meet to discuss Spurs games, in amongst various more risqué topics. They skirt the boundaries of taste and decency most of the time, which is one reason I like it.

Flav explained to me how advertisers come calling once a podcast has a modicum of success: 'If you have a podcast of a significant size, generally you'll get approached by an agency selling an aggregated audience [to advertisers]. Because it's football, there's so much money that comes in through betting. About 80 or 90% of the deals we get offered are bookies. The rule of thumb for a podcast is that we would charge twenty to twenty-five dollars per thousand listens.'

For *The Fighting Cock*, which was garnering between 15,000 and 20,000 listens per episode at time of writing – and most likely more by now – that works out as up to $500 an episode. It's a handy bit of income for Flav that helps him do what he loves – talk about Spurs – for a living rather than as a hobby. Indeed, since I first spoke to Flav, William Hill has become the podcast's official betting partner. (To his credit, Flav spends much more time than some counterparts pointing out methods that problem gamblers can use to get help.) For an advertiser, the sums of money involved in sponsoring *The Fighting Cock* are chicken feed, a slip of the accountant's pen. But that money works hard. Advertisers can zero in on a highly engaged audience that already has an interest in sport.

Some deals are more lucrative. *The Totally Football Show* is one of the most successful football podcasts, thanks to the calibre of its guests and the popularity of its host, James Richardson, an urbane, knowledgeable and funny football journalist. He got his big break fronting the 1990s football show *Gazzetta Football Italia*, introducing the latest Serie A clashes from Italy, typically while sitting at a table in a sunny piazza enjoying a gelato or a glass of Chianti. *The Totally Football Show* has racked up more than 60 million listens in its lifetime. It's a crude back-of-napkin calculation but, on the kind of terms Flav was talking about, that would equate to £1.5 million over the lifetime of the show, if every episode were sponsored by a gambling company. And *The Totally Football Show* isn't just sponsored by one – part of its content is devoted to it. Paddy Power's deal with the show means that one of its odds compilers gets five minutes on air per episode to talk about which bets are worth placing that week and why.

It's no different on the good old-fashioned wireless, where the voluntary code that applies to television has, mysteriously, never been in place. Gambling adverts can be heard at any time of the day on the radio, during the school run or in the middle of the night, with seemingly no controls in place to prevent children from being exposed. Some broadcasters take it further: talkSPORT frequently broadcasts live commentary of football matches. Such are its commercial deals with gambling companies that commentators will offer odds in between calling the play.

This is just another facet of the contemporary advertising landscape, which offers myriad routes into the minds of consumers, some of them so subtle as to be barely noticeable at all.

## DIRECT MARKETING

One of the most exciting aspects of modern marketing – from the point of view of a gambling company – is the ability to micro-target specific demographics who are more likely than average to be receptive to the product. People who've already demonstrated their interest in sports betting or online slots deliver a much bigger bang for your advertising buck. We've seen already that social media platforms can help with this. Another way is to simply purchase large swathes of personal information to gain an edge in the battle for gambling dollars. Just as we saw with Sky's AdSmart product, so-called 'data houses' harvest details on age, income, debt, credit information and insurance details, which they pass to betting affiliates. This helps the affiliates and the gambling firms to tailor their content and target people based on what they earn.

'Third-party data providers allowed us to target their email lists with precision,' a digital marketer told the *Guardian* in 2017.[28] The insider, who counted betting companies among his clients before leaving his agency, said: 'Lower-income users were among the most successfully targeted segments. We could also combine segments, i.e. we could target users who are on less than £25K a year, own a credit card and have three kids, via these providers.'

The data is sometimes gathered from raffle sites that offer cash prizes and gifts in weekly giveaways, he said. To apply for the prize draws on such sites, tempting for people with little money but a good helping of optimism, users must usually provide their name, date of birth, email and address. He claimed raffle companies would then resell the data, which customers may have unwittingly consented to via lengthy terms and conditions.

Advertising companies can then identify members of target demographics – often made up of people in lower-earning brackets – and use credit information to reach them. They were also found to have used a method called 'dynamic retargeting' to single out people who may not have gambled for a while and try to entice them to pick up the habit again.

A *New York Times* article in March 2021[29] detailed how Sky Bet had used data-profiling software to identify a lapsed UK customer as someone to 'win back', even predicting that he would be worth about £1,000 to the company if they could reel him in again. They'd used a company called iovation to gather nearly nineteen thousand fields of data about the devices he'd used to gamble and the locations where he'd done it. They'd used another, Signal, to trace his likes and dislikes, allowing them to tailor the offers made in an attempt to woo him back. Sky Bet knew, for instance, that he was likely to be receptive to gambling promotions that featured Las Vegas. 'They had taken his addiction and turned it into code,' said Ravi Naik, a lawyer who helped the customer uncover his data.

The reason firms do this is because customer retention is fiendishly difficult in the competitive British gambling landscape. One of the most effective ways to hold on to market share is by appealing directly to individual gamblers via a more one-to-one conversation.

When a customer opens an account, the firm immediately places them on a marketing list unless they make it clear that they want to opt out. What this means is a stream of emails, texts, even phone calls, offering 'free' bets and bonuses. In most cases such bets aren't free at all. You might get £10 without spending any money but you won't be able to cash out any winnings until you've placed more bets, with the stake often needing to be recycled many times. That condition gives the company several more opportunities to win your money and, crucially, keeps you in the habit of placing bets. These methods of communication are known as direct marketing and they crop up time and again in tales told by gambling addicts and penalties meted out by the Gambling Commission.

In his book *The Gambling Establishment*, long-standing gambling expert Professor Jim Orford refers to advertising methods that are 'questionable, if not legally then certainly ethically'.[30] He points to a study by researchers at Sheffield Hallam University of three thousand direct mail promotions sent out by sixty-seven promoters. They deployed tactics 'including the portrayal of gambling as glitzy and glamorous, the frequent use of sexualised images and the emphasis on friendship and socialising with appeal to young people [. . .] The main themes were an emphasis on skill and knowledge, which were mentioned three times as often as luck.'[31] The promotions avoided using the word 'gamble' or 'gambling', instead opting for euphemisms such as 'flutter' or 'punt', or simply 'bet'. They also highlighted rare instances of punters who'd had big wins: 'A lucky lady from Yorkshire is £150,000 richer after hitting the jackpot on our Rainbow Riches slot! Could you be next to collect the pot of gold at the end of the rainbow?'

It's probably redundant to point out that the possibility of losing money never came up in these promotions. And, of course, these enticing messages arrived directly in the gamblers' email accounts or text message folders.

'That's the cynical part, that's where a lot of the horrible stuff has been added,' said Kim Lund, an online poker industry expert and founder of gaming consultancy Infinite Edge Gaming. 'A brick-and-mortar casino cannot show up at your doorstep at exactly the time you'd normally be at the casino and ask "Why are you there, why are you not here?" There they have so much responsibility for making something worse, for selling something irresponsibly that must be sold responsibly.'

Lund referred to the need for the industry to sell products responsibly. But in the world of gambling advertising, it hasn't historically been the companies that have been urged to be responsible – that's been left up to the punters. For much of the period since gambling advertising became legal, adverts have carried the disclaimer 'Please gamble responsibly'. It's even in Ray Winstone's script these days: 'I'm Ray Winstone and I gamble responsibly with bet365,' he tells us.

This, says Jim Orford, fits in with the way that advertising has created a narrative that casts gambling as nothing but harmless amusement. 'The biggest fiction is that commercial gambling is an ordinary entertainment business like any other,' says Orford, 'that all the industry is doing is providing an entertainment product that a few people can't use responsibly. That combination of it being entertainment, an ordinary business, and people being responsible for their own behaviour is a very powerful discourse that they promote and that the government has generally accepted. It's part of the reason it's taken so long to face up to the fact that this isn't an ordinary commodity at all. It's very dangerous and it's got much more dangerous because of technology.'[32]

That's not to say that the gambling industry doesn't nod to the dangers at all. In late 2021, just in time for the government's review of gambling laws, the industry announced plans for a new motto: 'Take time to think.' But until then, the dominant safer gambling slogan was 'When the fun stops, stop.' It was dreamed up by the Senet Group, a now defunct industry collective that worked on so-called 'responsible-gambling initiatives'. The phrase has invited a fair degree of ridicule. For a start, the word 'FUN' is printed in a significantly larger font than all of the other words, for no apparent reason. One could be forgiven for seeing the fun and little else. In fact, that's what academics at the University of Warwick think is going on.[33] Researchers from the university's psychology department asked 506 people, who said they were fans of Premier League football and also had experience of sports betting, to place small wagers after viewing adverts, some of which contained the warning label and some of which did not. They found that those who had seen the responsible-gambling message bet more often than those who had not. The difference wasn't statistically significant enough to show that the slogan was actually inducing people to bet more, but researchers concluded that it was certainly having no effect in the other direction.

The much-derided slogan sits alongside GambleAware's 'Bet Regret' campaign, which made its debut on a Sunday in February 2019 during the Manchester United v Liverpool game. The Bet Regret spot was sandwiched between adverts from bet365, Betfair, Paddy Power and Sky Bet, leading to criticism from campaigners who said the message was 'drowned out'.[34]

As for the industry's role in this, in 2020 the Betting and Gaming Council announced that its members would commit to making 20% of their adverts about safer gambling and the tools they offered customers to protect themselves, such as time-outs and spend limits. This was to be welcomed, no doubt. Nonetheless, it did not escape attention that these ads were still laden with company branding. In some cases, the cautionary message seemed to get lost somewhere between concept and execution. One, for the William Hill-owned brand Mr Green, showed a visibly delighted young woman apparently having a whale of a time setting deposit limits, ending with the slogan: 'Enjoy award-winning online casino with Mr Green.'[35] Another spot, for Sky Betting & Gaming's casino brand, listed the safer gambling tools on offer, concluding: 'That's why I play at SkyVegas.'

Sometimes, albeit most likely by accident, the safer-gambling message gets misused even more egregiously than that. In Safer Gambling Week 2020, the UK and Ireland Twitter account of PokerStars changed its official avatar to the Safer Gambling Week logo. That same week, the account tweeted an offer: £20 of free play when customers deposited £10.

It's incidents like this that make you wonder exactly whose interests are being served by safer-gambling messages, at least in their current guise.

## SO WHAT'S THE PROBLEM?

Most concern about the volume of gambling advertising in modern society stems from two premises: that marketing induces more people to gamble and that some of those people will develop a disorder, meaning more addicts and more suffering.

There are good reasons to suspect that the first premise is true. For a start, it's common sense: it *feels* true based on our understanding of how the world works. Gambling companies don't spend millions for the prestige of appearing on TV. They do so, like any other brand, because they believe they can win new customers, or lure them away from competitors. Market research tells them this works, or else they wouldn't continue.

Studies carried out for GambleAware suggest the common-sense view may be correct. In one of the studies,[36] subjects aged between eleven and twenty-four could identify more than seven out of ten gambling brands that they were shown. Not only did they recognise them but they talked about them too. More than four in ten of those aged eighteen to twenty-four and 22% of those aged eleven to seventeen had engaged with some form of gambling advertising in the past month, mostly through discussing it with friends or family. The same group of researchers found that the more people were exposed to gambling adverts, the more favourable they were to the industry and the more likely they were to gamble,[37] a finding backed up by a landmark review of twenty-seven studies.[38]

And what of the premise that more gambling means more

addiction? Again, we could start with the common-sense calculation. Logically, if a certain proportion of gamblers develop a disorder, whether we agree or disagree about how high that proportion is, more gamblers means more addicts. Again, though, there's no need to rely on instinct. Academics have consistently traced links between advertising and behaviour such as more frequent and riskier gambling. But there is no such thing as certainty in academic research of this nature; it is incredibly hard to determine why humans act the way they do.

And yet, by charting the rise of gambling advertising, it's possible to show how we have, in little over a decade, built a world in which it is virtually impossible to escape online casinos and bookmakers. This is a cultural sea change, fuelled by liberal regulation and technology, the effects of which are largely unknown. How will today's young adults, who've grown up in a society drenched in the language, imagery and culture of gambling, fuelled by technology that didn't exist when their parents were growing up, deal with an immersion they've learned to accept as normal? We remain, for the most part, very much in the dark about how this shift in advertising culture is affecting us and how it has affected gambling-related harm. It stretches the limits of credulity to imagine that such a profound transformation in our lived experience could have left us unchanged.

What seems clear is that it isn't loony do-gooders, Bible-thumpers and recovering addicts with an axe to grind who feel things have gone too far. A YouGov survey in 2021 found that 77% of adults support a ban on gambling ads on radio and TV before 9 p.m.[39] Only 14% opposed the most draconian option put to them, a total ban on all gambling ads, via any medium, at any time. Some in the industry see me as anti-gambling and I don't know that even I would support that measure – yet it appears that millions do. The British people know when they're being sold a bad deal.

We'll return to advertising, in particular its relationship with football, in Chapter 5. In the meantime, I want to examine phenomena that are part of – and work in tandem with – advertising. I want to explore the tricks and mechanisms that help gambling firms do more than just put themselves in front of our eyes, instead burrowing into our very psyche and emerging clutching pound notes.

# 3. BRAINHACKS, DARK NUDGES AND GAMBLING BY STEALTH

Is it really not possible to touch a gaming table without becoming
infected with superstition?

FYODOR DOSTOEVSKY, *THE GAMBLER* (1866)

Much as we like to pretend otherwise, none of us is immune to the
siren song of the advertising techniques described in the previous
chapter. But, susceptible as we are to the warm embrace of consumer
capitalism – or its vice-like grip, depending on your perspective – we
have also grown wise to how it works. When the voice-over artist
cheerily informs us that this luxury leather sofa is 'only four-nine-
nine', we know she is studiously avoiding saying the words 'five',
'hundred' and 'pounds'.

As well as our own layers of scepticism, we have regulators
keeping watch, ready to jump in and sanction the health supplement firm that claims its sugar pills fight cancer, or the beauty
company that suggests moisturiser halts the ageing process. Even
if such regulators weren't around, we are more informed, particularly on health matters, than we used to be. You couldn't claim that
'Guinness is good for you' any more, as appealing as the notion
of medicinal stout might be to some. Generations have come
and gone since cigarette company Lucky Strike boasted: '20,679
physicians say "Luckies are less irritating!"' That sort of thing feels
like satire now.

Brands have to work a lot harder and play their hand far more subtly to access our disposable income these days. Doing so is a particularly complex challenge in the era of on-demand subscription media, when customers can sign up to Netflix and, theoretically, never again have to put up with the irritation of having their TV series or film interrupted by a commercial break.

Gambling has always been a bit different to other consumer products, though. Coca-Cola advertises in the knowledge that you probably already know how it tastes. The occasional memory-jog will remind you why you like it and might lead you to buy more and to choose Coke over Pepsi when you do. It's a pretty simple equation. Bookmakers and online casinos do this too, of course. Campaigns – such as those Ladbrokes Life commercials – are about creating and reinforcing a coherent and memorable brand identity that punters feel speaks to their own personality.

But convincing a customer to choose your brand – and remain loyal – is only half the battle with gambling. Betting firms also need to persuade punters that they have a decent shot at winning some money even though – in the long term at least – they don't.

The gambling industry could not exist unless the bookmaker or the casino had a better grasp on the odds than the punter. That's not remotely controversial; indeed, it's the foundation upon which the industry is built, and it's a bargain that – unless they are completely delusional – the gambler enters into knowingly. They bet believing that they might just be the one who can upset the apple cart and beat the bookie, if not by judgement then by luck.

But it isn't just the odds that the bookie has a better grasp on. The industry knows its customers better than they know themselves. That fact is the essential truth at the heart of a profitable gambling industry, and it's an advantage that successful firms hammer home at every turn.

'There is a reason why gambling games are highly addictive and it doesn't have to do with winning money,' says Kim Lund. 'You don't get addicted by the opportunity to win money. There are very primitive psychological triggers.'

José Perales is an associate professor in the Mind, Brain and Behaviour Research Centre at the University of Granada in Spain. Like most people who study gambling psychology, he has read the Holy Bible when it comes to the design of gambling games: *Addiction by Design*, written by the cultural anthropologist Natasha Dow Schüll, associate professor in the Department of Media, Culture, and Communication at New York University. In it, she reaches the conclusion that the people who design these games marshal technology 'to delude gamblers'[1], tailoring the user experience to convince us to act against our own interests. The book charts how the industry has been able to use Las Vegas as a kind of giant laboratory. Perales told me: 'The psychology of gambling is not that complicated. They don't really need so much psychology or science, they try things and see what happens. You change something and if it works you keep it.'

The casinos of Las Vegas have, over the years, provided vast reserves of data on how best to part punters from their money. Perales suggests that the same thing is now happening with online gambling, to an even larger extent: '[Online] it's so easy to change something slightly, to change a feature and see how it works. Eventually they find something that works and makes people gamble more heavily or for longer.' He suggests that gambling companies don't necessarily know themselves exactly why a certain feature hooks people in or encourages them to bet again. All they know for sure is that, as Perales puts it, 'what works, works'.

The psychology may be 'primitive' and the tricks used to exploit it old hat to those in the know. But that does not stop them from working effectively, particularly when deployed in new ways, reimagined and tweaked to widen the gambling company's advantage and respond to changing consumer trends. Some people call this sort of psychological manipulation 'brainhacking', the art of using subtle techniques to affect cognitive function, changing the way we think and behave. So what are the tricks and how do gambling firms exploit them to take our money and convince us to come back, time and again, and let them take more?

## YOU ARE DELUSIONAL

The starting point is a fundamental facet of the human brain. We all experience and exhibit something called cognitive bias. Put simply, this means that we are irrational. We misjudge reality based on our flawed perception of it, rendering us liable to base our decisions not on evidence or factual analysis, but on subjective experience and intuition that has little basis in reality.

Gambling relies heavily on this and always has done. The quote at the beginning of this chapter comes from Dostoevsky's *The Gambler*, the experience of its protagonist, Alexei Ivanovich, rings true because Dostoevsky had frequented the gaming tables of Europe and developed his own gambling problem. Like several of the characters in the book, the Russian author laboured under the irrational belief that he, unlike the vast majority, was destined to upset the odds. 'It is true that only one in a hundred wins,' says Ivanovich, echoing his creator. 'But what does that matter to me?'[2]

Kim Lund has made a career out of game design expertise and has seen at first hand how cold hard probability defeats the illogical human mind every time. 'All gambling games are based on psychological triggers that mean they work,' he told me. 'The human brain is incapable of dealing with randomness because it doesn't have a cause and effect, it just is. We're obsessed with finding patterns in things that are random because that prevents us from going insane. We want to make sense of things.'

*The Gambler* is full of such delusions, of addicts who believe they have developed a system, monitoring outcomes and establishing patterns that aren't really there.

Philip Newall is an academic psychologist who has been studying dynamics like these for much of his professional life. He's also seen both sides of the equation, having previously been an online poker player. Unlike many forms of gambling, poker requires a high degree of skill; if your opponent is a bad player, they are unlikely to get the better of you due to luck, at least not over time. Newall enjoyed a degree of success because he had one type of game – fixed-limit hold'em, where all bets and raises are fixed at a certain amount. Understanding that form of poker as he did, Newall stuck to what he knew and, for the most part, only played against people he was sure he could beat. That background, coupled with his in-depth study of psychology, makes him well placed to explain what the industry knows about how our minds work.

Newall used to walk down Walworth Road in London, a high street replete with bookmakers' shops. He would pass William Hill, Betfred and Ladbrokes and notice they were all offering similar types of bet that went something like this: 'Manchester United to win 3–1 v Burnley and Marcus Rashford to score first.' This very common type of bet is known in the trade as a scorecast market. The scorecast bet requires a combination of events to occur at once, in this case the exact score, the winning team and the first goalscorer. As soon as you start combining probabilities of multiple events, the odds lengthen very quickly. This means that a scorecast outcome is pretty unlikely, so the bookmaker can offer what looks like a bargainous 15–1, knowing the chances of it happening are more like 50–1.

Bookmakers are sitting on a mine of information on their historical return from scorecast markets, and will have a good idea of the difference between the odds they're offering and their own calculation of what the real odds are. They don't publicise this for obvious reasons. That, in Newall's words, would be 'killing their own action', giving a disproportionate amount of information to the person on the other side of the bet. In poker the saying is 'Don't teach the fish' – fish being bad players you can easily take money from. Instead of teaching the fish, gambling companies try to ensure, through the types of bet that they promote most heavily, that as many people opt to gamble their money on more complex-probability scenarios, rather than sticking to simpler outcomes.

To go back to the comparison with Coca-Cola, it's as if the company were focusing its marketing efforts on advertising thimblefuls of Coke for £50 each, rather than bottles that cost £1. Nobody would go for that – it's obviously much worse value. But the more complex decision-making tree involved in gambling obscures the loss of value.

'People are paying more attention to the high pay-off than the probability,' says Newall, and gambling companies know this. According to Newall, a poker player dabbling in sports betting would look at the above scenario and calculate the expected value of the bet. They'd do that by weighing up the chances of it happening against the potential payout if it comes off. In poker they call this concept Sklansky bucks, after the poker theorist David Sklansky.

The Sklansky bucks on the Marcus Rashford scorecast bet are low, much lower than the cost of the bet. That's because the chances of it happening are small and the bookie isn't offering enough of a payout to make the risk of betting on it worthwhile, so the clued-up gambler probably steers clear. However, to the average person in the street, the idea of Marcus Rashford scoring the first goal to help Man United to a 3–1 win over Burnley sounds like a pretty plausible scenario. When a gambler thinks about that scorecast bet, they are picturing in their mind's eye an in-form striker opening the scoring in a routine victory over an inferior team. A standard Saturday afternoon, you might say. Perhaps the mental footage cuts at that point to a picture of themselves having a couple of hundred quid in their pocket to spend that week – who knows.

José Perales, who has studied the same phenomena as Newall, explains that this is the result of something called the 'representativeness heuristic'. He said: 'A heuristic is a rule of thumb, something you can use that works pretty well in your daily life but can convince you to make quite serious mistakes, especially when they're deliberately exploited, which is the case here.'

The football match scenario in question is something gamblers can easily envisage happening and which they may even have seen before. It *could* happen. But, as we have seen, the necessary confluence of multiple events means it is actually far less likely than it instinctively feels. There are many other outcomes that are just as likely, or much less likely, which could occur too.

Gambling companies are getting better and better at targeting this sort of weakness in our mental defences. Philip Newall tracked television adverts over two World Cups in 2014 and 2018, drawing on data collected by my *Guardian* colleague, the data journalist Pamela Duncan.[3] He found that standard home-draw-away bets (on the winner of the match) simply disappeared from one tournament to the next. These straightforward, easier-to-understand wagers featured in nearly 8% of adverts at the 2014 tournament but had dwindled to nothing at the next. By contrast, high-odds complex bets shot up from 4% to nearly 35%. The result? A very lucrative World Cup performance for the gambling companies. As the odds lengthen, the gambler's ability to calculate them weakens. 'The higher the odds go, the higher the house edge goes,' says Newall. 'Your average gambler is not paying attention to the probability but to the amount they could win, and as the odds get higher the probability of winning decreases more, resulting in a worse bet in terms of Sklansky bucks.'

Another inescapable delusion of the human mind is 'loss aversion'. This is the human refusal to accept that time, money or effort has been wasted. Rather than cut our losses and accept defeat, we expend yet more of those precious resources to show that it hasn't all been for nothing. It's why we might continue waiting for a bus that hasn't come for twenty minutes, even though we could probably walk home in ten. It's why warring nations have allowed more troops to die in unwinnable conflicts rather than concede defeat and risk acknowledging that those who have already died did so for nothing. It's a phenomenon well known to students of direct marketing – the controversial pyramid-style schemes in which people sign up to sell goods and sometimes stick with it for months and years, despite never making any money.

When it comes to gamblers, many would rather blame anything else than admit they have willingly joined a game so evidently rigged against them. 'You will see gamblers irrationally defend a casino,' says Kim Lund. 'I can be an addicted gambler and I can see an article written that criticises the casino for sub-par gambling-addiction remedies and even though I'm one of those addicts, I'll defend it. I am so afraid that all of this was for nothing that I'd rather defend the idea that it is something that it isn't than accept that all of this was pointless.'

Loss aversion is at the heart of one of the behaviours that clinicians and researchers use to identify gambling addiction: chasing losses. A punter chasing their losses keeps feeding money into the system, hoping that the big win that makes it all worthwhile is just around the corner. In the long run, it almost never is.

## DARK NUDGES

Gambling companies make more money when we behave like this, when we miscalculate the odds or succumb to loss aversion. It's why they push football bettors in the direction of scorecast markets rather than simpler bets. Any military commander knows that, once you've identified an enemy's weakness, you can – indeed must – exploit it.

The industry benefits from what is known as 'informational

asymmetry'. Online casino operators know everything about you – particularly in the internet age when they can track your online patterns of play and analyse the data in minute detail. The overwhelming majority of punters, by contrast, know very little about the company on the other end of the bet, how it operates and the reality of the betting markets being offered.

Emboldened by this knowledge imbalance, gambling companies are able to deploy techniques that are as old as the hills, but which are constantly evolving in the way that they are used. Philip Newall has coined the phrase 'dark nudges' to describe these weapons. The phrase is a nod to the 2008 book *Nudge*, written by University of Chicago economist Richard H. Thaler and Harvard Law School professor Cass R. Sunstein.[4] The book, a favourite of former UK prime minister David Cameron, draws on psychology and behavioural economics to examine how people in positions of authority can 'nudge' people into making decisions that benefit both them and society. The idea is that you can drive positive changes without needing to be openly coercive, which might only make people resistant. Of course, you can nudge people towards poor choices too.

'Clearly companies have an incentive to nudge people into making worse decisions, particularly in something like gambling which is a zero-sum game,' says Newall. 'You only make money when someone loses. You don't make money by having an informed person against you.'

Nor do you make as much money from people exercising caution. There are ways in which operators can nudge customers towards reckless behaviour. A study by the Behavioural Insights Team, the UK-based research agency sometimes known as the 'Nudge Unit', looked at how even measures geared towards safer gambling can lead people to make unwise choices.[5] For instance, operators offer their customers a 'deposit limit' tool, which sets a cap on how much they can put into their account. The idea is to set binding limits when you're rational, saving you from changing your mind at 3 a.m. when you're desperately chasing losses and liable to get into even deeper trouble and lose your shirt. Most firms offer customers a drop-down list of deposit limits ranging from small sums such as £5 to eye-watering figures such as £100,000 – tantamount to no limit at all. The Behavioural Insights Team's hypothesis was that people were influenced by what they saw on the screen. With bet365's help, they tested three options on 45,000 customers. One group was given the standard drop-down with a range of suggested limits, including very high ones. The second group was given a list of suggested limits, the highest of which was £250. Anyone wanting to go higher had to actively type in the figure they wanted. A third group was shown nothing but a free-text box, which they themselves had to fill in. The researchers then measured what deposit limit people set and how much they actually ended up spending. As they thought, the presence of sky-high 'limits' led the first group to set much higher daily deposit limits, about £1,600. The other two groups each set limits of £866 on average. Higher suggested deposit limits also seemed to lead to higher actual deposits over the next thirty days: £446 on average compared to £426 for the group who were shown the thriftier option. Intriguingly, though, those who had typed their chosen limit into a free-text box ended up spending least of all, by some distance, at just under £361.

In this case, the absence of any nudge at all is what led people to take less risk. It was only when pointed in a certain direction by the operator that they succumbed to the temptation to put more at stake.

I want to examine three key elements of human behaviour that the gambling industry exploits to make us act in ways that we otherwise might not. The techniques they use to tap into these psychological truths are both artful and terrible, marrying simplicity of concept with ingenuity of execution to nudge us into the dark.

## ILLUSION OF CONTROL AND THE GAMBLER'S FALLACY

A sports bet isn't a game of skill, nor is it entirely a matter of chance. Nobody will stake money on Liverpool losing 15–0 to Port Vale, because they have enough experience of the game to understand that this is as close to impossible as you can get. But in games that are entirely random, players exert no control at all over the success of their bet. Indeed, assuming that the game isn't rigged, nobody has total authority over the outcome. Gamblers often behave as if they do not understand this. Sociologists have observed dice players throwing softly when they want a low number and hard when they want a high one, for instance.[6]

In her seminal 1975 paper 'The Illusion of Control', Ellen J. Langer conducted a series of experiments that showed that our expectations of success in a game of chance vary, depending on factors that do not actually affect the outcome.[7] One of the variables that makes a big difference to how gamblers behave is the introduction of an element of choice. In one of Langer's experiments, subjects were given lottery tickets with an American football player on them. Some subjects got to choose which player they wanted, others were allocated a ticket at random. On the morning of the draw, everyone was asked how much they would be prepared to sell their ticket for. Those who had chosen their ticket demanded an average of $8.67, while those who had been allocated one at random were prepared to give it up for $1.96. Even though the choice of a ticket had no influence on which one would be the winner, those who had made a conscious decision were significantly less willing to abandon it.

Dr Steve Sharman, research fellow in the School of Psychology at the University of East London, is a specialist in gambling psychology. He explains what's going on: 'If you go into a casino and you're playing roulette, they show the previous outcomes. They might show so-called "hot numbers" or "cold numbers". A "hot number" is one that has come up a lot recently, while a "cold" one hasn't been seen for a while. By displaying them, the casino is inviting you to entertain the idea that previous spins of the roulette wheel have any effect on future spins.' This, explains Sharman, reinforces something called the gambler's fallacy, or the failure to appreciate the 'statistical independence of turns'. 'If I've got ten heads in a row, it doesn't make it more likely that tails will come up,' he says. 'But gamblers don't think like that.' Indeed, people in general don't tend to think like that.

I came across hot numbers while reporting on FOBTs too. Above the machines, betting shop staff would plaster a notice advertising which numbers had been coming up a lot lately on the machines' digital roulette games. This, says Sharman, 'reinforces that sense that you are basing your decision on something other than complete chance'. At that point, you're labouring under an illusion that you have some kind of agency, that your choices are based on information rather than complete chance.

José Perales points out that there are different kinds of illusion of control, although he calls it 'illusion of mastery', which I prefer for its poetic lilt. One type is related to the notion that some person or force other than ourselves is pulling the strings, and that our behaviour might be able to affect that force. That's something we can recognise in those who believe in the power of prayer, or simple superstition – don't walk under that ladder or you'll have bad luck. The other kind is a belief in our own abilities. That's something at play in those complex football bets we talked about earlier – the feeling that you know quite a lot about football so your instinct that

Rashford will nab the first goal in a 3–1 win is a decent shout.

The illusion of control is a psychological phenomenon that can be particularly effective among the cohort of people most likely to be problem gamblers: young men. 'The average gambler in Spain some years ago was a slot machine gambler who had been having problems with gambling for a long time, maybe with an average age of about fifty,' Perales tells me. 'The new customer is much younger, more educated, still male mostly.'

That's a socio-demographic profile associated with a different kind of mindset, with different vulnerabilities. Perales's contention is that these young, educated men are particularly susceptible to the mostly illusory notion that they are using their intelligence to get ahead.

'Their general reasoning abilities are pretty good. But that doesn't protect them from developing cognitive biases related to how gambling works. You can feed their sense of confidence and self-worth by making them develop the feeling that they can control much more than they really can. Designing the product in such a way that you increase the sense of control or the sense that you are learning something.'

As we've seen, this could work by displaying hot numbers or nudging bettors towards complex markets where they believe they are well informed. It also works with something incredibly simple like the mechanism of an online slots game. In some games you click on 'Spin' and the reels whizz round and stop of their own accord. In others, you can stop them at a moment of your choosing.

'It's very difficult to avoid the feeling that the physical process determines the outcome. But it's just a random-number generator,' says Perales. In other words, whether you stop the spin or you let the computer do it, it doesn't make a difference. But it somehow feels as if it does.

Natasha Dow Schüll offers even more deceptive examples in

*Addiction by Design*, including a game called Strike It Rich, in which players are invited to help guide a bowling ball on a screen.[8] While the game allows players to lift, move and aim the ball, its final destination is determined by a random-number generator.

The association of betting success with self-worth and self-esteem – a feeling that the illusion of control feeds upon – remains in effect even after the gambling session is over. Something Perales has been researching recently is interpretative bias, where we mislead ourselves about why something has happened. Imagine you lose £1,000 in a single day. If you accept that this was your fault, or you did something wrong, that's quite a significant moment in how you perceive yourself.

Accepting losses forces you to see yourself in a different light. Something that people with a gambling disorder are known to do is reinterpret events in a way that is not as painful for them, looking for reasons beyond their own irrational choice to stake too much money on a game whose outcomes cannot be predicted. 'It's not my fault, I did everything right and then something happened' is how Perales describes it. In this example, the illusion is that 'I did everything right' when no such dynamic exists. 'In probabilities, shit happens. It happens all the time.'

This reminded me of a conversation I had with James Grimes, a recovering addict who set up The Big Step, a charity and campaign group devoted to exposing and breaking the links between gambling and football. 'When I was nineteen I had a massive bet on Peterborough,' he told me. 'Their keeper, Joe Lewis, made a terrible mistake that cost me loads of money. I remember tweeting him saying he was awful and how much he'd cost me, that I've got no food for the week now.'

James's abusive tweet should have been a red flag that he had a severe problem. It was patently ludicrous to think that his loss had anything to do with the footballer, rather than with the unpredictable nature of the universe. What was that phrase? Shit happens all the time.

'At no point did I consider that stopping gambling was the solution,' said James. 'It was always that I know a lot about football so it's a matter of time before I pay all this debt off.' James was labouring under the illusion that he was in control, when nothing could have been further from the truth. His belief stemmed from the idea that he was pretty informed about what he was betting on.

Philip Newall recently looked at an innovation that appears to put some of the power back into the hands of clued-up punters but which actually does the exact opposite. Punters have always been able to build their own bets to some degree. A well-known example of this is Eddie Kirkland, who bet that his son Chris would play in goal for England before he was thirty, and won £10,000 when Chris came on as a substitute twelve years later. These days, social media has allowed firms to soup up this process. William Hill, for instance, invites punters to request their own bet through Twitter, using the hashtag #YourOdds. The feature, which is also present on the company's smartphone app, lets you put together your own scenario, suggest it to the bookmaker – and get given odds in return.

Newall found that the house edge on requested bets – in other words, the proportion of money staked on these markets that William Hill can expect to pocket – is 43.7%.[9] That's around ten times as much as a straight wager on home win, away win or draw. Request-a-bet is a feature that takes advantage of both the illusion of control and the representativeness heuristic. Not only did you decide what scenario you wanted to bet on, you painted a believable picture of it for yourself.

Indeed, the illusion of control often overlaps with other features of gambling psychology.[10] For instance, academic research has found that slot machine players typically adopt the so-called 'minimax' strategy.[11] The traditional slot machine that most of us picture in our mind's eye has one 'line of play', a single horizontal line along which, you hope, three identical pictures match to give you that jackpot moment. Modern online slots typically feature multiple lines of play. You can divide up your bet by placing amounts all around the screen. The minimax strategy involves placing the smallest possible bet on the maximum number of lines displayed on the screen. That means one of your mini-bets is more likely to pay off, although, of course, the majority will not. You can do exactly the same with roulette, placing one or two chips on lots of numbers.

The average payout from the minimax strategy is exactly the same as lumping everything on one line over time, yet the feeling of deploying a strategy gives the player belief in their own agency. The researchers found that the minimax strategy was more likely to result in players extending their session over time too. The illusion of control plays a part in this but so does something else: losses disguised as wins.

## LOSSES DISGUISED AS WINS

A win is a win and a loss is a loss, right? Not quite.

Make a simple bet on Tiger Roll to win the Grand National and you lose your stake if the thoroughbred throws his rider at the first fence. There's no hiding the fact that you've lost. That isn't always the case, though. One of the most common devices that gambling firms use to placate punters and keep them coming back for more are losses disguised as wins.

On a slot machine, you might deposit some money on Egyptology-themed game Eye of Horus, set your bet to £1 and spin. Most of the time you lose the stake. A small percentage of the time you spin and get more than £1 back. But one of the other outcomes is that you lose a portion of your stake, say 50p. At that point, an animated box flashes up saying 'Winner paid 50p'. 'Objectively you've still lost,' says Sharman. But the slot machine frames it as a win.

When players adopt the minimax strategy, as many do, that loss disguised as a win happens again and again, reinforcing the notion that they are experiencing multiple small wins when, of course, they are slowly siphoning money out of their own wallet. 'For me the [disguised losses] were what made FOBTs so dangerous and so addictive,' says Sharman. 'Depending on how you play, it's actually quite easy to "win" something on every spin. So it makes the gambler believe they are constantly winning a little bit.'

Gambling companies have an incentive to ensure you don't twig that you're steadily haemorrhaging cash, and that incentive manifests itself in the way games are designed. Typically, a machine might flash up with the same music and the same lights for a win as it does for a loss disguised as a win.

'The only feedback you might get is the lights and sounds,' says Sharman. 'So, if there's no difference between the feedback you get from a win and what you get from a disguised loss, that's a clever way of tricking the neurological circuitry.'

In a 2013 study by researchers at the University of Waterloo, Canada, the team managed to reverse the effect of losses being disguised by happy music.[12] Instead, they played 'negative' music over small losses. This might be familiar to players of early platform computer games: the sad music when your character steps on a bomb or falls down a hole – the comedy 'wah-wah-waaaah' of failure, if you like. When researchers played sounds like this with every loss, they noticed players stopped overestimating how much success they were having.

It stretched credulity to imagine that the researchers were the first to realise all of this. Game developers will surely have known exactly what effect these features had. I've heard tell of game developers giving presentations to industry executives, explaining how it all works, how to extract the most money out of people by tweaking features such as music and graphics.

In 2020, the Gambling Commission set up an industry working group led by game designers Playtech and SG Gaming to look into ways of making slots and other products safer. One of the results of the process was that the misleading happy music was abolished.[13] Of course, under pressure from the regulator, the operators hit upon this as one of the solutions because they knew exactly how it worked.

Sometimes, though, the companies game the very systems designed to inform and protect punters. By order of the UK Gambling Commission, betting terminals in high-street bookmakers, online casino games and slot machines all have to carry information about the average amount that players will lose over time. Put simply, this is how much customers win back on average, measured over tens of thousands of spins. If players win approximately 85p for every £1 they put in, the return to player is 85%. The Commission allows companies to publish this information in one of two ways. They can either describe it as 'return to player' or 'house edge'. Invariably they choose 'return to player'. After all, if you're the player, it sounds more benign that way.

## NEAR MISSES

This phenomenon is so well known that it has become a cultural cliché, illustrating that agonising feeling of 'so near yet so far'. The reels on the one-armed bandit spin, the first strip lands on cherries, and the second strip lands on cherries too. The third strip briefly touches on cherries . . . and then slides on – perhaps in slow motion – to the lemon, or the gold bars. Behind the meme lies a strange phenomenon.

'Near misses are very interesting in that they produce this strange bivalent response,' says Steve Sharman. 'They're consistently rated as being more unpleasant. People feel worse when they have a near miss than they do when there's a massive miss. At the same time, they make people want to continue gambling more.'

Recovering addict Martin Paterson remembers that effect all too well and how maddening it could be when he was playing FOBTs: 'If I was on twenty-eight it would give me twenty-nine. If I was on zero it would give me three.' Martin would try to physically shove the machine to move the ball in his favour, like you might with a 2p machine at a seaside arcade. 'That's the madness, trying to nudge a digital ball,' he said.

Sharman and his fellow researchers decided to test how gamblers react to two different types of slot machine near miss: the ones where the reel spins one place too far, beyond the 'payline', and the one where it doesn't spin far enough.[14] Interestingly, they found that when the reel doesn't reach the payline, the gambler is more likely to keep on playing, having apparently been on the cusp of the jackpot. But if the reel moves one place too far, it seems to dissuade people from continuing, almost as if the chance of a win briefly materialised and must now have gone for good. Yet, of course, neither outcome actually has any bearing on the result of the next spin.

Modern online slot machine games, with their multiple lines of play, are more complex than the old-school one-armed bandits. They move much faster too, in order to increase the rate at which they take your money. Both of these phenomena make it harder to spot near misses during regular play, but they're still there. Most slots have bonus features, an occasional moment where the opportunity to win a bigger prize comes up and the gambler pays closer attention, including to near misses. This is when today's slot machine gambler might be more likely to experience the emotional reaction to the perception that they almost won big.

Online casino and slots games are growing in popularity, taking nearly £3.2 billion from punters in the year to March 2020,

£800 million more than they did four years earlier. More and more people are being exposed to psychological effects such as the near miss. But dark nudges and psychological tricks are not confined to slot machines. Gambling companies have figured out that they can deploy the same tactic in football betting, a significantly more widespread activity that is growing even faster. While casino income grew by a third between 2016 and 2020, football betting doubled. Gambling firms have smartly transplanted the tricks of the casino to this rapidly expanding arena.[15]

'Paddy Power were one of the first to do it,' says Sharman, high-lighting a common offer pegged to accumulator bets. This type of bet, known as an acca, is slightly different from the scorecast, which invites you to guess multiple outcomes contained within the same game or event. The acca requires you to pick several results across multiple games and get them all right. It's one of those complex bets with long odds. Players typically place small wagers, knowing they'll probably lose but with a small chance of a high return, like a mini-lottery ticket.

The near-miss effect works here too. 'If you have a five-team acca and four teams win, you can get your money back as a free bet,' says Sharman. 'That's really focusing on those motivational properties. They're saying, "You were so close, have another go!" It's an obvious use of a psychological mechanism to encourage people to continue gambling.'

## HOUSE MONEY

The feeling that you're getting a good deal is another motivating factor that makes you more likely to bet. You've had something for nothing, or for less than you should have had it. But it's worth it for the house if it brings you back for a second bet at riskier odds.

One of the products that has emerged in recent years is 'boosted odds', where the bookmaker gives you much longer odds than you would usually get, say 15–1 that a good team such as Chelsea will beat a weaker Fulham side. Sometimes this will be on offer to new customers only, as a means of driving new account sign-ups.

The same phenomenon is at play with the 'free' bets and bonus spins that companies hand out. 'It's called the house money effect,' explains Philip Newall. 'People are much more risk-seeking with money they've won than with money they've paid in.'

We all like something for nothing and we're prepared to risk it too. If the house gives you a free spin, you've got nothing to lose. Except that such free bets and bonuses usually come with strings attached. You get them, for the most part, only on the condition that you'll 'roll over' the bet into a second or third one. Sometimes the bet has to be rolled over many more times before it can be withdrawn. The house money effect makes that whole process feel like a free ride. Of course, all the while you are becoming habituated to gambling, and you're more likely to return with your own money and to go on longer rides, this time at your own expense.

## BET IN PLAY: THE RISK OF NOVELTY

Competition in the UK marketplace is fierce – and the number of people interested in gambling is more limited than, say, the number interested in buying groceries. Operators have had to work hard to stand out from the crowd in what is probably the world's most mature betting market.

There's only so much you can do with snazzy branding and advertising, so the smartest and most successful firms occasionally come up with new ways to package up bets to make them seem attractive. Innovation is partly about customer acquisition, finding ways to get people to bet with you rather than with someone else. But product innovation also offers new opportunities to widen the gap between how attractive the bet looks to a punter and how sensible a wager it really is.

One of the more successful innovations of recent years has been the 'cash out' option, a common element of football betting in particular. Say you've put £10 on Tottenham Hotspur to beat West Ham 3–0 at odds of 10–1, meaning you stand to walk away with £100 if they do. With ten minutes left in the game, Spurs are winning 3–0 but you have a suspicion they might concede, ruining your bet. The bookmaker will allow you to cash out, to take some winnings now, but at less favourable odds. You get the certainty of the win, albeit smaller than the one you might have been in line for, while the bookmaker potentially saves themselves an even bigger payout.

The effects of this on the psychology of gamblers – and addicts in particular – is unknown, because the feature hasn't been around long enough to be studied in depth. 'You can cash out a bet and win less than you should have done, or at the other extreme you can cash out a bet that would have lost, so everything you get is a bonus,' says Sharman. 'We have no idea how that influences behaviour.'

We do know that cash out is just part of a wider phenomenon that has given experts cause for concern. Cash out is part of in-play betting, the brainchild of bet365. It is a genuinely game-changing product, perhaps the biggest innovation in gambling this century. Before the internet – and smartphones in particular – betting on football was mostly a matter of placing a wager and waiting until the game was over. Technology has made it possible to bet on anything at any time, with almost instantaneous results. Bets are no longer necessarily about who will win, or even score, but about something much more random, like which team will win the next corner.

Now, in-play betting is king. For bet365 it typically accounts for around 80% of revenue.

'There are lots of components of that type of gambling that we know are important in the development of problems,' says Sharman. 'There's lots of control because you're making a decision based on what you're watching. It's very quick – you can bet on who gets the next corner and the outcome can be resolved in thirty seconds. You can do it a lot, piling on different bets and games all the time. I'm not sure if everyone offers this but on bet365 you can modify your accumulator even after the games have started. We have zero clue how that actually impacts behaviour. The only people I'd suggest have an idea of the psychological impact of that are the gambling providers themselves. We're constantly playing catch-up.'

As ever, the technological innovation happens first and the re-action to it happens much, much later. Products are released onto the market without any testing to see whether they might be harm-ful. Gambling reform campaigners have called for a rigorous testing regime that could result in products being subject to different restrictions, depending on how dangerous they appear to be. So far, no such thing exists.

Sharman gambles now and then – not on something like FOBTs or online slots where there is a house edge, but on football, where he does at least have some hope of predicting outcomes. 'I had six teams in an acca and one let me down and I could feel the impact of these tricks even though I know how it's working.'

I've felt the same way while road-testing, for research purposes, a gambling app that I wanted to write about. All I needed for my five-team acca to turn £10 into £60 was for Celtic to beat Hiber-nian, usually a pretty reliable bet. Of course, they didn't, and I felt that irrational frustration, as if someone else was to blame, as if fate was being unfair to me.

If someone who doesn't bet and a psychology professor are both vulnerable to such emotions, what does that say for the rest of us, and for addicts in particular?

Recovering addict Adrian Howard, a civil servant from Blackpool, explained to me what rapid-fire in-play sports betting has meant for him: 'Before, you could enjoy a football match, sit there and watch it and that bet can't change. When the cash out option became prominent I wouldn't look and watch the game, I'd sit and look at that [the value of the bet] go up or down.'

## ADDICTION BY DESIGN?

There is a question mark over the extent to which gambling firms are deploying these techniques with precision. Some of these phenomena are so woven into the fabric of certain gambling products that they aren't so much being weaponised as just becoming a fundamental feature of gambling. If you're at a casino and you put all your chips on twenty-five, spin the roulette wheel and it lands on twenty-six, the only person you can blame for that near miss is Lady Luck, whatever the detrimental effects on you may be. It's a near miss, but not a manufactured one. It is self-evidently an intrinsic part of the game you've chosen.

It would, of course, be different if a digital game were designed in such a way as to make this happen more than is statistically likely. I have spoken to many problem gamblers who are convinced that this is the case, that the machines are rigged to push your buttons as much as you push theirs, to maximise near misses and capitalise on psychological factors such as loss aversion or the gambler's fallacy. I have never seen any evidence for this and such information would surely be closely guarded by any company unscrupulous enough to deploy it.

The same goes for the 'early win'. This is something that crops up again and again in my conversations with gambling addicts and is backed up by statistics. A 2019 report from the National Gambling Treatment Service, an umbrella term for several organisations offering help to addicts, found that 59% of those receiving treatment had experienced a big win at the start of their gambling career.[16] It makes sense that hitting the jackpot soon after you start gambling – or even within the course of a session – creates a memory of that sweet feeling that might drive you to gamble more and more, hoping to recapture the same taste. It's reminiscent of the horror stories parents tell their kids about drug dealers giving out free samples to get people hooked.

In the course of my journalism, I occasionally experiment with various gambling products so that I can get a better idea of what I'm talking about. On my very first go with online slots, using a game called Starburst, I had a couple of big wins. (Steady on, we're only talking a tenner here.) I don't know what would have happened if I'd carried on gambling but the return to player on that game was 96.09%, so it's a certainty that I'd have lost my winnings eventually. If it could be proven that firms were deliberately facilitating early wins on games of chance, that would be a serious and sinister brain-hack liable to foster addictive behaviour. For now, that proof does not, as far as I am aware, exist.

When it comes to online casino games and slots, Kim Lund feels that, for the most part, something less cunning is going on: that firms are simply watching what makes money and repeating it in a robotic process of trial and error by people with little affection for the actual games they offer: 'My main gripe with the industry is that it has, to a large degree, been run by people who don't love it, who treat them [gamblers] as dumb sheep. They see gambling as a commodity just like petrol: "We have a commodity – how do we sell it? What else can we sell them while they're at the gas station?"'

When the bosses have only minimal interest in the products, a disconnect emerges that obscures who is responsible for how the game affects the player. These days, gambling companies' websites are flexible – deliberately so. A skilled game designer can develop a slots game, plug it into an operator's platform and start getting paid as soon as people lose money.

'That's allowed people who think slots are interesting to build a boutique company and see if they can innovate. There's great work done that way,' says Lund. 'But it also isolates the developers from the customers and it isolates the company dealing with the customers from the product development. If the developer applied any psychological tricks to make the slots more appealing, by the time it ends up with the company that markets it, they can say: "We don't know, we have an open platform for slots and someone suggested we sold this, so we did." Then they sell it to the customer and the developer can say: "We have no idea what the effect is."'

The result is a self-perpetuating evolutionary mechanism that rewards the development of addictive content while absolving anyone from the responsibility for its creation or its impact.

In *Addiction by Design*, Schüll identifies this problem in conversation with game designer Randy Adams, sometimes described as the 'Michelangelo of Slots'.[17] Asked to identify what makes the difference between a game being fun and it being particularly addictive, he said that it came down to how the game was built. But he stated that it was 'not intentional on our part, just the way it happened to evolve'. As with Lund's description of an architecture that allows everyone to avoid blame, Schüll comments that 'accountability for addictive behaviour jumped from one position to another, never quite settling'.

And Lund highlights one more feature that has emerged in online games in support of the notion that many companies have no real interest in the product they are producing, as long as it pays. If a gambler selects the 'auto-play' feature, rather than pressing the button to spin each time, they can set the computer to do it for them, up to a certain number of spins or a maximum monetary value. In theory this means you are placing a maximum limit on your loss.

But it's easy to lose track of what's happening, and big losses can stack up this way too. Some games allow you to bet up to £500 a spin and auto-play one hundred times. That's a cool £50,000 at stake while you cook dinner. Had you been in charge of each spin, you might have thought twice.

As a game designer, this sort of thing is anathema to Lund, like a musician recording an album only for someone to play it on fast-forward. It also makes it harder to argue that what you're selling is a normal leisure pastime. 'I enjoy playing *Top Gun* slots because I like the film, I get to hear the music, same for *Star Wars*, or *Game of Thrones*,' he says. 'But then [with auto-play] the slot is spinning so fast that none of that can be realised because you're not even aware it's happening. How do you decide at what speed you're basically eradicating everything that is good about your slot beyond the basic addiction-driven mechanism?'

The Gambling Commission banned auto-play as of 31 October 2021.[18] Again, it was the result of a consultation with industry operators, who knew exactly how dangerous it could be.

## GAMBLING BY STEALTH: LOOT BOXES AND SOCIAL GAMING

In the past five or ten years, the lines between gambling and other types of online activity have started to blur. I'm not much of a video gamer any more, so it was 2017 before I heard about a product that looked and felt like gambling but, technically, wasn't.

Social games are those moreish little time-wasters you see on mobile phones and social media, such as FarmVille and Mafia Wars. They're deemed 'social' because you can interact with other players, exchanging in-game items or sending each other messages.

Perhaps naively, I was surprised to find how many of these games were modelled on gambling or had gambling features integrated into their narrative, anything from poker to casino table games and online slots. There were no age restrictions – although some of the games said they were 'aimed' at people over twenty-one.[19] Nor did there seem to be any apparent restrictions on how appealing they might be to children. You could spend real money on in-game items that would help you progress but, crucially, you could not stake money on a chance outcome and win, meaning they were not gambling games.

One of them featured children's cartoon characters the Flintstones, while another was themed around the *Rapunzel* fairytale. A third was simply called OMG! Kittens. A Christmas feature in Jackpot Party Casino Slots was called Toys for Tots. After signing up to the app I received email reminders, sometimes twice a day, offering bonuses and other perks, much like the inducements on offer to customers of real gambling companies. After a 'win', players are invited to 'share free coins with your friends so they can win too!'

These games felt like training wheels for young people, teaching them to gamble in later life. That suspicion grew when I realised how many of them were produced by Scientific Games, a US-based company that manufactures FOBTs and casino games for major gambling firms. It reminded me of the chocolate cigarettes that newsagents used to sell when I was a kid growing up in the late eighties and nineties. They're rarely seen any more and unsurprisingly are banned in many countries after successive studies linked them to an increased likelihood of taking up smoking as an adult. But at least those were not manufactured by Philip Morris.

One of the most popular – and profitable – mobile games at time of writing is Coin Master, where a three-wheel slot is the driving mechanism of the game. The age rating for the game on Play Store, Google's pre-installed app store for Android devices, was 12+ at time of writing.

The nexus between gambling and games was among the emerging risks singled out in a 2017 report by the Gambling Commission. The regulator found that children who played social games were more likely to bet money on adult gambling products. 'Among young people who have ever played online gambling-style games, a quarter had spent their own money on any gambling activity in the past week, significantly higher than the average of 12% among all 11- to 16-year-olds,' the report found.[20]

Mark Griffiths, professor of behavioural addiction at Nottingham Trent University, told me that, much like those candy cigarettes, social games were the 'number-one risk factor' for children becoming problem gamblers, even if hosted on Facebook rather than on a gambling site. 'What games like these do is behaviourally and socially condition children from an early age to be into gambling,' he said. 'The thing about social networking games is that in the end you never lose. They set up unrealistic expectations of what gambling involves. If you win all that virtual money, you might think that if you'd been playing with real money you would have won too.'

Social games aren't classified legally as gambling, no matter how much they might look like it. The reason for this is that you can't take any money out of them as winnings, although, of course, you can put as much as you like in. The lack of a wagering dynamic means the games makers do not have to follow the same rules.

'I've seen social casinos do way worse things than gambling casinos,' says Lund. 'I've seen them do things like shifting the win rates of machines exactly when they want to so that suddenly you're winning. They massage you until you think it's worth it and then they shift it back again. They defend that by saying it's not real money, it's just for entertainment.'

While social games have raised concerns, another product of the gaming world has grown into a far more high-profile issue, and one that is yet to be resolved.

## LOOT BOXES AND SKINS

My *Guardian* colleague Alex Hern aired misgivings about loot boxes in a 2017 article that highlighted the case of a gamer who racked up a credit card bill of $16,000 while playing the video game Final Fantasy Brave Exvius (FFBE), a free-to-play game for android and iOS based on the popular Final Fantasy series.[21]

Alex explained it very well, so I'll let his words from that article speak for themselves.

'It's one of a number of games which use a similar system to reel in, and profit from, players,' he wrote. 'Unlockables – be they new characters in FFBE, new players in the FIFA football sims, weapon upgrades in the new *Star Wars* game Battlefront II, or car parts in racing game Need for Speed – aren't available for direct sale. Instead players buy, with real money or in-game currency, a random item or set of items, in what are termed "loot boxes". Players have no guarantee of what they'll get, and no way to guide the game into giving them something they need or want. The system is a sort of weaponised behavioural psychology, perfectly pitched to exploit all the cognitive weaknesses that make people so susceptible to addiction and compulsion. They pull all the standard strings of problem gambling: the desire for one more go, the misplaced belief that an unlucky streak must come to an end, the hope that continuing to bet will reverse the losses already incurred.'

Two years after Alex wrote that, the prevalence of loot boxes had soared, as computer games companies cottoned on to a way to boost revenue. Loot boxes and other in-game purchases massively expanded the revenue-generating life cycle of a game, boosting them beyond an initial purchase and into repeat transactions, as players paid to improve and prolong their enjoyment.

Researchers at the University of York studied 463 games on the desktop computer gaming application Steam and found that the proportion featuring loot boxes had increased from about 4% to 71% over nine years.[22] Having identified the increase, David Zendle, who led the team, wanted to know whether loot boxes might correlate with increased spending on traditional gambling. Could the rise of this new product spur problem gambling, or appeal to those who were already suffering?

An opportunity arose when he heard that a little-known game called Heroes of the Storm was due to release an update removing loot boxes as a feature of play. He recruited gamers and split them into groups. One group were gambling addicts, as defined by their score on the commonly used Problem Gambling Severity Index (PGSI) measure, which asks people about their relationship with gambling. The others were not. Zendle measured how much they all spent on the game before and after the removal of loot boxes. The addicts stopped spending on in-game purchases when the loot boxes disappeared. The ordinary gamers carried on spending via more straightforward, non-randomised purchases. One group appeared to be interested largely in gambling-style products, the other in features that enhanced the video gaming experience.[23]

'Everywhere you measure it, you get it,' Zendle told me. 'If you measure someone's problem gambling and how much they're spending on loot boxes, you find a correlation between them. The more severe their problem gambling, the more they spend. It's a correlation but it's a very robust correlation.'

Despite the commonalities between loot boxes and gambling, they aren't treated in the same way. In a 2019 evidence session before MPs, Gambling Commission boss Neil McArthur cited 'significant concerns' about loot boxes. The difficulty for the regulator, he said, is that the law does not currently classify them as gambling products. This is because, in the jargon used by the Commission, items contained in loot boxes are not 'money's worth'. In other words, game developers did not allow players to 'cash out' by exchanging the items for real money. There are two problems with this approach, one that the Commission identified and one that it did not.

The Commission has acknowledged – and sought to address – the emergence of illicit third-party sites that have sprung up to allow the sale and purchase of in-game items.[24] This means that any kid playing a video game can stake a small amount on a loot box, win big, and then exchange the item for a higher amount than they wagered. The mechanics of this transaction are no different from regular gambling. You stake some money and potentially get money back. Your brain logs the experience of gambling and winning. There are real-world parallels too. As with the streamers who film themselves playing online slots, there are gamers who film themselves opening loot boxes, celebrating like jackpot winners when FIFA's loot box feature gives them Lionel Messi or Cristiano Ronaldo.

Yet, despite these gambling-like characteristics, the law doesn't see it that way. Zendle suggests this is down to a legislative blind spot that is unsurprising given that the law moves slowly and politicians are middle-aged or older. That idea of 'money's worth', he points out, is of questionable use to people who spend much of their time in a virtual world where traditional understanding of value – not to mention what constitutes currency – is breaking down. 'Money's worth is such a stupid concept,' he said. 'You can't get your money out of Steam's ecosystem, you can't turn it into a £5 note you can spend at Pret. The Gambling Commission is therefore not forced to acknowledge it as money's worth. But the idea that loot box contents do not have value does not take into account a lot of cultural factors.'

Steam has a marketplace inside it where gamers can trade items that they have bought or won. Zendle added up every purchase made on the portal and found just under £5 billion worth of trades. These trades show that in-game items have value, albeit in a marketplace isolated from traditional currencies.

The Gambling Act 2005 is frequently referred to as an analogue law in a digital age and this is a good example. The law does not account for the notion of a digital item having value because, in the marketplaces where such goods are exchanged, nobody is handing over real money.

In Belgium, loot boxes have been classed as gambling products. The result was that most video games companies simply withdrew them from sale rather than be forced to obtain a gambling licence and market only to over-eighteens. While parliamentarians in the UK seem minded to follow suit, the pace of change has been glacial and nothing had been done as of August 2021.

In her book *Games Without Frontiers*, noted gambling researcher Heather Wardle warns about the ever-closer relationship between gambling and games. 'Game developers, by borrowing from and incorporating more gambling-like features in their products, have either wittingly or unwittingly become agents for the further promotion and normalisation of gambling and its associated ideals within our societies,' she writes.[25]

We'll return to the convergence of gambling and gaming later in the book, when we look at the new frontiers and boundaries that the industry has in its sights. The blurring of the lines between the two is part of an emerging trend that politicians and regulators will need to grasp very quickly, in the way that one might argue they have failed to do with technological changes in the gambling landscape between the turn of the century and today.

Now, though, I want to turn to something much less subtle but hugely significant in how gambling established a hold on our society. If brainhacks and psychological tricks have functioned as surgical tools, the industry has used blunt instruments too. Of these, one of the most effective and dangerous has been the VIP scheme.

# 4. VIPS: VULNERABLE IMPRESSIONABLE PUNTERS

This is the end result of all the bright lights and the comp trips, of
all the champagne and free hotel suites and all the broads and all
the booze. It's all been arranged just for us to get your money.

ACE ROTHSTEIN (AL PACINO), *CASINO* (1995)

Many people enjoy the occasional drink, especially in the UK, a
nation not known for its temperance. Plenty have a favourite pub,
a 'local' where, if they show their face often enough, they might be
considered one of the regulars, perhaps on first-name terms with
the landlord. A select few may find themselves the lucky recipient
of a drink on the house now and again, by way of thanks for their
custom. There is, after all, nothing wrong with giving a little bit back
to the people who support your business.

But what if the pub landlord went further than that – a lot
further? What if they sent regular emails or text messages to their
biggest-spending regulars, offering freebies? Patrons of this hypothetical pub – let's call it the Dog & Duck – could be browsing
Facebook, texting a friend or shopping on the internet when up
pops a notification. 'FREE BONUS DRINK: Ice-cold gin and
tonic waiting for you on the bar right now!' It could even take the
form of a more personal message, something along the lines of: 'I
can't help noticing you haven't been in for a while. Would a free
drink or two fix that?' What if they even phoned you up with the

same entreaties? How much willpower would be required to resist such personal attention?

Alternatively, what if global alcoholic drinks companies were able to measure how much of their product you drank and reward the biggest spenders with gifts, such as a Christmas hamper or a day out at the FA Cup Final, all expenses paid? Would that increase the likelihood that customers drink to excess? Would it hinder alcoholics' attempts to get clean?

In practice, such a love-bombing campaign almost certainly wouldn't be permitted. Politicians and regulators are well apprised of the manifest dangers posed by alcohol addiction and have targeted the heavy discounting that renders alcohol artificially cheap. Drinks companies have long been wise to the importance of showing their commitment to responsible drinking. The Portman Group, set up in 1989, is the alcohol industry's social responsibility group and it keeps a pretty strict eye on its members to ensure they aren't promoting their products recklessly.

In any case, even if drinks companies or pub landlords could get away with brazenly aggressive sales tactics, the strategy might not be all that effective. On a cold, rainy night, the walk to the pub or the off-licence might be enough on its own to dissuade the more casual drinker. Partners, friends, flatmates or family members might ask searching questions of anyone who disappeared to the pub too often, returning very obviously the worse for wear.

Gambling, though, is different to drinking alcohol. Pubs and drinks companies rely on real-world customers making real-world purchases to keep the cash flowing in. But an online bookmaker or casino can take your bet instantaneously, at any time, from anywhere. You can gamble while your other half lounges on the sofa beside you, watching a series on Netflix. They would be none the wiser if you frittered away the money that funds your mortgage payments, or the savings meant for your children's inheritance.

With the rise of smartphones, online betting firms have been quick to capitalise on this immediacy of access. Through direct marketing, such as emails, calls and texts to customers, they are able to encourage punters to bet and see instant results. These messages come with incentives attached such as bonus bets, 'free' spins, or other special offers. And, if your custom is particularly lucrative, you might be awarded VIP status.

## RISE OF THE VIP

It's a label that conjures up images of a high roller gracing the tables of Monaco or Las Vegas, sharing witticisms with the casino owner over a Martini. If not James Bond flirting at the baccarat table, perhaps a film star, footballer or stable owner laying a big bet on the Grand National. The reality, in many cases, is a world away from that. For the most part, attaining VIP status has typically come down to displaying a tendency to lose large sums of money, whether you can afford it or not.

One industry insider, a betting tipster with genuine expertise in horse racing, has experienced first hand how bookies treat customers who win, compared to those who lose: 'I make money from betting because it's been my whole life and I've had every account I ever opened closed,' he told me. 'I opened an account with one operator, deposited money, placed a whole lot of bets and they lost. I got an email inviting me as a VIP client and an invitation to the darts the following Friday. The next day I had three bets and they all won. I had my VIP status revoked and my invitation to the darts revoked too.'

Far from being the preserve of millionaires and big winners, VIP loyalty programmes have, time and again, proven to be a honey trap for addicts on the brink of financial ruin and mental health breakdown. In fact, the schemes are cited in roughly seven out of ten sanctions issued by the Gambling Commission against companies who fail to meet their obligation to protect vulnerable people.

Between 2015 and 2020 alone, the Commission has levied sanctions against a string of firms for increasingly jaw-dropping transgressions relating to VIPs. At one time or another, almost every well-known name in betting has been implicated. It's hard to believe that these were the exception either. Far more likely, they are the tip of the iceberg.

## SIX OF THE WORST

### Betway

In 2020 the online firm that sponsors West Ham United Football Club paid a record £11.6 million settlement for accepting millions of pounds of stolen money from high-spending VIP customers, some of whom were displaying clear signs of gambling addiction.[1]

One customer shovelled over £4 million to Betway, despite the firm's internal systems having flagged the account twenty times as a potential risk. On each occasion, staff took the gambler's word as evidence of their source of funds. The customer's details were even referred to Betway's board of directors, who decided to allow the gambler to keep playing, and the account was only closed after the police contacted the company about it.

Another customer deposited £1.6 million and lost more than £700,000 over three years, despite being unemployed. Betway also accepted £494,000 from a customer who had eleven different accounts with the company and had previously signed up to exclude themselves from gambling, the voluntary measure offered to people struggling with addiction. In total, the company allowed £5.8 million of stolen money to flow through the business, the Commission found.

'The actions of Betway suggest there was little regard for the welfare of its VIP customers or the impact on those around them,' said Richard Watson, executive director at the Gambling Commission.

Betway's CEO, Anthony Werkman, said the company had no interest in profiting from stolen funds and had improved its systems and shut down its VIP programme. 'Betway takes full responsibility for the small number of historic cases which have led to this settlement. We have fully cooperated with the investigation and will take further proactive steps to ensure all recommendations and findings are implemented.'

## Gala Coral

In 2016 the Commission found that systemic failures in Gala Coral's systems had led to it taking hundreds of thousands of pounds from a VIP problem gambler who was using the proceeds of theft to feed his habit.[2] The bookmaker had relied on 'uncorroborated' suggestions that the man was independently wealthy, when in fact he had stolen £800,000 from a vulnerable person. Gala Coral paid out £880,000 in a voluntary settlement but proved no less attractive a business for it. Later that year, Gala Coral was taken over by Ladbrokes in a deal worth £2.3 billion.

The company said it had stopped doing business with the man before it was aware of any police investigation, adding that failures in its controls had 'for the most part' already been addressed the previous year. It also claimed to have beefed up its anti-money-laundering team, improved training and introduced new tools to tighten up customer checks.

'Due to the unique circumstances of this case and the impact upon the family of the amount stolen by the customer, we have agreed with the family to make an *ex gratia* payment to them equal to the customer's losses,' the bookmaker said.

## William Hill

In April 2020 the *Daily Telegraph*'s consumer 'champion' Katie Morley took on the case of siblings who'd discovered that their mother had gambled away £88,000 with William Hill.[3] She had struggled with both alcohol and gambling, and towards the end of her life had developed severe liver disease that left her brain-damaged.

William Hill had made her a VIP member, inviting her to Ascot and a Stone Roses concert.

When the siblings complained to William Hill, the bookmaker told them they had no claim for a return of the money, which is where Morley came in. She checked medical records, establishing the 'significant' nature of their mother's alcoholism-related brain damage. 'The thought of her schmoozing and boozing with William Hill staff who wanted her to place big bets made my skin crawl,' wrote Morley in her column for the newspaper.

Thanks to Morley's help and tenacity, the pair eventually secured a repayment from the bookmaker, but only after a lengthy procedure that saw the company do everything it could to avoid coughing up.

A William Hill spokesman said: 'We are extremely sorry for the situation that arose in respect of the customer referenced. During the time that the customer was with us we saw no indication of any health issues or incapacity. We subsequently found out the position with regards to the customer's health – and following a meeting with the family we agreed to return the customer's funds to them. We take safer gambling very seriously and are committed to using the newest technology and processes to help us to track potential markers of harm and safeguard our customers.'

## LeoVegas and Casumo

In 2019 I spent several days poring over the betting records of a forty-two-year-old recovering addict who adopted the pseudonym

Katie. She had been a successful accountant but had struggled with gambling addiction and ended up losing £125,000 with the online casinos LeoVegas and Casumo.[4] What neither Katie nor I could understand was how the companies' internal systems didn't flag her up as displaying signs of problem gambling behaviour.

She had used nine credit cards. Her losses included a £54,000 deficit racked up during an all-night spree when she'd been allowed to place bets of more than £380,000 on one website in a single session.

Katie, who told her story to me and to BBC Radio 4's *You and Yours* programme, consistently displayed behaviours the Commission said should alert betting companies to problem gambling. These included making dozens of failed deposits – where her banks refused to let her place bets – and cancelling the withdrawal of winnings at the last minute to plough money back into casino games.

Both companies made her a VIP customer without implementing affordability checks and showered her with 'free' spins. Casumo offered her complimentary tickets to events at Wembley Arena even as she gambled away the proceeds of her high-level job. To add insult to injury, internal communications among Casumo staff revealed that an employee had called her a 'prick' after she later complained that the company had not stepped in earlier.

LeoVegas declined to comment on Katie's case but said that it 'takes safer gambling very seriously, and follows strict policies and procedures to ensure compliance with our legal obligations and our licence conditions'. Casumo also said it could not comment on Katie's case but insisted some of the details were 'incorrect', although it declined to elaborate.

## MansionBet

One of the more staggering examples of company negligence I've seen – and it's a crowded field – involved MansionBet, an online firm that has built its brand recognition in the UK by sponsoring football teams such as Tottenham Hotspur and AFC Bournemouth. The case involved a gambler whom I'll call Max. MansionBet accepted Max's redundancy payout as proof that he could afford to place thousands of pounds in bets, and then rewarded him with VIP perks for doing so.[5]

The payout was a five-figure sum and, to MansionBet's credit, when Max deposited £8,000, the VIP manager did at least ask for reassurance that he could afford the bets. They were 'a large chunk of your annual salary'. In fact Max did not have a salary; he had a fast-diminishing redundancy cheque and no full-time job. Yet the manager cheerfully accepted his verbal assurance that he had other work, and dished out more free bets in return. In a telephone call, a recording of which was shared with the *Guardian*, the VIP manager said: 'I can tell them [MansionBet's responsible-gambling department] he's received the settlement, he's managing it responsibly and he's got other work. The thing is, we don't even want to do it but we have to do it because the UK gambling regulators make us do it. As a thank you for clearing that up, there's a £100 free bet for you. I hate being intrusive but I'll always reward you if you give me proper answers.'

When I asked MansionBet for comment at the time, they said: 'This case has been reviewed thoroughly by senior management due to the extensive nature of the contacts by the customer, and we are satisfied all conclusions drawn are in line with our regulatory requirements. MansionBet disagrees with the characterisations of the incidents in question, as put forward by you in your questions.' It did not offer further explanation.

## Playtech

The consequences of unfettered VIP schemes don't get any worse than in the tragic case of Chris Bruney. Like Jack Ritchie, he was a young man who took his own life while in the throes of gambling addiction. His is among the most harrowing stories of gambling addiction that I have ever heard.[6]

Just twenty-five years old, Bruney lost £119,000 in five days in 2017 with online casino Winner.co.uk, which kept happily accepting the staggering sums. Despite the fact that Bruney was already handing over breathtaking amounts of money, the company was relentless in the way it pursued him to keep betting more and more, offering him free gifts such as an Apple Watch and asking no questions about where he had found the money to deposit tens of thousands of pounds at a time.

Days before he died, the promising young engineer's personal VIP manager had encouraged him to 'have a go'. He received a £400 cash bonus a matter of hours before he took his own life and yet another bonus, worth £500, arrived shortly afterwards. In his suicide note Chris blamed gambling for his descent into despair.

Initially it seemed as if nobody would face any sanction at all for the way Chris was groomed even as he slid into the abyss. Playtech, which owned Winner.co.uk, forfeited the licence held by the division, a tiny part of its multibillion-pound empire. The result, after an eighteen-month Gambling Commission investigation, was that the company admitted its failings and made a £620,000 charitable donation, far less than the £3.5 million it would have paid out if it hadn't shut down the Winner brand. It was only after intense pressure from the media, most notably the *Daily Mail*'s Tom Witherow, that the company – perhaps mindful of its name being dragged through the mud – agreed to increase the donation to the full £3.5 million.

Claire Milne, Playtech's interim chair in May 2020, said: 'Mr Bruney's death was a tragic event and our deepest sympathies go out to his family for their loss. We sincerely apologise and take full responsibility for the regulatory breaches identified by the Gambling

Commission. The failings occurred in a business that is now closed. We have since invested significantly in making sure these types of breaches do not happen again.'

## WHAT MAKES A VIP?

The circumstances of these cases vary. While most of the so-called VIPs I've listed are men, they range from young to old, from relatively wealthy to people of modest means. But until Bruney's death hit the headlines, more than a decade after the UK put in place its gambling laws, all of these VIP cases had one thing in common. Not once did they trigger any more thoroughgoing examination by regulators or politicians of the schemes themselves. Instead the authorities focused narrowly on individual incidents where the conditions of gambling licences had been breached. What they never addressed was the question of whether the very existence of VIP programmes, or the way in which they were structured, was inherently dangerous. Nobody was asking whether VIP schemes created an incentive for companies to put vulnerable people at risk. Nor was there ever any examination of whether the acquisition of VIP status was driving addicts towards ever more dangerous behaviour. To understand this, we need to know how VIP schemes work and what those who know them intimately have to say.

The most important thing to remember about VIP punters is that they are not selected because they are wealthy. As in the experience of the veteran bettor quoted at the beginning of this chapter, they are picked out of the crowd because they lose, because – in effect – they are walking cash machines.

In February 2019 the *Daily Mail* published an investigation after its reporter Tom Payne infiltrated bet365's Gibraltar-based training centre.[7] While the existence of VIP schemes came as no surprise to anyone familiar with the gambling world, Payne's first-hand experience offered a revealing glimpse into how the company separated VIP punters from the rest of the herd, marking customers for special treatment as soon as they hit a 'net loss threshold'. In other words, a person (P) becomes very important (VI) by virtue of how much cash they haemorrhage.

Once a VIP is made, they become a pretty reliable source of future revenue. Guaranteed sources of income are the stuff of dreams for company finance chiefs. It isn't just about boosting the top line, although that's obviously the main attraction; it's also about certainty, about the freedom to invest and build the business, in the knowledge that you aren't suddenly going to face a cash shortfall. It makes sense, therefore, to invest small sums in order to lock down reliable revenue generators.

The story of one recovering addict I interviewed in 2019 has always struck me as a succinct summation of the VIP dynamic.[8] Phil Worrall, a thirty-three-year-old from Nottingham, had had VIP status with several companies and described to me how it could trigger a vicious cycle: 'The more you bet, the more you'll get given free bets and the more likely that you give it straight back. It keeps you coming back. You might think you've got no money left but if you get an email saying you'll get a £50 free bet if you bet £50 of your own money, you find a way to scrape it together. It's a little hook back in.'

A former VIP with Paddy Power, who asked to remain anonymous, explained how this self-fulfilling prophecy relied on a fiction that was all too easy to believe and which fuelled an increase in risky bets. 'You don't realise at the time that you are actually funding the enhanced bonuses rather than being given preferential treatment. I found myself betting high stakes that I couldn't afford just to ensure I qualified for free bet bonuses.'

Such customers will usually be allocated their very own VIP manager tasked with keeping punters happy, keeping them betting and, most importantly, keeping them from defecting to a rival. The VIP manager isn't any old job. It takes a certain skill set. They need a head for figures in order to calculate the value of a customer and weigh that up against the value of the incentives they might be offered to secure their custom. Sometimes that will be based on internal company norms but a good VIP manager may have discretion to go the extra mile. They need patience, because people who bet a lot can be emotionally volatile when they lose, demanding ever-higher free bets or cashback on losing wagers. Charm is another essential virtue when convincing people to part with their cash.

Job adverts posted on online recruitment portals make no bones about what the role entails.[9] One advert for a 'VIP executive' to work at Gala Bingo's online business, part of the GVC-owned Ladbrokes Coral group, stated that candidates would be working to increase 'overall player lifetime value and the revenue contribution for the VIP player base'. Applicants for the job were told they should contact their VIPs on a regular basis and 'reach out to lapsed VIP players to try and reactivate dormant accounts'. The inherent risk of targeting lapsed gamblers is dealt with in rather peremptory fashion, with a line saying that all of this should be done while 'following the responsible-gambling guidelines'.

A separate advert for Foxy Bingo, also part of GVC, goes one step further than simply 'reaching out' and strays into the territory of analysing customers psychologically, then using these findings to extract money from them. The posting explains that VIP managers should be able to 'identify triggers' that help the company extract maximum value from customers. They should also be able to spot players who 'have the potential' to become a VIP.

A third advert gives some insight into how to go about inspiring loyalty. It calls for staff to help oversee 'business crucial' VIP gamblers at Betfred, including the planning and hosting of 'hospitality events and [. . .] rewards campaigns throughout the year'.

Some recruitment listings raise more questions than they answer. One, for a VIP support representative at the online site 888 Casino, says staff may be required to 'undertake special projects'. It does not mention what these might be, nor does it mention responsible gambling or protection of vulnerable people. It does, however, insist on 'promoting the interests and welfare of the company at all times'.

Once they've got the job, VIP managers have typically been trusted to operate independently in order to keep their VIPs happy. This, for the most part, involves dishing out a dizzying array of freebies and perks, staying in touch with their customers via friendly emails, text messages and even phone calls. For those who don't gamble, or not at the level that warrants any special treatment, it is impossible to imagine what this sort of personal service must be like, or how it might affect one's gambling. Ordinary people don't experience this kind of bespoke service in many areas of life. No matter how many bags of oven chips you buy in Tesco, they're not going to take you to the FA Cup Final.

## LIFE AS A VIP MANAGER

In the years I've been covering the gambling sector for the *Guardian*, it has never been all that hard to find stories about how VIP schemes have fed on, or even fuelled, problem gambling. Such is the volume of harm done by the schemes that, if you wait long enough, desperate punters will simply come to you. It has proven less easy to make contact with the people on the other end of the arrangement – the VIP managers themselves. Some industry insiders have been forthcoming, though. None of them are anti-gambling, for obvious reasons. They've worked in the industry, they consider themselves to know right from wrong and they believe, for the most part, in what they do.

Geoff (not his real name) has worked in the industry for decades.

The first point to note, he says, is that it isn't reasonable to condemn the notion of rewarding customer loyalty in gambling. The industry is, he says, a legitimate enterprise that should be able to look after good customers if it sees a benefit in doing so.

'We had some elderly customers who you got on with. Sometimes we'd want to give them a ring to see if they were OK, if you hadn't heard from them for a few days. You couldn't because it could be taken the wrong way and we were wary of that. But at Christmas, regular customers would get things like a hamper, or some salmon, things like that, as a way of saying thank you for your custom. Some people would say even that's too much. I'm not quite sure where I stand with that but if customers have been with you for six years, and you have no concerns they're spending too much, it feels innocent enough.'

But Geoff has seen at first hand how the VIP structure can motivate people in the industry to overstep the mark in the interests of keeping the money coming in, particularly when they are paid on commission or offered bonuses for getting clients to spend more.

'There was a big punter with a share in a racehorse. He had an account and his VIP manager bought a share in the same horse so they could be at the races with him while he was punting. One of the other lads there said: "This guy is not interested in the horse or being mates with you, he's just here in an official capacity." The bloke [VIP manager] overheard it and set on him [physically attacked him]. He was worried about losing his commission.'

Another former gambling company employee, who also did not want to be named, explains how less volatile VIP managers conduct their business: 'The more proactive VIP managers will give out bonuses or try to meet the VIPs and take them out, form a relationship. They might take them to the races, a meal or a show. They'll know if this guy's a football nut, he might appreciate going to a game. Anything to create more loyalty. I remember at my last company, some of these VIPs were maybe a bit lonely or what have you and one of these people's hobbies was gardening. The VIP manager gave her an exotic plant. She understood who that player was and understood what she'd like. It went down really well. They do that because it makes them money. Bear in mind that some of these VIPs can make or break your business. We had a guy who would drop a million pounds a year, so taking people for a snazzy night in the open that might make them more loyal, that's doing good business.'

There are more subtle ways to keep gamblers happy. In early 2020 a *Guardian* reader got in touch to share screenshots of WhatsApp messages with his VIP manager. In the overwhelming majority of cases I have dealt with, both the gambler and their VIP manager have been male. Conversation typically revolves around sports, betting and little else. Each calls the other 'mate', despite the client–customer relationship that underpins the dialogue.

Here, though, the VIP manager – working for online betting company 10bet – was a young, good-looking woman. Her WhatsApp messages were friendly to the point of flirtation, peppered with emojis and light teasing.

'I have some awesome news [smiley emoji],' she wrote. 'I've spoke with my boss since we talked yesterday and from today on I'm your new account manager [champagne bottle emoji]. If you're interested, I can send you an email with all of my details so you can find me when you need me or you have questions.'

The gambler responded that he was 'delighted' because 'you're incredibly easy to chat to'.

'Hehe, glad that you think like that [smiley emoji]. It means that I'm good at my job. It may seem a bit silly but I want to know a bit more about you, so I've prepared a small survey.'

She went on to ask him about whether he had pets, what his dream job was when he was growing up, his favourite food and drink and his favourite event. She joked about sending him a 'flying carpet' to take him on holiday. He answered the survey and got a £50 free bet in return.

'You're far too kind,' he said.

'Should I take my free bet back?' she teased.

Sometimes the approach is a little less sophisticated. In 2021 I interviewed Andy May, days before he was imprisoned for four years after defrauding his employer and spending £1.3 million of the proceeds on gambling.[10] His VIP manager at Betfair, where he lost £437,000 before anyone thought to verify the source of his apparent riches, became concerned about Andy. His fear was not that Andy was betting too much or too often, nor that he had stopped altogether or defected to a rival operator. No, the concern was that he was not betting enough.

Putting it bluntly, the VIP manager wrote: 'Long time no speak. I noticed you are depositing less than previously, is everything OK?'

Whether VIP managers are flirty or brusque in their bedside manner, they don't apply this kind of pressure out of an innate enthusiasm for their job. Typically they are paid not just a salary but also a commission linked to the amount their clients spend. Just like social media tipsters, VIP managers have an incentive to make sure you lose money.

Some firms have found a way to incentivise their punters in the same way, to make even VIPs not only lose money but work for the pleasure. In late 2019 members of Paddy Power's VIP programme received an email explaining the new 'mates' rates' programme. The idea was that you referred a friend to their VIP scheme and were rewarded for doing so. All you had to do was introduce them to your VIP manager and you'd stand to benefit if they signed up. Perks included a £100 bonus on the next three monthly anniversaries of your mate joining the scheme. If they remained a VIP after ninety days you were entitled to a bottle of champagne and a bonus of up to €2,000. Why groom new dupes when you can have the existing ones do it for you?

When companies spot big-money opportunities, recruitment methods can be even more astonishing. One of the first gambling addicts I ever spoke to in great detail was Antonio Parente,[11] known as Tony. His case was also among the most astonishing I've come across. Unlike many in the VIP category, Tony genuinely gambled large sums, tens of thousands of pounds at a time and more. On one occasion, according to court documents, Paddy Power staff labelled him a 'wild man' after he staked £548,000 in a single day.[12] Tony had enjoyed modest success in Dubai, working in the property industry. He had made his own money but it wasn't nearly enough to fund such astronomical wagers. Such was the ferocity of his gambling habit that he had begun to steal from the clients whose money he was supposed to be investing in real estate. In the end, he has conceded in court, he defrauded more than twenty people – including his own sister – of around £5 million in total. The proceeds were used to fund hundreds of thousands of pounds' worth of wagers with Ladbrokes, Paddy Power, bet365 and William Hill.

In 2017 Tony was convicted of a £77,000 fraud against a former employer, an automotive company, but he escaped a custodial sentence. He has otherwise avoided prosecution. Some of his victims have been remarkably understanding about his addiction and have refrained from seeking a prosecution or suing him. In at least one instance, the fraud took place in Dubai and was only discovered after he had left. With Tony's help the victim, businessman Amarjeet Singh Dhir, turned to the courts to reclaim some of his lost funds from Paddy Power, who he said should have been aware that Tony was a gambling addict who could not afford such sums.

Proceedings exposed the parasitic relationship between VIP managers and their clients.

The court heard[13] that Paddy Power had struck a deal with a couple called Tony and Ericka Carroll, 'VIP introducers' who were paid to woo Parente to defect from Ladbrokes, where he had been gambling before, and to keep him sweet thereafter. Parente was given a £20,000 signing-on bonus, as well as free trips to the Grand National and Premier League football games. The Carrolls, under the terms of their deal with Paddy Power, were entitled to 25% of his losses thereafter, with the payments never to fall below £5,000 a month – a retainer, in effect. According to the *Daily Mail*, which covered the case in depth, they made close to £100,000. The Carrolls have not responded to a request for comment, while Paddy Power has indicated that the sums involved are lower, although it is legally prohibited from saying how much lower.

Whatever the outlay on recruiting Parente, it was more than worth it. A little over a year after signing Tony up, he had gambled away £347,000.

The judge, Mr Justice Griffiths, concluded that: 'Paddy Power knew that it was dealing with a compulsive gambler who could not afford what he was doing, and Paddy Power did not really care.' But, unfortunately for Dhir, he did not find that the victim was entitled to compensation from the company.

The international chief executive of its parent company, Flutter Entertainment, conceded that the case was a 'significant source of embarrassment' for the bookmaker. That ought to be an understatement. The VIP scheme, as described in the High Court, was an elaborate system that incentivised the exploitation of an addict, who turned to crimes that harmed multiple victims.

In a House of Lords select committee evidence session in 2020, gambling bosses described the system of incentives for VIP managers rather more delicately.[14] William Hill boss Ulrik Bengtsson admitted that 'there are people in the organisation who are measured on revenue' – although he insisted that this system was tempered by strict rules on preventing addicts from becoming VIPs. The bosses of bet365 and Paddy Power admitted the same.

In their final report the Lords wrote: 'Despite the care which they profess to take about affordability checks, we find it hard to see how the incentive of higher pay or bonus can fail to tempt staff into putting numbers of players and great amounts wagered above customer safety.'[15]

## BEING A VIP

I got to know Tony Parente long before details of his relationship with Paddy Power emerged, when he was not yet ready to go public with his entire story. He feared prosecution, something he has only been able to avoid because of his high-profile effort to help his victims reclaim their funds from bookmakers. Before Paddy Power wooed him, Tony was a Ladbrokes man.

He told me what it was like to be a VIP. As his addiction spiralled and he started betting with stolen cash, Ladbrokes lavished him with corporate hospitality.[16] They offered him free tickets to Arsenal games, four tickets to see the Floyd Mayweather v Marcos Maidana boxing match in Las Vegas, and an invitation to the company box at Royal Ascot. On one occasion the company agreed to pay for business-class return flights from Dubai to London, worth more than £2,000, so that he could attend the North London derby between Arsenal and Tottenham. Fortnum & Mason hampers arrived at Christmas and, on his birthday, a gift of £3,500 credit in his betting account. The enticements continued to pour in during and after a five-month period when he managed to stop betting.

Text messages between Tony and his VIP manager show that the latter – perhaps incentivised by the same mechanisms that would later enrich Ericka Carroll at Paddy Power – had scant regard for the rules. The conditions of having a UK gambling licence include a requirement that companies check their customers' source of funds. The idea is to be sure they are not betting with stolen money, as Tony was, or gambling more than they can afford.

In one message the VIP manager wrote: 'Don't know if you know about this but there is a new law in place imposed by the Gambling Commission to have on file provenance of funds from its top customers.' He asked Tony for a bank statement, 'to comply with the regulator's policy'. When Tony didn't reply, the VIP manager wrote: 'Don't worry mate won't need this now.'

As Tony wrestled with his addiction, a fresh text message from the VIP manager arrived that read: 'Just checking no issues your side mate as notice you haven't played with us for two weeks.'

After once again receiving no reply from Tony, the VIP manager wrote: 'Morning mate, I've put a £5k bonus in your sports account for you.' A few weeks after the text messages, he lost £60,000 in one day with the bookmaker.

Tony could be classed as a genuine high roller, given the amounts he was betting. But most VIPs aren't.


## HIGH ROLLER OR LOW EBB?

The experience described by Joe Wright (whose name has been changed to protect his anonymity) illustrates how VIP status often arrives not when gamblers are living the high life but rather when they are approaching their lowest ebb. He had been in the military and used to visit the bookmaker's with his army pals every week, where they would lay small bets on football accumulators. This type of bet is typically a massive long shot, where you bet a relatively small amount on a series of outcomes. In the unlikely event they all come in, the returns can be huge. This had all seemed like harmless fun, but when Joe left the army his betting escalated.

'It was probably out of boredom,' he explains. 'I'd lost that thrill and buzz you get being in the military and I had a lot more time on my hands.'

As with many gambling addicts, Joe traces the origin of his

problem back to a large win rather than a loss. 'I had £20,000 to my name in savings and I got to a point where I had £45,000 to £50,000. I was always betting on online sports, mostly football but as time went on it developed into tennis and basketball and things like that. The funny thing is, at that time, it was quite calculated. I would only bet on big games I knew about. But by the end of it I was betting on anything. During that six-month period where I started getting worse and worse, I won a lot. I'd become addicted and I didn't realise it. It got to the point where even though I had £40,000 and most of it was winnings, if I lost a tiny amount I had to go and get it back.'

In 2012 Joe was living with his partner in a rented house. Days before Christmas, he squandered every penny he had. 'She was making dinner for us and I was sat in the living room betting on my phone constantly. I'm a Manchester United fan and at the time they were pretty good. I think they went a goal down to Sunderland and I was down to £17,000 at that point, from £45,000, and I lumped it all on one bet for United to win. Not long after, they went 2–0 down. I remember being distraught but I couldn't show it to my partner because she just didn't have a clue how bad things were. I instantly had to pretend like nothing was wrong when inside I was distraught.'

As gut-wrenching as that was, things soon got much worse. Joe no longer had much spare cash but he had a good credit report and wasn't in debt. It was easy to get a current account overdraft and loans from high-street banks. By 2016 he was close to £30,000 in the red and the only source of ready money was payday lenders offering small sums at exorbitant interest rates.

When Joe was winning, nobody had offered to make him a VIP. But once he became a serial loser, an offer arrived from the company. The firm is one of the UK's best known, but unfortunately cannot be named here because Joe signed a non-disclosure agreement with them, a means of silencing the industry's victims that we'll return to later.

'I got an email telling me they were delighted to say they wanted me to be a VIP member,' says Joe. 'I didn't think much of it – it was just marketing. But things progressed from there and I realised it was a pretty big deal. I was getting crazy bonus bets and rewards [money back] on my losses. They had a scheme where over a week, depending on how much you've staked, you'd get a certain amount as cash on the Monday. Not even a free bet, just cash. If you'd staked £20K in a week, you'd get £500. I was quite regularly getting that. If I had a period of time away, usually because I couldn't get the money to gamble, I'd get an email out of the blue with a £300 free bet. This is when it got really, really bad and my mental health started to be affected. It wasn't ideal before but from that point on it was more than just a gambling addiction. I didn't feel well. I couldn't control it. Even when I won I wasn't happy.'

The online casino never asked Joe if he could afford to bet so much. Even the most basic checks of his rapidly declining credit rating would have revealed that something was amiss. 'I was clogged with payday loans. I had so many outgoings with essential bills, but also the loans, that on some occasions I'd get my wages and I'd think, right, I need to try and win with this to pay off bills and have money for the month. And then my wages would be gone in a weekend, so not only did I not have the wages, I couldn't pay those outstanding bills.'

Joe tried to stop gambling but would always return. And there were always inducements on offer to do just that.

'Christmas 2016 stands out. I'd stayed away for about two or three months, off the back of a really heavy loss. I'd told them in an email I was staying away from gambling, that I'd been to see a GP. On Christmas Eve they said they'd missed me and if I made a deposit of £600, they'd match it.'

When we think of a VIP experience, what Joe went through

probably isn't it. But the allure of free bets is catnip to someone suffering from a gambling disorder. They are able to secure a level of personal service that suggests an element of luxury that doesn't match the image of someone who is suffering.

## WHY VIPS MATTER

The sort of bespoke attention lavished on VIPs might seem like something that goes on at the fringes of the industry, a drop in the ocean in the context of a gambling company's annual business. Perhaps I've reinforced that idea by suggesting that VIPs actually aren't all that 'important', in that – in many cases – they aren't wealthy. That may be so but VIPs are, in some ways at least, a big deal. The schemes have grown to such an extent that by 2019 they made up a sizeable proportion of some businesses' overall income.

That year I submitted a Freedom of Information request to the Gambling Commission, more in hope than expectation, asking for any data the regulator might hold about VIP schemes run by UK-licensed firms. It turned out that the Commission had collected data on VIP schemes from nine companies but had, for whatever reason, decided not to share it. The companies were granted anonymity but are understood to be among the UK's largest and best known. The numbers, compiled for an internal report held by the Commission, were shocking even to me.[17]

In one case, an operator told the Commission that while only 2% of its customers were VIPs, they accounted for 83% of deposits made on the site. A tiny cohort of high-spending punters, people who lost significant sums, were keeping that company in profit. That was the most extreme example but other firms also reported striking numbers. One took 58% of its betting account deposits from VIPs who accounted for just 5% of its customer base, while a third business accepted 48% of deposits from 3% of customers.

Another section of the report cited evidence that VIP gamblers are more likely than ordinary customers to be addicts. The Commission estimated that there were 47,000 VIPs in Britain, with about 8% of them thought to be problem gamblers. This is more than ten times the rate among the wider public.

The report did not say how many of those VIPs fell under the 'at risk' category, one level below the generally accepted 'problem gambling' classification. Previous studies have found that the 'at risk' group is usually much larger than the out-and-out 'problem gambling' group. They may not be deemed addicts but they – and those around them – can still suffer significant harm.

The Commission highlighted a concern that algorithms used by gambling companies to track betting patterns were far better at identifying people who might be worth granting VIP status to than they were at spotting gamblers losing control. As former sports minister Tracey Crouch put it to me: 'You would expect that companies who basically live and die through algorithms could actually step in when they see people that are gambling for six hours in the middle of the night.'

The regulator's report on VIPs outlined the options it was considering to rein in the schemes. One was to ban them altogether.

That hasn't happened. Instead, in September 2020, the Gambling Commission gave the industry another chance, after putting together a working group to examine the role of VIP schemes. It drew up some new rules, such as forcing companies to do affordability checks before making someone a VIP and banning membership of the schemes for under-twenty-fives. The working group was led by Entain, the owner of Ladbrokes and Gala Coral, which changed its name from GVC in late 2020. Entain had derived 38% of its UK profits from VIPs, according to the report I'd obtained earlier that year.

The changes were greeted warmly by the Betting and Gaming Council, suggesting the trade body's members found the changes pretty easy to live with.[18] Some companies have rebadged their schemes in light of the scrutiny they have faced. In May 2020, Paddy Power VIPs might have noticed that the emails they received no longer came from the VIP team but from the Relationship Management team. Quite the change.

'This is everything that is wrong with the gambling establishment and its allies rolled into one,' said Matt Gaskell, consultant psychologist for the NHS Northern Gambling Service. 'This is why marking your own homework and light-touch regulation of a harmful industry doesn't work.'

As of August 2021, the government was still considering whether to ban the schemes altogether, as part of its major review of gambling laws. It may become law in 2022 but too late to help many of the so-called VIPs already driven to despair.


## BOTH SIDES OF THE FENCE

I want to tell one last story in this chapter, not because it is extreme – although it is – but because it encapsulates how people on both sides of the VIP fence can easily get hurt.

Mike got into gambling through his first love, horse racing. He had always wanted to be a jockey and even spent time at the British Racing School in Newmarket, one of the most prestigious training centres for aspiring jockeys.

'I [did] about six weeks and realised I probably wasn't going to be good enough. The alternative was shovelling horse shit as a stable lad on low pay so I made the decision to go [to] college and uni after getting decent GCSE results. I found a job working in a betting shop and became a shop manager. That led to me working out in Malta on what they call an elite trading desk. These were not the very top VIPs – the footballers and celebrities – but mid-range punters, who could ring up and speak to a dedicated team.'

Mike quickly progressed onto the main trading desk, compiling odds and trading prices. 'There was all this info flying around, bets coming in from trainers, big owners, jockeys' agents and footballers, all placing big-money bets. At the time I was twenty-three, thinking, "I'm flying here." I felt like a little kid in a sweetshop. In hindsight, being exposed to it so young was the worst thing that could have ever happened.'

Every day, he was surrounded by screens showing football, horse racing and other sports, with an opportunity to place his own bets at any given moment. Increasingly he began picking up on information that came in from what industry people called 'warm' sources – well-informed people who place smart bets based on detailed knowledge rather than emotion.

'One of the major problems I had is how the trading room was run. The trading director used to say things like, "You guys should be paying me to work here, the amount of money you could be making, betting on the info that comes in."'

But in practice, even people with an advantage over other bettors can't keep beating the house.

Mike's wages would arrive in his account on a Friday and could be gone by the next day. He was living off payday loans yet somehow hiding his problems from colleagues and his friends and family. What he didn't know was that the environment was taking an even greater toll on one of his colleagues.

'Greg was slightly younger than me,' explains Mike. 'We shared a flat for about eighteen months. We weren't mega-close but we would go out for a drink after work. We'd started on the desk at the same sort of time and our careers were going along at the same time. He'd be full of beans on payday and then two days after he'd be sat on the sofa, barely able to put food in the cupboard. I knew that he had gambling problems but I was dealing with my own issues.'

One evening Mike came home from a night out to find residents of their apartment block gathered outside the building and Greg's broken body lying prone on the ground.

'He didn't leave a note but it was obvious to me what had happened,' says Mike. 'We'd all got paid a decent bonus. He got £7,000 and span it up to £14,000. Then he lost it all the next day. That evening he jumped off our apartment block. I was the first person on the scene that knew him. It was all at the age of twenty-three, twenty-four. It was a lot to take in. Greg's dad, who died shortly afterwards, obtained his bank records and betting account information with one of the online firms he was gambling with. The figures were eye-watering. Pretty much every penny he had earned had been spent on gambling.'

One might have expected a period of introspection to follow at the company that had employed both of them. It didn't.

'They paid for the memorial and there was a race named after him but for me that was just guilt money. There was no aftercare or lessons learned, everything was business as usual. One of the company bosses even said that it would be best if his family thought his death was due to drink or drugs rather than gambling. If it was public knowledge that Greg had killed himself due to a gambling addiction, it wouldn't look good for the company's profile. I was off the next day trying to come to terms with it and my boss was asking the other guys in the trading room why I wasn't at work. I don't remember being offered any support or counselling. It was as if it never happened. About a year after Greg died, I needed help and I went to the trading director. I don't think I could pay the rent. I was in tears, about to hand my notice in. I said I was in trouble, I'd gambled too much. It wasn't that they'd get me help with mental health services or GamCare. He said, "I'll lend you the money", and everything would be back to normal. I was a racing form analyst who'd do races that he would bet off. If I went, he'd lost that source.'

The attitude, he says, was symptomatic of the environment in which he worked and the way the company took advantage of its customers.

'I feel disgusted with myself thinking about it. There would also be messages going around about punters, saying, "This guy's a mug, he's a self-exclusion waiting to happen, lay whatever he asks for, he's an absolute wagon" (wagon was the slang term used for a customer who was losing heavily – wagon shunter . . . punter). We had a small business intelligence team at the time but that would just flag up accounts that were unprofitable, people we were losing to. Anyone winning lifetime over a certain amount, we'd get rid of or restrict them. Anyone who was a big loser, the VIPs, punters classified as really good for the business, could have what they want. There was no analysis of punters who were losing big sums or those that could potentially become problem gamblers. And the frustrating thing is, all the data was actually there.'

The ethos extended to staff members like Mike and Greg.

'It was as if there was something up with you if you weren't punting.'

Eventually the company brought in a betting ban for staff but Mike says it had nothing to do with welfare or lessons learned from Greg's death by suicide. 'The company owners carried out an audit and interviewed former staff. They found out that the trading director was using inside info and passing it on to his associates before the company had [a] chance to react to the info first. It was affecting the company's ability to trade the prices and they were losing money. I keep in touch with some of the guys I was on that elite desk with in the early days. I ended up with a gambling addiction myself, Greg killed himself. Another guy has an addiction and is going through treatment and there's one more who's working to get six figures back from one of the big online companies who failed to adhere to their own social responsibility rules. We've all started on that elite desk at a young age and most of us have developed gambling addictions. That can't be a coincidence.'

Eventually Mike got a job elsewhere but it was far from the end of his problems. In fact they got worse. He remained in the betting industry, taking well-paid jobs first with a company in Leeds, then with a major gaming technology firm at its office in London, and then in Singapore. He would sometimes spend his increasing salary ostentatiously, such as on trips to South America. Family and friends thought he must be doing well. But with each bump in pay came the opportunity to place larger bets. In Singapore he would get home from work in the evening in time to bet on horse races in the UK, laying out tens of thousands of pounds at a time.

'Over the lifetime of the account I'd deposited over £160,000 in less than two years, with net losses of over £75,000. My wages plus any money I could get hold of from loans and credit cards went into that. The only interaction [from gambling companies] was offering me free bets if I hadn't had a bet for a few days or inviting me to big race meetings and football matches. I was never asked about affordability at any point.'

He left Singapore in 2018 with close to £100,000 in the bank, thanks to a hefty bonus and contract gratuity from the company he worked for.

'I went travelling, to South America, to get my head sorted and get a fresh start. I could have bought a house, started a business in the UK . . . but I found myself in Brazil, in one of the greatest countries in the world to see things, [and I was] spending time in backstreet betting shops and on racetracks frittering money away.'

On his return to the UK, Mike moved back to Yorkshire, where he had grown up. It was there, in July 2018, that his addiction nearly ended in the same tragedy that had befallen his friend.

'I'd had to borrow some money off my parents and couldn't pay it back. The shit was hitting the fan and the excuses were starting to run out. That day I planned to kill myself. Although on the outside I'd had a good career, it had affected me in other ways in terms of relationships, family, wanting to have kids and things like that. I hadn't met anyone to settle down with and I didn't go out and meet new people because I would just isolate myself gambling all the time. I was anxious in groups and didn't want to join in nights out. I'd also seen the damage that addiction had done to children and I thought, "I don't deserve to have kids." I thought if the second half of my life is going to be worse, what's the point of having a life?'

Mike drove out to Malham Tarn, a lake that must surely count as one of the most beautiful spots in England. He looked over the water and contemplated what lay ahead. 'My mind was everywhere and I was just going to walk into the lake and try to drown myself or something like that. I was stood on the shore where you look out at this beautiful setting. One minute I'd be fine and then I'd burst into tears again, thinking how worthless I am, I should end it now. I got back into my car and was driving, thinking, "Just crash your car into a wall." Then I'd get it together again.'

He phoned the Campaign Against Living Miserably (CALM) helpline from his car and briefly felt better but soon the despair overtook him again and he drove to Filey Beach and walked up towards the clifftop on the Flamborough Headland coast, battling the urge to take his own life. He rang a good friend and broke down, telling him everything. The friend arrived within an hour and took Mike to A&E. In a matter of days, he'd told his friends and family everything and had signed up for intensive treatment at a residential rehab centre for gambling addicts. He still struggles sometimes but he is alive.

'People at the top don't know, or maybe they don't want to know. I'm not anti-gambling but I want to do something, if anything for Greg.'

# 5. THE GAMBLIFICATION OF FOOTBALL

The great fallacy is that the game is first and last about winning. It is nothing of the kind. The game is about glory, it is about doing things in style and with a flourish, about going out and beating the other lot, not waiting for them to die of boredom.

DANNY BLANCHFLOWER (FOOTBALLER,
NORTHERN IRELAND AND TOTTENHAM HOTSPUR, 1954–64)

It matters more when there's money on it.

SKY BET

A visitor to the House of Commons on 9 January 2020 might have come away with the impression that gambling had hooked its claws into football overnight. Politicians of every stripe rose to their feet in the historic chamber to denounce the industry's pernicious influence on the national game.[1] Several of them had rarely, if ever, spoken on gambling or football before. The catalyst for their outrage was a deal between the Football Association and bet365 – as well as six other gambling companies – that gave the betting firms the right to broadcast matches played in the FA Cup, the world's oldest and most fabled club football competition.

Under the terms of the commercial arrangement, games that hadn't been selected for broadcast by one of the major television channels could be streamed live on the gambling companies' websites, available to any customer who signed up. If your team wasn't on the TV and you wanted to watch them play, you had to open a betting account. This was a far cry from what dewy-eyed troubadours of football punditry still sometimes refer to as the 'romance of the Cup'. Rather, it was a naked customer acquisition strategy that put the cart before the horse, betting before football.

The FA Cup deal was variously described as 'distasteful' by former sports minister Tracey Crouch and 'the most egregious example of how money is ruining football' by Labour MP Justin Madders. Conservative Jackie Doyle-Price said it was 'abhorrent' that such a deal should coexist with the FA's public support for its president Prince William's mental health campaign.

Even the prime minister threw his not inconsiderable heft behind the outcry. 'This is a matter for the FA but we believe it should reconsider its deal with bet365,' said a spokesperson for Boris Johnson, the leader of a Conservative party more used to espousing the merits of the free market than publicly rapping corporate knuckles. Speaking to the *Daily Mail*, that self-styled media bastion of Conservative morality, a government source elaborated: 'It is for the FA to deal with, but you should call a bad business a bad business.'[2]

Nor was it just grandstanding MPs who had something to say on the subject. Claire Murdoch, national mental health director for the NHS, lamented 'another own goal from the gambling industry'. Gary Lineker, the England striker whose career was characterised by an exemplary record of fair play and good behaviour, aired his annoyance on Twitter, calling the deal 'all kinds of wrong'.

Yet for all of the performative outrage on show, there was precious little acknowledgement that football and gambling had long since been deeply enmeshed, to a degree that now seems almost irreversible. It is essentially impossible to watch football without being not just exposed to but drenched in gambling imagery and invitations to partake. Streaming deals for a few FA Cup games, while they might have attracted attention, are the least of it.

I'll explore how we got here and what the effect of this symbiotic relationship means for the game. But first let's consider this relationship from the point of view of the people who, in theory at least, matter most: the fans.

For match-going football supporters, the past twenty-five years have witnessed profound change. Some elements of the fan experience remain much as they ever were – the fruity language, the sudden herbal waft of the turf en route to your seat, the long, snaking queues for the toilets. Others are significantly altered, often in a positive way. Crowds are more diverse in racial and gender terms, and the low-level threat of violence is – if not quite a thing of the past – far less evident than it once was. In the more modern grounds you can even read emails via the stadium Wi-Fi, should you be so inclined. At the new stadium of my beloved Tottenham Hotspur, you can enjoy battered tofu and a craft beer, rather than the traditional pie. Perhaps unsurprisingly, the whole day out costs a hell of a lot more than it used to.

But one of the biggest changes over that quarter-century period has been one of the least noticed. Where gambling was once a relatively incidental feature of football, it has quietly become both integral and inextricable. Back in the 1990s fans might have played the football pools or placed a bet in a high-street bookmaker's or even at a booth inside the ground. Today, though, gambling is rather more prominent. As a thought experiment, I considered how that might manifest itself for a football-mad household on a typical matchday. Let's call them the Cole family.

## A DAY IN THE LIFE OF THE FOOTBALL FAN

9 a.m. – Over breakfast the Coles listen to the talkSPORT radio station for previews of the day's fixtures. Each advert break features a commercial spot for bet365. During games broadcast on the station,

commentators reel off live odds in between describing the action. Perhaps one or both parents already have an account with a bookmaker. If so, they start receiving emails or texts offering the latest odds and perhaps a bonus bet.

11 a.m. – The youngest member of the family, nine-year-old Jared, is adding new stickers to his Panini album. Every footballer pictured prominently on the front cover is wearing a shirt with a betting sponsor. The word 'bet' features five times on the cover alone and many more times inside the sticker pack itself. Of the 636 Panini Official Premier League 2020 stickers, 270 feature a betting logo. Perhaps Jared reads the BBC's *Match of the Day* magazine. The May 2019 issue featured fifty-two gambling logos in sixty-eight pages.[3]

11.30 a.m. – In the living room, older sister Lana is playing the FIFA 21 video game. She selects Wolverhampton Wanderers, who advertise ManBetX on their pixilated shirts, versus Bournemouth, sponsored by MansionBet. She stops briefly to check Twitter, where Arsenal's official account is tweeting an ad for its betting partner, bitcoin-gambling specialist Sportsbet.io.

12.30 p.m. – Burnley's Turf Moor stadium hosts the first televised game of the day, versus Aston Villa. The oldest part of the stadium, formerly called the Cricket Field Stand, is now known as the Ladbrokes Stand. The home team's shirt is sponsored by LoveBet, while Villa players have the logo of W88 emblazoned on their chests. This year, for the first time in more than a decade, there is no gambling advert at half-time – the result of the industry's whistle-to-whistle ban. However, during the match itself, advertising hoardings display gambling logos and slogans on a rolling basis.

3 p.m. – It's time to leave for the match, an afternoon kick-off. Jared and Lana listen to a football podcast on the train. *The Totally Football Show* is their favourite so on it goes, via Spotify, which displays a graphic indicating that the podcast is brought to you 'in association with Paddy Power'. Halfway through, the programme

is interrupted for a few minutes of chat about the latest odds from a Paddy Power employee who intersperses betting promotions with tepid banter. If the kids prefer a different podcast, they might choose one of the club-specific ones offered by sports publication *The Athletic*. Its betting sponsor of choice is bet365, who don't just buy an advert slot but provide a script read out by the familiar and trusted voice of the podcast host.

4 p.m. – The Coles pass several high-street bookmakers' shops on their way to the ground, with window displays prominently advertising odds on first goalscorer and accumulator bets. Billboards display adverts for Virgin Bet and one of London's famous double-decker buses trundles past, with a long banner ad for BetMVP on it. If they are Stoke City fans, they will soon see the bet365 Stadium looming towards them on the horizon. Fans of a club in England's second tier are gearing up for a game in the Sky Bet Championship, while Scotland's top flight is the Ladbrokes Premiership.

4.30 p.m. – Mum buys a programme for the kids. Each edition features, on average, 2.3 actual gambling adverts and a further thirty-eight instances of 'incidental' exposure to gambling brands, such as action photographs showing shirts or pitchside hoardings. Young Birmingham City fans might have enjoyed the Spot the Difference competition. One of the answers is the logo of online casino 888. A quick check of Twitter to see who the manager has picked for the line-up might, if the Coles are Tottenham fans, reveal a tweet from the club's official account, no less. The tweet is sponsored by William Hill yet it somehow ends up on the BBC's live match updates feed, despite the state broadcaster's ban on commercial advertising. The stadium announcer reads out the names of the players, an announcement also sponsored by William Hill, whose logo flashes up on the big screen to the 62,000-capacity crowd. The bookmaker's exclusive deal with the club might explain why anyone using the Tottenham Hotspur Stadium Wi-Fi is blocked from their account with Ladbrokes and other competitors.

5.30 p.m. – The whistle blows. If the Coles are watching West Ham v Newcastle United, then the visitors' shirt is sponsored by Fun88. The home side have a comprehensive deal with Betway that means the online casino's name adorns not just the players' chests but every single pitchside hoarding too. It is impossible to watch a second of the game without seeing Betway's name. At half-time, there are Betway booths on the concourse.

7.30 p.m. – On the way home, while waiting for the bus or train, the kids open the LiveScore app (owned by the same company as Virgin Bet) to see results from the rest of the Premier League and maybe an update from Italy's Serie A or Spain's La Liga. Ads for Betfair, Virgin Bet and bet365 scroll across the bottom of the screen repeatedly. If they're Arsenal fans, they might watch the infamous YouTube channel ArsenalFanTV for some reaction from irate fellow supporters but not until they've sat through an advert for Betfair, featuring the actor Clive Owen.

10.30 p.m. – Mum and Dad – and maybe the kids if they're lucky enough to be up that late – watch highlights of all the day's games on *Match of the Day*. On the non-commercial BBC there are no adverts but the on-screen prevalence of pitchside hoardings, shirt sponsors and other promotional opportunities means gambling logos are still everywhere they look, effectively advertising for free. Should there be any evening games or highlights, they can expect to see gambling promotions fronted by managers such as José Mourinho and Harry Redknapp, or ex-players such as Peter Crouch and Michael Owen. By midnight on matchday, barely a minute has passed when gambling isn't on sale as part of the football experience.

# WHY GAMBLING TARGETED FOOTBALL

It wasn't always like this. Fans have always bet on football, of course, but the way that the game lives cheek by jowl with gambling is a relatively new phenomenon. It hasn't come about by accident; rather, the state of affairs we know today has been orchestrated by commercial enterprises motivated by the opportunity for profit. Those vested interests have taken advantage of a potent cocktail made up of three major components: the liberalisation of laws on gambling adverts, the rise of mobile connectivity and the increasing number of games broadcast live.

Let's rewind a little. My early football education came in the late eighties and early nineties. As a child, when very few games were aired and the internet was still new-fangled gadgetry for nerds, I would hungrily devour the sports pages of my dad's newspaper. I'd absorb every word and statistic with the obsessive zeal of the typical football-mad kid, poring over league tables and picking a favourite in each division, including overseas and outside the top four divisions. To this day I still look out for the results of Rangers, Cambridge United, Bayer Leverkusen and Barnet and feel a faint flicker of pleasure if they win, although I've long since forgotten why I decided to root for them. I'd even scan the pages that showed the FTSE 100 share prices, checking to see whether Tottenham Hotspur's stock had gained a penny or two. In those days, a slight bump on the FTSE was about as good as it got for a Tottenham fan.

One football-related section of the newspaper had an impenetrable aura of mystery around it, though: the football pools. The pools are a means of betting that asks you to predict which matches will end in a score draw. Entry was cheap and, given the long odds on getting multiple results right, the prizes were potentially very large. In 1994, when I was eleven years old, 10 million people played the pools every week, in addition to those who bet on football in high-street bookmakers' or by telephone. To get to the point: the popular appeal of having a flutter on the football is nothing new.

But football in the nineties was a completely different animal to what we know today. The internet was yet to light the fuse on an explosion of technological innovation that spawned thousands of opportunities to bet on football, twenty-four hours a day. Satellite television had not yet developed to the extent that almost every game was broadcast. Gambling still had relatively little impact on the game itself, nor a great deal of visibility within it.

When gambling did crop up as a major subject matter in football discourse, it was thanks to an unusual scandal, something that potentially posed a threat to the very integrity of the game. In the mid-1990s several players, the most notable among them Liverpool goalkeeper Bruce Grobbelaar, were accused of match-fixing – specifically, of accepting money to rig games on behalf of Asian betting syndicates. None of them were ever convicted. Grobelaar later lost a libel battle with the *Sun* newspaper, which had printed the accusations.[4]

Even by the 2005–06 football season, the same year the Gambling Act received royal assent, just one Premier League football team bore the name of a betting company on its shirt. Middlesbrough's deal with an up-and-coming online casino called 888.com was the only one of its kind. By the 2019–20 season, betting company logos adorned the kits of half of the twenty top-flight clubs, with the figure rising to seventeen out of twenty-four in the second tier of English football, the Championship – or, to give it its full title, the Sky Bet Championship. Between the two top tiers of football, shirt sponsorship by gambling companies is worth an estimated £110 million at time of writing, although the exact value of the deals isn't publicly disclosed.[5]

That's just the tip of the iceberg.

I spoke to a sports marketing executive with unparalleled experience in the English game about what has changed since the days when Middlesbrough were the only team with a betting sponsor. He spoke on condition of anonymity and I shall call him Eric: 'Their [gambling companies'] focus in the early noughties was not necessarily football, it was horse racing and the traditional focuses for the gambling industry,' he said. 'But the internet made access – and the ease of reaching the audience and processing the bet – much easier. Secondly, there was the relaxation of the regulation. At that point, there was undoubtedly a stepladder effect in terms of the growth, not only the volume of betting but also the number of companies that were becoming involved.'

Gambling firms suddenly had not just the permission to get involved in football but also a massive and growing incentive to do so. Technology, particularly smartphones, allowed them to take bets in huge volumes and with high frequency, while football gave them the platform they needed to bring the activity into the mainstream. This led to the rise of a new breed of gambling company, such as bet365 and Sky Bet, technology-focused businesses that relied not on convincing hardcore, high-spending gamblers to switch to football, but rather on persuading the legions of football fans to bet where perhaps they had not done so in the past, particularly via the new in-play products that allowed swift bets during the course of a match.

Richard Flint, who would go on to become CEO of Sky Bet, recalls the early days of that growth, when Sky was just looking for more ways to monetise football via its broadcast rights to show the Premier League. 'We were never focused on high rollers or VIPs. It was all about another thing that customers could do around live sport that Sky wanted to participate in and, yes, make money from, something that adds to the thrill of watching sport.'

The reward was a sustainable and lucrative business model based on huge numbers of mostly modest but regular bets, placed by an army of casual football fans, many of them pretty new to betting.

'That pivot to football was because it's a much more popular sport,' said Eric. 'The volume of guys who think they know about football and can beat the market – or just see it as entertainment – grew enormously.'

## THE FOOTBALL MARKETPLACE

With growth came an increasingly competitive, sophisticated and lucrative market that is still evolving at pace.

Eric likened shirt sponsorship deals to a 'spot market', much like the way some commodities are traded, with prices determined in a frantic auction-style process that takes place during a fairly brief window in April and May, as clubs look ahead to the next season. It isn't just about front-of-shirt deals either. There are myriad other entry points, from space on the sleeve to major broadcast deals, or several minutes per game on pitchside hoardings.

'These things are all monitored by people with stopwatches, who will assess what that would cost you if you had to buy that airtime from broadcasters,' Eric told me. 'The rights owners know that, the agencies know it and that is what establishes the market.'

Academic research has revealed more about why that market has become so sophisticated. Deals for shirts and LED hoardings are so lucrative because even non-commercial broadcasters such as the state-funded BBC have unwittingly ended up working as proxy advertisers for bookmakers and online casinos.

Rebecca Cassidy is a professor of anthropology at Goldsmiths, University of London, as well as one of the UK's leading gambling industry experts and the author of *Vicious Games*, a must-read book exploring the rise of the industry. In 2017 she published findings that were, to many people, entirely counter-intuitive. Gambling, her research found, was in some cases more heavily promoted on non-commercial TV than on channels that showed adverts. In a study of three episodes of the BBC's flagship football highlights programme, *Match of the Day*, Cassidy found that gambling logos or branding appeared on screen for between 71% and 89% of the show's running time.[6]

Despite the fact that Sky runs adverts entirely devoted to gambling brands, the research found that the percentage of screen time enjoyed by gambling firms during a live football broadcast on Sky could be as low as 68%. That figure was for a game between Tottenham Hotspur and Manchester United, neither of which were sponsored by a betting firm.

There are several reasons why the BBC can end up as a more efficient advertiser, despite not charging companies for the pleasure. For a start, Sky's live football programmes typically feature long periods of pre- and post-match analysis in the studio, during which gambling logos hardly appear at all. Much of the game itself is shot from a distance, allowing viewers to visualise patterns of play, thus minimising the visibility of branding. But highlights shows, including *Match of the Day*, tend to include close-up and slow-motion shots in which billboards and shirts are much easier to make out. What's more, each episode of *Match of the Day* features multiple post-match interviews with managers, conducted in front of background hoardings festooned with sponsors' logos.

Even in Safer Gambling Week, when firms in the industry gather to pat each other on the back about their efforts to limit harm, the bombardment continues. In 2020 I watched a game between Fulham and Everton that featured one ad for Safer Gambling Week on the pitchside hoardings, alongside three for Betway, TLCBet and bet365. With no fans in the stadium due to the Covid-19 pandemic, a huge tarpaulin was draped over the seats, promoting BetVictor. This is part of what has been called the 'gamblification' of football, the gradual saturation of the game.

These days, simply buying space on shirts and pitchside hoardings has become rather a stale tactic. Increasingly, the gambling industry is demanding more imaginative bang for its buck – not just a few inches on a shirt but a place within the firmament of football culture, and in extreme cases within the action of the game itself.

In September 2017, during a David-and-Goliath FA Cup match against Arsenal, Sutton United's portly goalkeeper Wayne Shaw was filmed stuffing a pasty into his face while sitting on the bench during the game. Sun Bets had been running a market offering 8–1 odds against him doing so. In the aftermath of what came to be known as 'Piegate', Shaw was fined £375 and banned for two months by the FA for breaching its betting rules. He resigned from the club, which in turn was directly affected by the affair when, during a later match, it had to field an outfield player in goal, rather than Shaw, due to an injury to the first-choice goalkeeper.

The Gambling Commission fined Sun Bets owner Tabcorp £84,000 over the stunt, as well as for a separate offer of odds on someone streaking during the game – something the regulator said could have encouraged an illegal act. Some fans saw it as a hilarious bit of banter. Others found the whole thing distasteful, even disrespectful to the competition. Rather less amusingly, as the Gambling Commission discovered during the course of its investigation, Tabcorp had also allowed more than a hundred gamblers who had tried to exclude themselves from gambling to open duplicate accounts and carry on betting.[7]

Paddy Power Betfair took a rather more subtle approach than Sun Bets, rolling out its own publicity stunt under the guise of opposition to the number of gambling shirt sponsors. Huddersfield Town players took to the pitch for a pre-season friendly wearing shirts with a huge Paddy Power logo on them, larger than is allowed by the rules on kit design. The gambling firm claimed it was only a hoax, intended to highlight its support for removing betting sponsors from football shirts. The FA didn't see it that way and fined the club £50,000.[8]

Neither Sun Bets's Piegate nor the Paddy Power stunt had much of an impact on the game, but perhaps they just weren't being ambitious enough. In 2019, a year after it was fined £2 million for failing to protect a vulnerable gambler, online casino firm 32Red helped bankroll the return of record England goalscorer Wayne Rooney to English football, with Derby County. He was even allocated the number 32 shirt, helping cement the brand's name in the minds of fans. Rooney was accused of 'selling his soul', while former sports minister Richard Caborn – who had been instrumental in pushing through the 2005 Gambling Act – described the arrangement as 'crass'. The Bishop of St Albans even weighed in on behalf of the Church of England, accusing a 'national treasure' of sullying his brand and setting a bad example for kids.[9] The affair illustrated the extent to which gambling was no longer confined to hitching its wagons to football, but was now wresting control of the reins too.

## WHEELER DEALERS

The temptation for players and clubs to play ball with the gambling industry – even in the face of reputational risk – is understandable when you realise the kind of money on offer. Indeed, what I'm about to explain will show that the nation's football clubs, beloved by millions, are not just complicit but actively eager participants in taking as much of gamblers' money as possible.

The value of individual sponsorship deals isn't typically disclosed, although the information often leaks out. But a 2019 court case offered detailed insight into how lucrative even relatively minor deals can be, how they get done, and how keen both football and gambling executives are to sign them. In the case, a company called Winlink Marketing sued Liverpool FC for £1.125 million, claiming that it was owed this money for its role in brokering a

£15 million deal that saw BetVictor become the sponsor of the team's training kit.[10]

The claim was ultimately dismissed but the detail that emerged during the proceedings illustrated some truths about the business side of the game that fans love. Giving evidence for Winlink, marketing agent Mark Dixon gave an assessment of how much clubs were charging betting companies for the privilege of being associated with them; Liverpool, he said, had charged its official betting partner £1.5 million in 2014, a sum that had risen to £9 million by 2020.

At one point, Dixon said, he had offered Liverpool £880,000 on behalf of BetVictor, which wanted to sponsor the LED advertising hoardings around the ground, only to be rejected. Liverpool, he said, were now in talks with the likes of Betfair and Marathonbet and would accept nothing less than $1.3 million for just three minutes of LED time.

Dixon's claim to a finder's fee was thrown out largely because the judge determined that the sponsorship arrangement between BetVictor and Liverpool had been brokered not by him but by sponsorship guru Raffaella Valentino, a veteran of gambling tie-ups at both Manchester United and Chelsea, who gave evidence in the case and who was described as credible by the judge.

One by-product of the case was that emails from Valentino emerged that underline how gambling companies have come to view football clubs – as little more than cash machines. In an email to BetVictor boss Andreas Meinrad, with whom she had a long-standing working relationship, Valentino told him that 'you get to virtually own Liverpool Football Club (with almost 400m fans in Asia!)' for an investment of £4.5 million per year.

I'm not a fan of the phrase 'let that sink in' but it seems appropriate here. 'You get to virtually own Liverpool Football Club' is not, I'm sure, something that fans of the club would enjoy hearing.

In a subsequent message she let slip information that reveals even more. Having previously acted as an independent broker of marketing deals for Premier League clubs, Valentino was now working directly for Liverpool. In the course of that work, court papers show, she had obtained access to figures about Liverpool's previous gambling sponsorship deal, with Marathonbet. Among the statistics she leaked to Meinrad about Marathonbet were the following:

- Campaigns linked to Liverpool accounted for 8.3% of all of Marathonbet's UK first-time depositors in 2015;
- 53% of Liverpool fans who opened an account went on to place a deposit.

In other words, football sponsorship didn't just work, it was actually an integral plank of Marathonbet's efforts to build a business in the UK. But the UK was only the half of it – perhaps even less. Valentino repeatedly stressed Liverpool's reach in Asia, which she said could open future opportunities to acquire new accounts there, as well as 'extending UK customer lifetime'. When BetVictor eventually confirmed its willingness to sponsor Liverpool, Valentino reported to the club that 'Asia and [Liverpool manager] Jürgen [Klopp] are big factors' in BetVictor's decision. She also told Liverpool that BetVictor wanted former striker Michael Owen thrown in, forcing him to ditch his deals with other betting firms. At time of writing Michael Owen is still advertising for BetVictor, although Klopp ceased plugging the brand after the FA suggested his 'tips' might be construed as gambling advice. Valentino earned a 'substantial bonus' for her work on the deal, court papers show.

The bonus was worth it for all concerned. Not only did BetVictor need Liverpool but Liverpool needed BetVictor. They each had something the other wanted. The football club had loyal fans interested in sport and the gambling company had money to help fund Liverpool's transfer activity. It was a match made in heaven.

That isn't the end of the extent to which football clubs and gambling companies have aligned their interests. People who bet on football, particularly those who have experienced mental health problems or financial difficulty as a result, might be surprised and upset to know that the club they support may well have benefited directly from their misery. According to several industry sources, clubs now routinely take a cut of the losses racked up by any customer who signs up via a partnership with the club. You may recall some of the deals involving affiliates and VIP managers, who introduce you to a betting company and pocket a percentage of every penny you lose. According to multiple sources, football clubs may be doing just the same.

I spoke to one veteran of the online gambling world who has held senior sales and marketing positions with major players, including one household-name gambling company. 'I met with dozens of football clubs and we tried to introduce the idea,' he told me. 'They [football clubs] didn't bite as much back then but now everything they're doing, they're tracking, and doing a revenue-sharing deal.'

Another senior source with more recent knowledge of the industry confirmed that revenue-sharing deals were commonplace. 'Football clubs are very much bedded in,' he said. 'But they'll never declare it.' He used Tottenham Hotspur as an example, although I should stress that he did so because I told him about my allegiance rather than because he has any knowledge of a real-life commercial arrangement involving the club. The situation that follows is fictitious and used only as a hypothetical illustration of how such an arrangement with a football club might work.

'Take Tottenham, for instance. In the programme it'll say: "Sign up, put the code SPURS1 in." As soon as that code goes in, that client will be tracked for life and Spurs will get a commission. So when football clubs stand up and are holier-than-thou [about gambling] – as they will do in a few years' time – they all earned money on commission.'

There is a good real-world example too. In 2009 bookmaker Victor Chandler, later renamed BetVictor, agreed to become the main sponsor of two-time European champions Nottingham Forest for a 'significant six-figure fee'. Famously, Chandler himself offered to pay the cost of season tickets for fans who opened an account, should Forest win the league. That never happened, a stroke of luck that Chandler said saved him £6 million. There were other hidden benefits for the company.[11] 'Victor Chandler has plans for promotions and benefits for adult season ticket holders and fans purchasing the new home and away shirts,' the press release said.

In the course of researching this book, I met someone who had seen first hand what that meant. Like the sources above, they would not talk about it on the record, for fear of how business associates and colleagues would react. 'As part of the deal Chandler had access to Nottingham Forest's database of fans, season ticket holders and anyone who bought merchandise online. They would send out betting promotions and offers. In return Nottingham Forest would receive a small percentage of the customer losses.'

It's a sobering thought. The club that you devote so much time, passion and energy to, not to mention money, lining its pockets with your gambling losses, with the losses of fans who may be facing financial ruin. The same clubs eagerly promote initiatives such as Mental Health Awareness Week while their hands are in the wallets of people who may be struggling with addiction. In summer 2021 I wrote to all clubs in the Premier League, several in the Championship and both Celtic and Rangers in the Scottish Premiership, asking if they still have, or have ever had, a commercial partnership involving a revenue share with a gambling company.

The majority declined to comment. Some asked for more details about my enquiry, or promised to look into the matter, and then went strangely quiet.

This sort of hypocrisy is the inevitable result of a world in which football and gambling feed off one another. Some said no such agreement exists now but refused to say whether it had in the past fifteen years. I can only say with any degree of certainty that no such revenue-sharing arrangement exists at Crystal Palace, Newcastle United, Tottenham Hotspur and Manchester United.

## WHITE LABELS AND THE ASIAN REVOLUTION

In recent years this dynamic has been souped up by the arrival on the scene of a phalanx of Asian betting firms. As Raffaella Valentino mentioned in her emails to BetVictor and Liverpool, Asia is critically important to gambling companies. The continent is home to tens of millions of people who enjoy both betting and football. Yet in some jurisdictions, such as China, betting is prohibited other than through a small number of channels, state-run lotteries or land-based casinos that operate in ring-fenced jurisdictions, such as the island of Macau.

Illegal or not, this hasn't actually stopped gambling companies targeting those customers. In 2014, shortly before I joined the *Guardian*, my much-admired colleague Simon Goodley revealed how bet365 was operating a successful Chinese business, taking bets from punters who risked prison if caught.[12] Stoke-based bet365 isn't risking much by taking bets from Chinese punters. Nor is it prepared to reveal whether it does and to what extent. Its financial accounts say that disclosing a regional breakdown of income would be 'severely prejudicial to the group'.

Firms based in China, or in other Asian markets where betting is strictly controlled, don't have the luxury of being able to take their compatriots' money from the safety of Stoke. Advertising certainly isn't allowed either, of course, meaning there are relatively few ways for them to reinforce brand identity among those customers who are determined to gamble by any means, or who find a way to do so legally. Instead, Asian-owned firms in China, Thailand, the Philippines and Malaysia have latched on to European football leagues – the Premier League chief among them – as their route into the hearts and minds of customers. In 2016, such were the opportunities that leading sports marketing agency SportQuake opened offices in Hong Kong and Beijing to take advantage.

'People lose sight of the fact that the first World Cup outside South America and Europe was in 1994,' said Eric the sports marketer. 'You've now got huge numbers of fans in Indonesia, China, Thailand. That internationalisation is a key part of it. Now the international TV rights are equal to and sometimes larger than domestic rights. There's a massive and eager audience for football right across the globe and particularly within Asian markets. That's why the growth of those Asian [betting] companies became so prevalent.'

The result has been an influx of betting sponsors in football that most English fans have never heard of and will probably never use.

In his in-depth investigation into Asian sponsors in 2021, *The Athletic* journalist Joey D'Urso highlighted a 2019 friendly between Wolverhampton Wanderers and Newcastle, held in the city of Nanjing as part of efforts to recruit fans in a country of 1.4 billion people. Both teams had to ditch their usual sponsors for the day due to China's betting prohibitions. They used guest sponsors instead, changing their shirts for that game only. If that's faintly farcical, D'Urso raised concerns that are more serious.[13]

For a start, any new Chinese fans who watch those teams play in the Premier League and are enticed to gamble as a result risk jail. Furthermore, the deals those firms do in order to get that visibility are opaque at best, meaning clubs often have little idea of who they're doing business with. Most Asian firms who sponsor English teams do not have a UK gambling licence and some don't even have functioning websites that UK punters could use. Instead, they take advantage of the so-called 'white-label' system. It works like this. The overseas betting firm, perhaps from China or Thailand, does a deal with a firm based in the UK or in a middle-man territory with privileged access to the British market, such as the Isle of Man or Malta. That middleman company already has a licence to operate gambling services in Great Britain. Mostly, the Asian company isn't interested in taking bets from British punters but it needs to piggyback onto the licence-holder in order to gain permission to advertise on football shirts. That way it can reach punters back home, entirely legally.

While the Gambling Commission permits white-label firms to exist, it has previously voiced concern that some do not have sufficient money-laundering controls in place and do not carry out sufficient due diligence to ensure that the websites they rent their services to don't have 'links to criminal activity'. In practice, neither the regulator nor the British public knows very much at all about some of the firms.

The white labels offer the opportunity to launch an operational gambling platform in the UK, but these companies' only interest, typically, is in marketing themselves to bettors in Asia whom they otherwise could not reach. Yet their presence in the UK market has an effect on the British gambling landscape. It creates competition for sponsorship space that helps drive the value of betting sponsorship inexorably upwards. It also adds to the ubiquity of gambling in football and increases the clubs' dependence on it, strengthening their resolve not to part with the revenue. It helps knit gambling and football ever-tighter together.

# THE MORAL MAZE

Football is full of moral grey areas, though. In that respect, the 'money first, questions later' relationship with gambling isn't new. Some of the biggest clubs are owned by oligarchs who obtained their wealth by questionable means, or petrostates where women are oppressed, migrant workers are abused and homosexuality is illegal.[14] Some of the world's most adored football superstars have committed heinous acts and got away with little more than a rap on the knuckles and a fine equivalent to a few weeks' wages. Many fans put aside their moral compass to scream obscenities at other grown adults of a weekend. The sums of money involved in the game – and its importance in the lives of so many people – make moral compromise almost inevitable.

The more we encounter these moral quandaries, the further gambling elbows its way into our relationship with football. I've already explored the inexorable rise of gambling advertising since the 2005 Act. A big part of that has been the growth in new and non-traditional content created by fans. YouTube channels like ArsenalFanTV and club-specific podcasts attract a relatively small but very engaged, fiercely passionate audience. These shows are fantastic recruitment grounds for gambling companies looking for more targeted ways of reaching audiences and – as Flav Bateman from *The Fighting Cock* explained – it makes sense for fan-run media outlets to fund themselves this way.

As we've seen, pretty much every fan podcast now has a gambling sponsor, typically bet365 or Paddy Power, although Betfred has been moving into that space too. It has become habitual for presenters to read advertising scripts themselves, rather than voiceover artists being used. This makes it much harder for people involved in the game to distance themselves from the gambling money.

I spoke to a football journalist I greatly admire who found himself in the uncomfortable position of being contractually obliged to flog gambling products on air, despite personal misgivings: 'We have a team who organise all of the commercial deals for the podcast and they literally tell us what the deals are and send us scripts to read out for the ads,' he explained. 'I feel bad about it, to be honest. I wish I didn't have to do it and feel weak for not saying no. I think there is just too much gambling advertising and I think in ten or twenty years people will look back at it like we do with tobacco in cricket or snooker. I do feel like a bit of a wanker for just reading it out so I try and read it out in a sombre voice, which is completely fucking pointless.' He emphasised that maintaining an untroubled conscience in the world of football is always likely to be a losing battle: almost every aspect of the game is compromised by the source of the money that supports it. 'It's really difficult to take a moral stance on everything but I do think it's grim how the Premier League is used and how clubs are happy to push this stuff on people all the time, given how addictive it is and how much damage it can do to people's lives.'

For a podcast presenter – relatively well paid by national standards but certainly not filthy rich – the pressure to do what their employer wants is considerable. Max Rushden, who presents the *Guardian Football Weekly* podcast, took the unusual step of backing out of a deal to promote gambling in 2020, after sounding out opinion from listeners. But not everyone will feel financially secure enough to turn the money down.

It's less clear what pressing need there is for players, coaches and even clubs to push betting products, given how awash with money the game is. Coaches such as José Mourinho and Harry Redknapp have promoted Paddy Power and BetVictor respectively. Outside the UK, global superstars Cristiano Ronaldo, Neymar Jr and Zlatan Ibrahimović have all hawked gambling products at one time or another. Mourinho's net worth is estimated at $100 million, Ronaldo's at close to half a billion dollars. The football authorities have nothing to say about this and that's a reasonable position to take. Athletes and their coaches are individuals, at liberty to strike their own commercial deals to make the most out of their talent, whatever anyone else might think about it.

But the gambling industry doesn't just do deals with football clubs, managers and players; in some cases it owns them too. The most prominent example is Stoke City, owned by the Coates family, who have soared up the list of Britain's richest people thanks to the meteoric growth of their bet365 empire. They may be the most high-profile but they are by no means the only ones. In 2009 professional gambler Tony Bloom – nicknamed The Lizard for his ice-cool demeanour when playing poker – bought Brighton & Hove Albion. Bloom had made hundreds of millions of pounds from property investments, sports betting and poker. He now runs Starlizard, a sports betting company whose business model is something akin to a hedge fund. Where hedge funds use complex algorithms, in-depth knowledge and big data to make money from investments, Starlizard does much the same, except with sports betting.

So successful was Bloom's model that one of his former employees, Matthew Benham, followed suit, buying his boyhood club, Brentford FC. There is no suggestion of impropriety in the ownership of a football club by gambling industry tycoons. Nonetheless, it feels like something of an ethical minefield, both in terms of the wider issues this book is probing and in the context of the mid-1990s match-fixing scandal. It wasn't long ago that household-name sports stars were accused of doing the bidding of betting companies, to the detriment of the game. Now betting companies own entire teams, both literally and, in the case of Liverpool and BetVictor, figuratively. Yet we assume issues of sporting integrity will never arise.

This relaxed attitude to ownership is particularly surprising given the swift action taken in other areas where potential conflicts of interest have emerged.

Footballers Daniel Sturridge[15] and Kieran Trippier[16] were both hit with bans by the Football Association, in 2020 and 2021, for 'passing on inside information' about their upcoming transfer moves. In effect, they were punished for telling too many people, some of them friends, that they had got new jobs. Clearly any improper betting activity on such matters is not to be condoned, but it seems odd that there should be no similar misgivings about those who make a living from betting companies owning football clubs, with all of the information they are privy to as a result.

As I've said, football's reluctance to take issue with gambling's place in the game makes sense when you consider the amount of money coming into the game from betting firms. But what gambling gives with one hand it takes with the other. A third of adult English Premier League fans and two-thirds of young ones say they watch an illegal football stream at least once a month, according to a 2020 article in marketing media outlet *The Drum*. 'You'd fill Wembley Stadium (capacity 90,000) around 79 times with the average pirate audience of an EPL game,' wrote John McCarthy.[17]

This trend is a threat to one of the main sources of money in football: broadcast rights. The Premier League sold its rights from 2019 to 2022 for more than £9 billion. The sum would most likely have been even higher were it not for the large number of fans who weren't paying the approved broadcasters but were instead going through illicit streaming sites that let them watch for free. Some of the larger sites operate from Saudi Arabia – one reason that the Premier League successfully opposed a takeover of Newcastle United by a Saudi entity in 2020.

Association with streaming sites may have been enough to scupper the purchase of a football club but it was not enough to dim the allure of partnerships with gambling companies, even though they have been among the most eager purchasers of space on those illegal streaming sites. Research conducted for the European Commission by White Bullet, which tracks the infringement of intellectual property, estimated that 43% of all adverts on websites that stole other people's IP were for gambling firms. Major brands guilty of doing this included bwin, owned by London-listed Entain, although I am confident that banner ads for nearly every well-known gambling company have appeared on such sites at one time or another. By far the worst offender was the Russian site 1xBet, which at time of writing has a partnership with FC Barcelona, the Spanish side that styles itself as *més que un club* (more than a club). Tottenham Hotspur, Chelsea and Liverpool all had deals with the company previously. At least, they did until it was accused of several other questionable activities, such as taking bets on children's sport, showing live streams of cockfighting and promoting a casino with topless croupiers.

In 2021 White Bullet kindly provided me with updated information. Their statistics showed a decline in major gambling brands advertising on pirate sites offering illegal football streams, but the numbers were still significant. Globally, there were 616 million adverts from gambling companies on 1,276 sites infringing sports rights such as the Premier League. Those sites earned about $2.7 million thanks to the practice, but the impact of lost viewers on the value of legitimate sports rights is likely to be significantly higher. I can't share the names of all the companies that were among the worst offenders, at White Bullet's request. The company advises clients who, for the most part, don't want their brands to appear on such sites but find it hard to avoid due to the complexity of buying advertising space on the internet.

Even if one accepts that argument, the presence of gambling advertising on illegal streams means that the very companies who claim to give with one hand, via sponsorship deals, are taking with the other by supporting piracy, unwittingly or not. As far as I'm aware, the football clubs and the broadcasters who lose out as a result have never kicked up a fuss.

Yet the powers that be in football have continued to defend the sport's ties to gambling in the face of criticism from campaigners, MPs, recovering addicts and fans. The FA, which looks after the laws of football and the national team, is perhaps the sole exception. It ditched a £4 million-a-year partnership with Ladbrokes in 2017, terminating the four-year deal after just one, amid concerns about gambling's increasing influence.[18] But in the parts of the game where the big money is, that concern doesn't seem to be matched. In a 2020 statement on its website, the EFL described the relationship as 'long-standing, with a collaborative, evidence-based approach to preventing gambling harms of much greater benefit than that of a blanket ban of any kind'.

In an interview shortly after he got the job in early 2020, Premier League chief executive Richard Masters said: 'We're certainly not sniffy about it; it's up to our clubs whether they want to have their own gambling relationships.'[19]

## THE PLAYERS

This laissez-faire attitude might be less surprising were it not for the evidence of gambling-related harm affecting people within the game itself. Gambling addiction is no respecter of wealth. We tend to be concerned about whether people with relatively little disposable income are gambling too much, but it can become a problem for rich people too, including footballers. This is true all the way from the lower leagues to the very highest level.

According to the Sporting Chance charity, set up by former England and Arsenal defender and recovering alcoholic Tony Adams, in January 2021 the number of athletes referred to their clinics for gambling addiction overtook the number seeking treatment for drugs and alcohol problems for the first time.

The list of footballers who've opened up about their toxic

relationship with gambling is long and growing by the day. You could put together a pretty serviceable team composed of players who have wrestled with gambling to some degree. From David James in goal to Andros Townsend on the wing and Steven Caulker in defence – even Michael Owen and Wayne Rooney up front. Peter Shilton, who has played more times for England than any other footballer in history, has spoken of his own struggles, while ex-Aston Villa and England midfielder Paul Merson has fought a prolonged and painful battle with his gambling habit. Despite knowing this, Merson's employers at Sky continued to allow his face to be used in adverts for Sky Bet, only stopping after a public backlash.[20] Even Gordon Taylor, the chief executive of the Professional Footballers' Association – a former winger – has fallen victim.

The problem can easily start at the much less glamorous, less lucrative end of the footballing spectrum, though. Richard Paxton was a promising youth player at Darlington between 2000 and 2002. There had been gambling addiction in his family – a common factor in those who develop a problem themselves – and the messages he had received in his early years were only reinforced in the dressing room as a youngster.

'When I was sixteen, I looked a bit older than I was. I'd go into the dressing room and I'd be sent to the bookie's by the first-team players. Sometimes I'd go in with thousands of pounds to put all these bets on. After I'd been in to collect a few winnings, that was me hooked. I was sitting in the stand with all these bets, running down at half-time to check the score. It wasn't even my money but I was getting the buzz. If they can do it with thousands of pounds, I can do it with a few quid. Before you know it, I'm the one putting thousands of pounds on.'

The habit nearly ruined Richard's life. It could have ended it.

# THE NET RESULT

As I've found again and again, there is no cast-iron evidence that can confirm beyond doubt a causative link between the way gambling is marketed and the effect on people in the real world. The industry benefits from a hypothesis that is more or less impossible to prove. In 2021 the Betting and Gaming Council made much of a report by Ian McHale, a professor of sports analytics at the University of Liverpool, which found no evidence that gambling sponsorship caused people to gamble more or to do so in a way that caused them harm.[21]

It's a hard one to stomach. The common counter-argument I've heard from pretty much anyone I've spoken to about this subject is that gambling companies wouldn't sponsor football if it didn't work. The figures tell their own story. Between April 2015 and March 2016 operators made £578 million in gross profit from football punters. Over the same period in 2019 and 2020, that figure had ballooned to £1.1 billion.[22] A portion of that increase is likely to be due to difficulties the Gambling Commission experienced, until relatively recently, in obtaining reliable data about which revenue came from which sport. But even adjusting for that, there's little doubt that football betting as an activity has become significantly more popular. Some of this will be down to the opportunity for in-play betting created by smartphones. But there is compelling evidence to suggest that the visibility of gambling within the game is playing its part as well. I refer to some of these studies about advertising in Chapter 2, but one piece of research chimed with my real-world experience of being a football fan in the 2020s.

Dr Darragh McGee of the University of Bath spent two years on a research project that drew on the experiences of two groups of fans aged between eighteen and thirty-five, the key target demographic for gambling marketing in football.[23] As McGee analysed the groups he was working with, he found the intensity of the online gambling culture in football had affected them deeply. Many young men had come to view casual betting not just as normal but actually 'vital to their enjoyment of sport', something Sky Bet celebrate in their advertising slogan: 'It matters more when there's money on it.'

'When I was younger, I couldn't wait to get home from school to see Man United playing in the Champions League,' twenty-seven-year-old Callum told McGee. 'Now, I'm sat there thinking about what I should be betting on tonight. I can't remember the last time that I just watched the game like a real fan.'

'If I back corners, I won't even want to see goals,' said Tom, aged thirty-one.

McGee highlighted the increasing pervasiveness of 'odds talk' in peer group chatter about sport, something that the industry has replicated in advertising campaigns focused around groups enjoying the game together while discussing their bets. 'I'm a nodder,' declares the protagonist of a recent Ladbrokes advert. 'Up to the football, down to the app, like a dog on a dashboard.'

This ad was eventually banned in July 2021 by the Advertising Standards Authority, which said that it depicted gamblers' 'detachment from surroundings, preoccupation with gambling and mood swings (including highs and lows, irritability and shortness of temper)'. By that time, the spot had been showing for months already.[24]

I've seen the nodders myself, not just in pubs and living rooms but even in the stadium, where fans have spent considerable time, money and effort to see their team. A few rows in front of my regular seat at Tottenham Hotspur, I noticed a man pull out his phone every few minutes, ignoring the game going on in front of him, to check the progress of his bets on that day's fixtures.

My lifelong love affair with football – one that developed without gambling – makes it hard for me to understand this. Is the game not enough for you? Would you like to give your seat up to someone who actually wants it?

I'm not the only football devotee who struggles to wrap their head around the nodder phenomenon. In 2021 former Scottish Conservative party leader Ruth Davidson presented a Channel 4 documentary called *Football's Gambling Addiction*, returning to journalism, the career she had before entering politics. Davidson, a lifelong Dunfermline Athletic fan and a handy player herself, interviewed fellow politicians as well as footballers and campaigners but was particularly struck by an afternoon watching a game with some young men. Their conversation hinged not so much on the intricacies of the game in its own right as on how events on the pitch related to their open bets.

'They're having discussions about whether a blocked shot counts as a shot,' she said. 'They're begging for a corner, not because they want their team to score but because they need four corners per half to go with their accumulator.'

Those lads were old enough to open betting accounts but still relatively young and certainly impressionable. But what of even younger people, those not legally able to gamble but who are still exposed to football on a regular basis?

Researchers led by Dr Rebecca Cassidy from Goldsmiths conducted a study of ninety-nine children and seventy-one adults to test their recall of major brands. They found that more than three-quarters of eight- to sixteen-year-olds believed that betting was a normal part of sport and nearly as many thought gambling on sports was a normal thing for adults to do. While they couldn't legally stake any money online or with bookies, some of those interviewed expressed clear intent to do so in future, or admitted that they were already doing so with friends.[25]

'It's normal for under-eighteens to bet with friends,' said one thirteen-year-old. 'I put £2 on Man U with other young people.'

One eight-year-old told researchers that 'if they love football, it [betting] is part of wanting their team to win.'

What's more, the researchers thought it likely – based on previous research into tobacco, alcohol and gambling – that high levels of exposure could lead to higher levels of consumption on the part of both children and adults.

Again, we lack definitive proof that this is what's happening. It may well be obvious that football is drenched with gambling imagery but we cannot say for certain what effect this is having. We can only guess at it and perhaps err on the side of caution. We could even accept that there doesn't need to be proof that gambling's role in football is harmful, so long as enough people who love the game feel uneasy about the relationship, or feel that it sullies the purity of our enjoyment of a sporting contest.

In the inimitable words of Ruth Davidson: 'I'm not a puritan, it's just gone too fucking far.'

She's not alone in feeling that way. A survey commissioned in 2020 by the campaign group Clean Up Gambling suggested that fans were getting sick and tired of the omnipresence of betting firms in the game they love.[26] One-third said they were put off spending money on their team's shirt if it had a betting sponsor, while a clear majority of 59% felt that there were too many teams sponsored by gambling companies. Some clubs are beginning to fight back, whether it's because they've listened to their fans' point of view or taken their own moral stance unbidden.

James Grimes's charity The Big Step campaigns for football clubs to cut ties with gambling. His story of gambling addiction has parallels with those of some of the addicts who spoke to Darragh McGee for his study and some we'll hear from later in this book. 'Football was my life in every aspect,' James has said. 'It was my job, my career and passion. I played it and watched it . . . It was everything.' Once he started gambling, that became the 'focal point' of his life, and he struggled with an addiction that has left him with a mountain of debt that could take a lifetime to clear.

But he has turned his addiction into a force for change, making it his mission to help wean football off the gambling teat, touring the country on sponsored walks to stadiums and trying to convince clubs to renounce gambling sponsorship. It's hard, though. Many of those clubs have become reliant on the gambling dollar. They may want to change but they can't.

'I've spoken to clubs and been in a situation where I'm talking to the head of their community scheme who asks me to keep my voice down because we're next to the head of marketing,' said James. 'There are well-meaning people [in football] who can't do what's right for the long-term health of fans because of the hold the gambling industry has over football.'

## CAN FOOTBALL WEAN ITSELF OFF?

There's no getting away from the fact that gambling has a hold on football because parts of the game have become reliant on the income it provides. According to Ruth Davidson's documentary, gambling's direct sponsorship contribution to football is more than £100 million a year, while around £200 million goes to broadcasters who pay for rights to air games and also promote the sport in other ways.

The cash doesn't just go to filthy-rich mega-clubs either. As former sports minister Tracey Crouch reminded me, money from gambling 'goes into grassroots sport, goes into women's sport, goes into disability sport and everything else'.

Indeed, the relationship of reliance tends to get stronger the lower down the league you go. As keen as gambling firms are to associate themselves with the game, they don't actually have the muscle to do the biggest deals, at least not yet. At time of writing, none of the top six clubs in the Premier League have a gambling sponsor on their shirt because they can all attract sponsors with even more financial heft. Manchester United have Chevrolet, part of the global automotive behemoth General Motors, Liverpool have the Asia-focused banking firm Standard Chartered and Chelsea are sponsored by mobile phone company Three. But once you move down the hierarchy of English football, gambling companies have established themselves as indispensable. That's one reason why the game's powers that be remain vehemently opposed to measures restricting gambling sponsorship.

'When you get into the Championship,' Eric the sports marketer explained, 'more than 40% of perimeter [pitchside hoarding] income is gambling. For many of those clubs that's one of the key sources of revenue. Similarly with shirt sponsorships. You could [sponsor] Nottingham Forest for £150K, it's not a huge amount of money. But for a club turning over £15 million to £20 million it's significant.'

But Nottingham Forest's shirt sponsorship deal actually provides a lesson in being careful who you accept money from. The two-time European champions were, like Queens Park Rangers, until recently sponsored by Football Index, the self-described stock market of football. Launched in 2015, it styled itself as a stock market for football fans, offering them the opportunity to buy 'shares'. The shares would go up in value if the players did well and those shares would also pay 'dividends' – regular cash payouts. The site became a mecca for football fans, mostly young and male, who had found a way to quantify their footballing knowledge with money and feel like hotshot City boys playing the stock market. If you felt like you'd spotted the next prospect in the German leagues, you could buy shares in them and prove to your mates that you were right all along when their stock went up and you made a return. The only trouble was, the whole edifice was built on sand.

In order to keep people interested, the site had to pay traders 'dividends'. But real dividends are underpinned by companies with assets and actual cashflow. The 'shares' in football players that Football Index traders owned were, effectively, just bets on whether a player would do well or not. Those bets could be bought and sold, as if punters in a bookie's were exchanging betting slips with one another. A bookie does not pay you dividends on your bets; they either come in or they don't. As one industry insider put it: 'They were effectively offering 20–1 on 2–1 shots.'

Football Index knew the model could not hold and eventually slashed the dividends on offer. What it didn't reckon with was the resulting exodus of fans, which ultimately forced it into administration, owing thousands of customers millions of pounds.[27] Administrators found that there was enough cash to repay funds deposited in customer accounts, but the same could not be said of the value that 'traders' believed they had built up in their share portfolios and the dividends they believed they were owed. These were bets and considered 'sums at risk'.

The fallout was noisy and the effect far-reaching. Football Index's legions of devoted fans were equally angry and mournful, lashing out at the company's directors while hoping beyond hope that the pastime they loved could somehow be resurrected.

The Gambling Commission came under fire when it emerged that the regulator had been repeatedly warned that Football Index was a house of cards, many months before it failed. The government launched a review into what had happened.

It was yet another example of how football's love affair with gambling does not come risk-free. Given the presence of that risk – not to mention the possibility that the government will one day legislate to curb or ban gambling sponsorship in sport – shouldn't clubs be looking for alternatives?

Football finance expert Kieran Maguire, author of *The Price of Football: Understanding Club Finance*, says smaller clubs have shown that, if they're well run, they don't need to depend on gambling money. 'The reason why clubs in the English Football League have such significant financial problems is down to poor cost control, it's not determined by revenue,' he told me. 'What we have seen again and again is that every time clubs have been given additional money, they spend all of it and a little bit more on higher player costs, so I don't have a lot of sympathy. Two-thirds of teams in the Championship are sponsored by gambling companies but by definition, one-third aren't, and those clubs can survive.'

Ruth Davidson made the comparison with alcohol when we spoke after her Channel 4 documentary had aired. 'We had this exact argument when we took Carlsberg off Liverpool shirts, Tennent's off Celtic, Newcastle Brown Ale off Newcastle United's. Everyone said we can't do without alcohol sponsorship. But you know what, we did.'

So far, the highest-profile club to ditch a gambling sponsor on moral grounds has been Everton, while Swansea City in the second tier and the likes of Luton Town and Tranmere Rovers have done the same. But with the pandemic having dealt a crushing blow to the finances of many clubs, it feels less likely than ever that football will take the big step voluntarily.

'Whilst gambling is allowed to be the highest bidder, it will be,' James Grimes told me. 'I can't point the finger at clubs for taking money, especially now when they're in such a precarious state. The gambling industry is relatively recession-proof and will be able to offer money where other industries won't. So it has to come from government and it's up to them to propose things that replace that income.'

Football finance experts have suggested alternatives, should the gambling punchbowl be taken away. Options include a levy charged on all sports bets, much like the one that funds horse racing. Clubs and leagues, some have suggested, could make better use of the legal rights they have over intellectual property, things like club badges and player imagery, extracting cash from betting firms who want to use them.

In a 2020 report members of the House of Lords put forward proposals that would see clubs given a grace period to find alternative sources of income, before being subject to a blanket ban that would send gambling sponsorship – on shirts, at least – the way of tobacco.[28]

Many people in football and gambling now believe that some sort of a crackdown is inevitable. Short of a total ban on all gambling-related sponsorship in the game, new curbs would likely meet with little opposition from the largest gambling companies, who – as we have seen – aren't that interested in the eye-catching front-of-shirt deals. It would likely prove a popular, headline-grabbing policy for a government that will need it as it navigates a tricky path to post-pandemic economic recovery.

Until and unless that happens, football and gambling will remain one of the most prolific partnerships in the game.

# 6. ADDICTION, 'AFFECTED OTHERS' AND SUICIDE

A person can compose a symphony or write a book while smoking
– indeed, it might even be essential to the process. But gambling is
all-consuming in its pointlessness.

DOMINIC LAWSON, *THE SUNDAY TIMES* (2013)

Addiction is the gravitational force around which everything else in this book revolves. It lurks in the background of most conversations about gambling regulation, the elephant in the room that calls into question the decision by the Labour government in 2005 to treat a potentially dangerous pastime as if it were any other leisure activity.

It is also what motivates most of those who seek reform of an industry they believe has grown into a malignant, even parasitic, presence in society. Were it not for gambling's addictive properties, there would be much less reason to ask whether the industry needs to be brought to heel.

The horror stories have become grimly familiar, notable among them the sad death of Jack Ritchie, who seemingly had the world at his feet until his gambling addiction robbed him of hope. Among the many harrowing tales I've heard while covering the gambling industry, Jack's death – not to mention his parents' incredible campaigning efforts – is the tragedy I always reach for when inspiration and impetus are in short supply. He was twenty-four when he died, around the same age I was when my journalism career began. The parallels between our lives – both young men from relatively affluent backgrounds, with loving parents and apparently everything to live for – is not lost on me. I cannot help thinking about the life that might have been for him, had he not been consumed by addiction.

Jack's story is difficult to read about but it is not unique – not even that unusual. The suicide of young engineer Chris Bruney in 2017, detailed in the chapter on so-called VIPs, is just as difficult to hear. Like Jack, Chris has become a symbol for something larger, a cautionary tale around which the campaign for gambling reform has coalesced.

In Chapter 3, on brainhacks and technology, we saw how the gambling industry has invested a great deal of time, money and energy into designing products with the express intention of hooking our brains into repetitive cycles of play. Unlike some addictive products that are innately habit-forming due to their potential for physical dependency, gambling can be – and has been – specifically designed and refined to be habit-forming. While many people are able to manage the effects of such lures successfully, the gambling addicts I've known have told me that they could not, making it impossible for them to step away from the abyss.

Suicide is the most extreme outcome of a descent into gambling addiction but it is not the only one. Witness the gamblers who steal to feed their habit, leaving their victims in turmoil and landing themselves in prison. Or what about the casual punters turned hardcore addicts, racking up huge debts through payday loans and ending up bankrupt, plunging their families into destitution? Time and again gambling addiction destroys relationships, thwarts careers, curtails opportunity and breaks up families.

These stories are emotive and it's both understandable and entirely appropriate to feel a powerful response to them. Gambling has, on many occasions, been described in terms that some in the industry and the libertarian commentariat have considered hyperbolic. Fixed-odds betting terminals have frequently been labelled 'the crack cocaine of gambling', something crack addicts and those suffering from drug addiction might well feel uncomfortable with. Addiction has been termed an 'epidemic' too. That can feel ill-considered, and even faintly distasteful, in the light of the deadly global pandemic that has recently reshaped our lives.

That's not to say that there is anything inherently wrong with using direct and evocative language to illustrate a nuanced topic. Everyone uses colourful language to make their point from time to time. A predilection towards evocative phraseology is particularly evident among those who seek to change people's minds – MPs, gambling reform campaigners, those who have lost loved ones and, yes, journalists and authors. The subtitle of this book – *How Gambling Conquered Britain* – does not seek to imply that bet365 boss Denise Coates launched a coup from Gibraltar and now sits atop a throne made of casino chips and crumpled £20 notes.

But if she had, it's fair to argue that a sizeable portion of the throne would have been built on the backs of addicts. A House of Lords select committee found that around 60% of industry profits come from just 5% of gamblers.[1] As we learned in Chapter 4, those figures can be even more dramatic, with one operator taking more than 80% of its revenue from the 2% of its customers who were made VIPs. According to a presentation at the Alberta Gambling Research Institute's annual conference in 2016, citing multiple studies, gambling addicts account for between 15% and 50% of the industry's revenue.[2] Admittedly that's a wide range. What's clear is that gambling companies active in the UK today owe a significant – if not precisely defined – share of their income to people who are suffering from harm, as well as visiting harm upon those around them.

When we talk about gambling addiction in terms that implicate the industry, we need to be on solid ground about what it is we are describing. What exactly is it? That isn't always easy to nail down, but there are some good places to start.

# WHAT IS GAMBLING ADDICTION?

Understandably the term 'problem gamblers' makes many recovering addicts feel uncomfortable. Not only does it reduce a living, breathing human being to the status of a 'problem' but it also suggests that the issue lies solely with the gambler rather than with the way in which potentially dangerous products are designed and marketed. In addition it risks glossing over the seriousness of the addiction, diminishing its standing in relation to other disorders and pinning the blame on the victim. We do not usually refer to 'problem drinkers' or 'problem drug users'. We talk about alcoholics or drug addicts. Failure to use a similar approach with gambling risks underplaying its potential severity. There are synonyms, whether it's 'gambling addiction', 'disordered gambling', or even 'ludomania', if you're feeling fancy. With apologies in advance, I may still refer to 'problem gambling' from time to time. It has relevance not just in common parlance but in academic and clinical circles, not least in the NHS and the Royal College of Psychiatrists, as well as the Gambling Commission.

When the annual NHS Digital Health Survey measures the extent of problem gambling, it does so using two scales. The first is the DSM-5, the fifth iteration of the *Diagnostic and Statistical Manual of Mental Disorders*, which came out in 2013.[3] The second is the PGSI (Problem Gambling Severity Index), developed for use in a wider analysis of societal impacts, rather than within a clinical context. They work in similar ways, namely by asking people questions about how they feel and about their actual behaviour. This ranges from something as simple as how often the subject gambles to more complex and subjective questions such as whether they have ever lost a relationship or a job because of it. A person's responses make up their score and a threshold determines whether they are deemed to be a problem gambler. On the DSM scale, five and above is the watermark, and for PGSI – the metric that is probably most widely used now – it's eight and higher. These formal criteria are useful for research and monitoring purposes – something we'll explore a little later. But there is only so much we can glean from cold hard statistics. Knowing that someone has a PGSI score of twelve offers us no real insight into their lived experience or the impact their disorder has on friends, family and wider society.

Historically, gambling addiction hasn't been very well represented in our cultural and political lives – certainly not in the way that substance abuse has been. Take popular drama, for instance. I remember any number of soap-opera storylines about alcoholism and drug use on *EastEnders* or *Coronation Street*. It is only in recent years, amid a gathering storm of discontent about the spread of gambling, that popular drama has started to draw on real-life stories documented in the media and elsewhere. The result is a deficit of understanding, a time lag that means gambling addiction is neither well understood nor afforded the same degree of concern. This is a mistake. Gambling addiction can be every bit as harmful as substance abuse, something that isn't always appreciated because its effects are not as empirically evident. Indeed, this cloak of invisibility is at the root of what makes it so pernicious, so difficult to quantify, and so hard to stop.

## AN INVISIBLE WRECKING BALL

Prof. Henrietta Bowden-Jones is one of the UK's foremost addiction experts. She is an honorary professor in the Division of Psychology and Language Sciences at University College London and honorary senior visiting fellow in the Department of Psychiatry at Cambridge University. In 2019 she was awarded an OBE for services to addiction treatment and research. The early part of Bowden-Jones's career was spent treating people with severe substance abuse problems. 'These were people born into addiction and who died in addiction, whose kids were on methadone when they were born,' she recalls.

In 2008, a year after the Gambling Act came into force, Bowden-Jones founded the National Problem Gambling Clinic. Just over a decade later she found herself expanding the clinic's remit to offer specialist treatment for children who gamble. Few people, if any, know the problem gambling landscape like Bowden-Jones. She highlights two things in particular that make it unlike anything else. The first is that a gambling disorder is often completely invisible, even to someone with her practically unrivalled expertise.

'If I see someone with an alcohol disorder or a drug addiction, certainly as someone who treats these things, I can see it. You know something's not right. Even more so when they're using the substance and they're intoxicated, but even when they're not there will be physical signs that someone can pick up. With gambling you don't. In fact, often what you're presented with is a very positive, dynamic individual full of plans.'

Bowden-Jones grew fond of the gambling addicts she treated, precisely because of the unusual way in which their disorder manifested itself.

'They happened to be some of the most fun and interesting people; their personalities were rather optimistic. They were people who went to gamble to buy clothes for a new baby. They were people who, with the best of intentions, would mess up every time. So I just fell in love with my patients.'

The flip side of that positive trait – one to which I can attest in my far more limited experience – is that their struggles can remain hidden for a long time, preventing them from seeking, or being offered, help. The average person being treated by one of the UK's National Gambling Treatment Service (NGTS) providers has wrestled with their addiction for ten years before seeing someone, according to figures released in 2020.[4]

'The relatives we speak to who have really suffered feel they've been duped into situations they would never have walked into,' says Bowden-Jones. 'You can keep it secret for a long time and the shame and the guilt come later when things are already falling apart. Whereas it's extremely harmful, that harm is not always visible.'

Recovering addicts know this all too well.

'There were times when my girlfriend would be asleep in bed next to me and I'd be on a casino site, usually roulette,' said Chris Murphy, a former addict who now works for the Sporting Chance clinic, aimed at athletes who have suffered from addiction. 'I'd have a YouTube window up so that if she woke up I could switch over, so she thought I was watching that on my laptop.'

Civil servant Adrian Howard managed to keep his wife in the dark even as he amassed debts of £45,000 while earning a salary of little more than half that. He said: 'Unless you're very close to that person and you know them intimately, I don't think there are any telltale signs, really, apart from being distracted all the time. And being skint. My wife probably knew something was going on but could never get to the bottom of it. She knew we were out of money but there was always an excuse, always a reason. I'd never say it was for gambling. I'd never say I'd blown the lot on the bookies.'

Throw a generational divide into the mix and it can be particularly hard for loved ones to peel away the facade to expose the turmoil beneath, as Jack Ritchie's parents know all too well.

Unlike Jack, former VIP Phil Worrall survived his darkest days. His parents were aware that he gambled a lot and suspected he had a problem, but they were not necessarily equipped with the technological know-how to realise just how difficult it might be for him to avoid temptation. 'They knew I was betting online but if you don't really know how the internet works or you don't have a smartphone, you don't know I can access bet365 while I'm going to catch the bus,' he said. 'My friends would come round my house to play [video game] FIFA in the evening and me and a friend have gone on Paddy Power roulette and lost money at 1 a.m. That's not something my parents would be aware of. That's not a thing in their world, being on online gambling at one in the morning.'

Alongside the difficulty in identifying it, another uniquely perilous aspect of gambling disorder is that, by its very nature, it is financially destructive and often rapidly so. Substance abuse can, of course, have serious consequences for one's bank balance. But unless you are extremely rich, or on one hell of an improbable winning streak, problem gambling *almost invariably* does. Bowden-Jones points to 'the destruction it causes of families, the children of gamblers who leave homes because they are hounded by debt collectors, move homes ten times, get bullied because they don't have clothes. There are children of alcoholics with dreadful lives, awful childhoods for reasons like violence and neglect. But it hits hard in a family when they've got no money to eat.'

As Dr Steve Sharman of the University of East London points out, that financial element becomes a self-fulfilling prophecy, because it means there is always – potentially, at least – more fuel for the fire. 'With alcohol, tobacco or illegal substances, there's only a finite amount of that substance that the body can take,' he says. 'The person is going to drink a certain amount and pass out. With gambling there isn't that physical stop line. You only stop when you've got no money left.'

The point at which a gambler has no money left is flexible. There is always a way – beg, borrow or steal – to procure more funds. And that is exactly what addicts will do, as we saw in Chapter 4 with the story of Katie (not her real name), who in 2019 told me she'd used nine credit cards to rack up losses of £125,000 with online casinos LeoVegas and Casumo.

That's far from unusual. Payday loans, charging usurious interest rates, are a common avenue for gamblers desperate for funds. Paul Jones, a thirty-nine-year-old recovering gambling addict, told me in 2017[5] that he twice took out high-interest payday loans by telephone in front of Ladbrokes staff at a branch in Birmingham. He said that they not only knew he was taking out the loans but even ran his debit card through the machine for him, to check whether the money had arrived in his account.

In 2020 the NGTS painted a statistical picture of the financial mire into which gambling can drag people. Of those being treated, 45% had amassed debts of more than £5,000, were bankrupt, or were going through a debt repayment scheme. They had spent a median average of more than £2,000 in the month before entering treatment, a sum similar to the average British person's monthly salary. Around one in eight had lost a job.[6]

According to figures I obtained from the government's Insolvency Service, which collects data on people who go bankrupt and businesses that go bust, there were more than two thousand insolvencies between 2010 and 2019 in which gambling was cited as a cause (although it should be noted that this category also includes 'rash speculation' such as unwise get-rich-quick investment schemes). Sometimes the source of funds is particularly illustrative of how low someone can be brought by addiction. One of the most troubling cases I've encountered is that of Liam McCarron.[7] Liam was a relatively successful businessman in Birmingham, until a mistake during a routine medical procedure left him severely disabled. His movement is impaired, as is his speech. It is extremely difficult for anyone who isn't used to communicating with Liam to understand what he says. The NHS compensated him financially for the error that left him in this unenviable situation. But in the course of a few short years Liam had squandered it all in Birmingham bookies'. He was even helped along the road to self-destruction by staff who knew that he could no longer work and was gambling with the proceeds of a one-off, fast-diminishing compensation payout. 'The money I used to gamble was intended to be for my ongoing living costs and care needs, which are significant,' he told me in a statement written with the help of his family.

Gamblers don't only lose money, though. Often they lose partners, friends and family into the bargain. More than a quarter of those who were treated by the NGTS in 2019–20 said a relationship of one form or another had broken down.[8]

Phil Worrall remembers an evening when gambling won out over an urge that most young men feel more strongly than almost anything else: sex. 'There was one night in my room at uni and I was there with a girl I really liked. She was sitting on my bed talking to me, saying she was really ugly, those things that girls do when they want attention and affection. And I'm thinking "Will you shut up" because I wanted to get some bets on the golf tomorrow. I was looking at who'd won and who'd lost and if I could get a bet on the next day. Maybe it would have happened, maybe it wouldn't . . . but I was too busy.'

Money and relationships don't exist in separate bubbles, of course. Adrian Howard's insatiable appetite for more funds made him, in his own words, a 'scumbag' who could not help but destroy personal relationships. 'You alienate people,' he remembers. 'I lent [borrowed] a lot of money off close friends with the intention of paying them back when the bet came in. But it didn't come in. I lost a couple of good relationships. One was an old friend I'd been to school with, I'd known him probably seventeen or eighteen years, I'll probably never ever get that back. That relationship is lost.'

'I've lost good friends, asking them for money,' admits Martin Paterson. 'I put my daughter in the position where I'm asking her for money and not telling her mum.' Martin would frequently quarrel with his son, partly as a result of his addiction. When his son died of a heart attack, the last words they had exchanged had been in anger. 'I had no time for him,' says Martin. 'I was there but I wasn't there.'

Sometimes gamblers lose their freedom too. Problem gamblers

are over four times more likely to go to prison during their lifetime compared with the average member of the population.[9]

The Howard League for Penal Reform points out that, unlike substance abuse, a gambling addiction is rarely treated as a mitigating factor in sentencing. All too often judges view a perpetrator's spending on gambling just as they would splashing out on Ferraris or holidays in the Maldives, meaning potentially lengthy sentences.

'What we're finding is that there's a real lack of knowledge within the criminal justice system as regards crime and problem gambling,' the Howard League's director of campaigns, Andrew Neilson, told me. One of the issues he highlights is that magistrates will sometimes use the Proceeds of Crime Act to confiscate assets from gambling addicts who have committed crimes to fund the habit. 'A piece of legislation designed with drug dealers in mind is being used against families. They're in prison and the family is being pursued for a confiscation order, when actually the money that was stolen was just ploughed into gambling to try and win back the debt the person was in in the first place.'

In 2019 Ben Jones from Nottingham was jailed for three years for stealing £370,000 from his employer, a cake decoration company.[10] He used the money to gamble with Betway. Steve Girling from Norfolk was jailed for four years after stealing £1 million from his former employer, Premier Education Group.[11] Andy May, the 'VIP' who told me his story days before he was jailed for four years, was another.[12] These are just a handful out of dozens of similar stories about gamblers who turned to crime when they had no other recourse to funds.

To most people, orchestrating a theft of such magnitude feels unimaginable, even when we know that the perpetrator is an addict. That's because it is impossible for a non-addict to really understand the strength of that compulsion. Gambling addiction is often completely hidden and powerfully destructive – an invisible wrecking ball sweeping everything before it, yet with the same pernicious hold over its victim as physical addiction. Even those suffering from it may not see it coming.

## WHAT DOES IT FEEL LIKE?

The sensation that Martin Paterson described – being 'there but not there' – is common among disordered gamblers, who often report symptoms that we are more used to hearing about when discussing alcohol or narcotics addiction. Indeed, Martin recounts a tale that sounds an awful lot like the classic scare story of drug dealers offering free samples outside the school gates.

'I got into fixed-odds betting terminals soon after they first came out in the first years of the twenty-first century. I got hooked during a demo week. When they [FOBTs] first came in, the bookies were getting everyone to try a free spin. It was a tournament, everyone who came in was allowed a £50 free spin. It gave you the impression that you were winning. When you got onto the real money, they already had so many people hooked.'

Most of us are familiar with that feeling of craving, whether it's nicotine, alcohol or something more common such as chocolate or salty snacks. Gambling addicts feel that too, but for the act of getting their next bet on.

Chris Murphy would have visions of his next session when he wasn't able to gamble: 'Even when I wasn't gambling, as a result of losing all my money there'd be this romantic daydream of the next session, this building of anticipation that this time I'm going to win. It was a feeling of romanticised anticipation.' In the midst of a serious session, Chris describes an out-of-body semi-catatonic experience, more akin to what you might associate with the intoxication of substance abuse. 'I remember being stood at a FOBT and it must have been a trance-like state,' he says. 'I'd been in front of this one machine for seven hours. The thought occurred to me that not only had I not had anything to eat, drink, or been to the toilet, but that I'd not felt the need. My mind was that obsessed that it didn't feel normal feelings like hunger and thirst.'

Marathon stints on FOBTs are far from one-offs. In 2017 a report by GambleAware found that seven gamblers had lost more than £10,000 in a day on the £100-per-spin machines. Given that FOBTs allow a spin every twenty seconds, the fastest you could lose £10,000 is in theory half an hour – but that would require a losing streak so statistically improbable that it can be discounted. In reality, plenty of those sessions will have lasted hours. Indeed, GambleAware found that one gambler had lost £13,777.90 – more than half the UK's national average wage – in a seven-and-a-half-hour sitting.[13]

In *Addiction by Design*, Natasha Dow Schüll refers to the Las Vegas casino industry's term for measuring these stints, known as 'time on device' (TOD), going on to explore the intricate techniques – some of them recounted in Chapter 3 – that game designers use to maximise the metric.[14] The result, she found, was 'the zone', a concept she returns to throughout the book. It sprang from a description given to her by a video poker addict named Mollie, who referred to being 'in that machine zone'. Mollie's characterisation was much like the 'trance-like state' that Chris Murphy speaks of.

'It's like being in the eye of a storm, is how I'd describe it,' she said. 'Your vision is clear on the machine in front of you but the whole world is spinning around you, and you can't really hear anything. You aren't really there – you're with the machine and that's all you're with.'

Matt Gaskell, consultant psychologist for the NHS Northern Gambling Service, explained to me what's going on in the brain, or at least a truncated version of a very complex process. 'It works through what's called the reward pathway in the brain, creating a hyper-exaggerated response of desire, motivation and focused attention,' he said. 'At the same time, the part of your mind which you'd rely upon to put some impulse control in place or weigh up decision-making – in the pre-frontal cortex – effectively goes offline. That part doesn't evolve until you're about twenty-five, which is why we're so worried about children.'

Whether adult or child, being in the zone can alter perceptions of reality. Chris Murphy's fantastical notions prevented him from recognising that it was he – the man tied to a machine for most of the day – who had the problem, rather than everyone else. 'I used to look out of the window and see people doing things like walking the dog, riding a bike or walking around with friends, and I used to think they were the losers because I was in there and was going to win this brilliant life. Why isn't everyone doing this?'

Problem gamblers sometimes speak of being entirely consumed by the need to bet, planning their lives around it, to the exclusion of everything else.

'It becomes a twenty-four-seven job,' Phil Worrall explains. 'You tell yourself you're doing it because it's easier than work but you're never switched off except for when you're asleep. When I was doing my degree it was more important to me than that. I'd bet first and do my degree second. I might not be logged in to my account but I'd be mentally logged in. Effectively it became me, I became gambling. That's what it does to you.'

One of the low ebbs that Adrian Howard describes is even more astonishing, particularly to parents who aren't familiar with the depths of addiction. 'Take my daughter's birthday when she turned five. We had a party at our home and had friends and family round. I don't remember that party one little bit. I was sat on my phone placing bet after bet, not interacting with anyone else, not taking anything in. I'd slope off somewhere else, spend time in the bathroom where I wouldn't be bothered.' It was a symptom of how little control Adrian had left. 'I'd bet on Venezuelan under-twenty-three footy at half past three in the morning and set my alarm to wake up and bet on that.'

As I've mentioned before, I'm not a gambler and I have, for whatever reason, never felt the buzz that even a casual punter must enjoy. Yet I recognise some of the situations these young men describe. I've been Phil, in my room with a girl at university, wondering what might happen. I've been a football fan at social events, feeling the urge to look up the score – albeit for sporting reasons rather than to check on a bet. I've been a smoker, knowing that I needed a cigarette but not fully registering that it was nothing more than dependency that made me feel that way. That was a physical addiction. But one experience that feels the most akin to the gambling addict's urge – to me, at least – is being unable to tear myself away from my smartphone. I doom-scroll endlessly through Twitter, check my emails, sometimes get the phone out and look at it without really knowing why. It's an itch, one that many of us feel these days.

In some respects, the only thing that makes it possible for me to empathise in the first place, not being a gambler myself, is the shared personal experience – of having been a young man, one who is really into football. Indeed, most of the gambling addiction story is told through the eyes of young men because they are the demographic that displays by far the highest rate of problem gambling. Men are more than twice as likely to be problem gamblers, with about 0.8% of them suffering from the addiction as opposed to 0.3% of women.[15] Of those in treatment within the NGTS network in the year to the end of March 2020, 75% were men.[16] That makes it easier for me to look at the gamblers I've met and put myself in their shoes.

But women therefore made up 25% of those being treated by the NGTS, and certainly women have been closing the gap in recent years – up from 19% in 2015–16. What's more, they appeared to suffer increased difficulty with gambling as the UK went into coronavirus-related lockdowns in 2020. The proportion of women self-excluding through GamStop was 26% in March 2020 but rose steadily to more than 31% by September, exceeding 50,000 sign-ups.[17]

Leanne Reynolds, whose name has been changed at her request, is one of those women who developed a gambling problem during the pandemic. She'd previously enjoyed bingo, which is disproportionately popular with women, but when lockdown hit she tried out online slot machines. The thirty-nine-year-old from Dunfermline had a monthly income of just £411 – her welfare cheque from the state under the Universal Credit system. She signed up with one of the best-known operators, whom I cannot name here, and quickly became hooked.

'I don't know what it was, whether it was the gambling, the boredom or just the curiosity,' she told me. 'But it's like everyone says, it's at your fingertips twenty-four-seven. I signed up, got the promotion that was happening, something like £30 matched with deposits or free spins.'

Within the first thirty days she had spent her Universal Credit money. When that ran out, she turned to other means.

'There were payday loans, money that my mum gave me, taking out phone contracts for two years and then selling the phones.'

She ended up in debt to mobile phone companies and payday lenders, money she'll likely be paying back for many years.

At times she won money but could not bring herself to withdraw it. 'The minute I got it, I deposited it straight back again.'

Leanne describes herself as having been in a trance for nearly two months, a slave to the allure of the games she enjoyed. Her description offers an insight into the twisted logic of addiction and the effect that the tricks described in Chapter 3 can play on the mind.

'One of the games they've got is called Slingo – it's a cross between a slot and a bingo machine. Let's say you pay £2 and get ten balls for your stake. If you don't get anything, you have to buy more balls, but the nearer you get to the full house, the dearer the balls are.

By the time you're waiting on one or two numbers, it can be £350 a ball. You're sitting there and thinking about this ball that's costing you £350. By this point you might have spent £850 already. Just say it's the wrong number. Do you write it off or buy another ball in the hope that you win £500 back? It's still a loss but it's not as big a one as if you hadn't clicked to take the ball. It's a loss but it's a win to a gambler. What they're capable of doing and the way they work with your mind is unbelievable.'

Leanne suffered from a sleeping disorder already and her obsession with slots meant she would stay up all night, locked into cycles like these.

'The sessions could last four or five hours. Normally I'm the kind of person who's always fidgeting about but when you start on that, anything can happen around you and you don't notice. You don't eat, drink, go to the toilet. You're just focused, in a trance.'

Leanne was on Universal Credit yet was able to gamble thousands of pounds at a time. The operator in question has acknowledged no wrongdoing. Worse, Leanne feels, they have displayed precious little concern for her well-being.

'They basically said they'd exhausted the procedure and there'd be no further correspondence. If you're at the end of your tether, it's enough to make you go and jump.'


## AFFECTED OTHERS

Stories like these may be rarer than those affecting men but evidence of a growing problem among women suggests they may become more commonplace. And there is one cohort in which women are much better represented, a category that has become known as 'affected others'. The internal mental struggle that disordered gamblers go through can, as we've seen, remain veiled even to those who know them best. Eventually, though, other people get sucked into the path of a tornado they did not know was coming. They, in the lingo of gambling disorder, are the affected others.

A survey by pollsters YouGov in 2020 found that affected others may number as many as 3.4 million.[18] Of the 9,008 people receiving treatment via the NGTS for problem gambling in 2019–20, 13% – an increase from 10% in 2015–16 – were classed as affected others.[19] A typical problem gambler affects at least six other people, according to a 2017 article published in the journal *International Gambling Studies* by four Australian academics.[20] That sounds like a lot of people but it makes sense when you hear the stories of those who have lived through it.

Julie Martin, fifty, spoke to me in November 2020. Although she came across as an eternal optimist, the exhaustion caused by the burden of her husband's addiction over many years could be heard in her voice. Julie first realised that her husband had lost control of his gambling when their children were eight and twelve. 'I was naive,' she told me, 'and I just wanted to help him because he was my world. I spent two years making myself extremely ill borrowing from Peter to pay Paul, swapping credit cards, borrowing money off my family, just to cover up everything he was doing.' With her husband's descent into ever-deeper addiction came mood swings and even violence. 'He alienated my parents so they couldn't come here any more. My mental state was abysmal because I was stressed and in a mess. In the end it accumulated to the extent that he assaulted me. He also left very threatening messages on my mobile phone, to the point that he was arrested for harassment. But he was bailed to this house, which meant me and the kids had to leave, we were practically made homeless. We went to live with my parents twenty-five miles away. The children couldn't go to school, I couldn't go to work.'

It's easy to see how quickly friends and family become collateral damage in a gambling addiction. With Julie's help, her husband got his life back on track and, for several years at least, the family held together. Soon, though, the cracks began to emerge again.

'We went away on our last holiday in the summer of 2019 and it became apparent he wasn't putting his mobile phone down very much. I saw then that we were losing him again, but this time with online [gambling]. In October last year I found that he had gambled away our savings. It was all gone, about £15,000. I've had to use everything including some of my children's savings to keep this house over our head. I've told them I'll get it back to them.'

Julie is now in the position of having to shield her children from the worst of the addiction fallout. She works twelve hours a day with dementia patients, a challenging environment at the best of times but even worse in the grip of a pandemic in which infections in social care settings are rife. 'Financially I have no choice. I've asked him for a divorce and to sell the house but he currently owes £50,000 on a car and we have £40,000 on the mortgage, which is all we've got left on it. I'm liable for half of both. I can't lose £40,000 when I need to move on with my future. I'm stuck, I'm trapped. He got a bit violent during lockdown and my children did witness it. But if he stands outside the front door and a neighbour walks past, he's his normal self. They'd never know what goes on in here. I should be doing what I need to do for my family but he absorbs everything. I'm dealing with dementia patients, being tested for Covid once a week, but I have to. Somewhere there'll be an end to it. I'm not sure where it is but I'll get there.'

Affected others are often trying desperately to limit the damage of circumstances over which they have absolutely no control. Yet feelings of shame and self-loathing do not respect logic. Julie told me that she still feels guilty when she thinks about the impact her husband's destruction of the family finances could have on her children. Despite having borne an incredible burden with superhuman reserves of strength, she still feels – completely irrationally – that she could have done more.

Stuart Monk, whose details have been changed at his request, knows that irrational feeling of guilt too. His son Grant developed an addiction that culminated in him losing £20,000 in two days. Stuart, a former schoolteacher, now feels ashamed of the anger he felt towards his son at the time, an emotion that, given the sums involved, would be completely understandable to many parents. 'I couldn't look him in the eye for six weeks, I was so angry. Never did I think about what he was going through, it was all about me and what it did to our family. It's only when I look back now thinking that it must have been absolute turmoil for him.' The anger, he says, stemmed in part from that lack of understanding, shared in broader society, of what gambling addiction can do to a person: 'If I'd known more about it, maybe I could have had a better plan in place. But I was making it up as I went along. If it was drugs or alcohol I would have had more of an understanding of how to deal with it.'

Stuart now tries to bridge that gap in understanding through a charity that runs courses designed to educate school-age children and their families about the dangers of gambling.

In cases where gamblers commit crimes in order to feed their addiction, the victims can be employers or business associates, as well as friends and family. In Chapter 4, I outlined the case of Tony Parente, who stole more than £1 million from clients of the property investment business he ran in Dubai. One of the victims of his theft, Amarjeet Singh Dhir, had to take to the courts to attempt to reclaim £1 million from Paddy Power, which lavished Parente with free gifts and inducements to bet even as he ploughed stolen money into their coffers.

Tony was spared the ordeal of incarceration but that isn't always how it goes. Earlier in this chapter I mentioned Ben Jones, who was jailed in 2019 after stealing £370,000 from his employer, a cake decoration company. His wife, Becky, learned the true extent of what he had done when he came clean about his thefts. She was thirty-seven weeks pregnant with their second child when she realised that she was facing the prospect of bringing up two young children while her husband, the man she had been with since she was fourteen, was behind bars. 'I was pretty distraught and hysterical – I just cried constantly. We were waiting for the police, wondering if they'd knock on the door. Every car that parked outside, we'd be checking the window, every knock on the door, living on the edge.'

Becky stuck by Ben, recognising that his misdeeds were the result not of greed but of a mental health issue – although, as detailed earlier, the judicial process does not tend to see it that way. He was sentenced to three years in prison, leaving Becky to look after the children. The couple decided to tell their eldest daughter that her father was away for work. 'When you're that age, it's murderers and robbers who go to prison. She doesn't understand that good people do bad things and she'd be worried for him too.'

There was some reason to be worried too. Ben found himself confronted by gambling even on the inside, which was particularly hard during lockdown, when inmates were confined to their cells for twenty-three hours a day. When a virtual version of the Grand National was held for charity, fellow prisoners voiced their anger at him for not taking part in the betting frenzy. During phone calls to his daughter from prison, Ben would have to pretend that inmates banging on the door and shouting for their turn on the phone were workmates messing around. Once, when she asked him what the weather was like where he was, he spun a tale about hot weather and hailstorms.

'She went and got her iPad and googled it,' said Becky. 'It turns out that somewhere in Africa there was this freak hailstorm, so then she thought she'd worked out he was in Africa. He got a friend to

Photoshop him into some wildlife photos. She's got these pictures of him with a lion.'

Their younger daughter knows even less of her father, recognising him only as a man in a picture and – occasionally – a ringing phone. 'She'll cuddle the phone. That's what Ben is to her, a voice on the end of the phone.'

Like Julie, Becky has had to draw on strength that she didn't know she had, simply to keep everything together and absorb as much of the impact as possible. Many people have been affected by Ben's gambling addiction – the managers of the business from which he stole, the couple's immediate families and their own two children. But it is Becky who has borne the heaviest weight on her shoulders, juggling her work as a midwife with looking after the children and managing the family's ravaged finances.

'This year has been the worst year of my life and I don't know how I've got through it. I can't tell you how I have but some days it's on an hour-by-hour basis. Initially the adrenaline gets you through but after a while I still wasn't sleeping, went off any food and there was this constant level of stress. I come home and I just want to have dinner, have a shower and go to bed. By the time everything is done it's 10.30 p.m. and I have no me time, no quiet time.'

Since Becky and I spoke, Ben has come home, reunited with his young family. But plenty of families have been torn asunder by gambling addiction, in the worst possible way.

## SUICIDE

For some addicts, the pain becomes so unbearable that the only escape route they can think of is to take their own lives. Over the years, I've spoken to many gamblers who considered suicide and a few who attempted it. I've also sat with the people left behind when the worst actually happens, trying – and undoubtedly failing – to conceive of such unbearable sorrow.

When Liz and Charles Ritchie lost Jack, they had to confront the most dreadful pain that any parent can imagine. But as they somehow navigated their way through that grief, they came to realise that their life-altering experience was replicated across the country. The charity they set up, Gambling With Lives, has helped far too many people affected by gambling-related suicide and has become one of the most influential campaign groups.

Proving a causative link between gambling addiction and suicide is notoriously difficult, partly because of what is referred to in medicine as comorbidity. People who take their own lives have often struggled with a variety of problems, perhaps multiple coexisting addictions or mental health troubles. That makes it hard to determine the extent to which gambling addiction led to their suicide. But we can certainly identify a link that suggests a degree of causation. Research commissioned by GambleAware and published in 2019 found that gambling addicts were significantly more likely than other people to have suicidal thoughts or try to take their own lives.[21]

A separate study by academics at Lund University in Sweden monitored more than two thousand people with gambling disorders and found a significantly elevated risk of suicide among participants, compared with the general population, over an eleven-year period. The study found that suicide rates increased nineteen-fold among men between the ages of twenty and forty-nine if they had a gambling problem, and fifteen-fold among men and women of all ages. The authors of the research said that, while the causes of suicide were complex and likely to involve more than one factor, their work indicated that gambling disorders were associated with far higher than average rates of suicide.[22]

According to calculations by Charles Ritchie, if the study is right then around 550 people a year in the UK – 9% of those who take their own lives each year – do so at least in part due to gambling addiction.

We can never know the thought process of someone who does take their own life and it's important to stress that there's often not just one cause at play. However, the accounts of those who have survived a suicide attempt offer a glimpse into how a recreational activity can end in death.

Martin Paterson, who described to me that feeling of being 'there but not there' during his addiction, comes from Coatbridge, North Lanarkshire, just outside Glasgow. It is an area characterised by poverty. It has twenty-two betting shops for a population of just 42,000, while nearby well-to-do Milngavie has just one, serving roughly the same population. Martin had wrestled with both alcohol and gambling addiction for many years before it all became too much for him.

'I attempted suicide in the car with a hose up the tube [exhaust], carbon monoxide. The day I decided to do that was the most relief I've ever felt. My family were sick of me, I felt worthless. Gamblers Anonymous wasn't working for me. I'd had many thoughts of it and the voices in your head will tell you: Do it. That got interrupted and the funny thing is it got interrupted at 2 a.m. by doggers. I'm here today because of a couple of wankers.'

The tragicomedy of Martin's story is what leaps out, but also the element of good fortune that saved his life. So too with Chris Murphy. His suicide attempt came after a destructive path of drinking and gambling that had seen him kicked out of college and in financial and mental ruin.

'I had a lot of debt, I'd been blacklisted from financial institutions, so I'd borrowed from friends and people you really don't want to borrow from, payday lenders and loan sharks. The walls were closing in. I looked at the money I had available and the most pressing debts and said either I'd win everything back or I'd take my own life. On this particular day I didn't hit one winning number, not one winning spin. I went home to where I lived in a shared house, four of us. I knew a friend of mine took sleeping pills. I went in and took what I thought were his sleeping pills, went out onto the moors and swallowed them.'

Chris had left a note that was found by a neighbour, who alerted his parents. Had the pills been what he thought they were, doctors later told him, he would have been dead by the time they arrived.

'I found out that they were hay fever tablets. I get really bad hay fever now and it's a bit of a reminder every time I sneeze in the summer.'

For Chris, something positive ultimately emerged from his suffering. His work with the Sporting Chance clinic has allowed him to help others confront their gambling issues and hopefully avoid ending up in the same desperate place. That option isn't available to everyone, though. Liam McCarron, who I mentioned earlier in this chapter, has attempted suicide on two occasions. The physical weakness brought on by his life-altering disability is all that has prevented him from doing so. There will be no new lease of life as a counsellor for him.

While the final thoughts of those who end their lives due to gambling addiction remain forever shrouded in mystery, it is often possible to discover some of what they see in the hours, weeks and months before their tragic deaths.

In a 2016 article, my *Guardian* colleague Jamie Grierson chronicled the circumstances that had led to the death of Ryan Myers.[23] As is so often the case, Ryan had told nobody around him about the turmoil engulfing his life. The only evidence his parents could find of him discussing his problem was in an online chat with a YouTuber who had spoken about his own addiction in video diaries. What's clear from their conversation is that Ryan was struggling with the gambling industry's ability to capitalise on addiction and profit from it.

'Finding it tough,' he wrote. 'What's making quitting tough for me is everywhere I turn there is some form of gambling advertisement. I go on Facebook and [see] Zynga Poker or Castle Jackpot. I go on Twitter and there is like £50 matched deposit, even buying a newspaper and just random advertisement, it's unbelievable.'

When Ryan died in 2014, nearly ten years after the 2005 Gambling Act, there was not yet a way for a gambler with suicidal thoughts to block themselves from all UK online gambling websites. Ryan's father told Jamie that his son's email account continued to receive promotions and adverts from betting companies even after his death: 'I wrote to one to say, my son has killed himself, can you stop sending stuff here. They sent me an email saying, as an executor of his will can you please send a death certificate and we'll look at his accounts.'

## HOW WIDESPREAD IS PROBLEM GAMBLING?

Given how extreme the consequences of gambling addiction can be, it's important that we measure how much damage it is doing to society. But, incredibly, fifteen years on from the Gambling Act, reliable information on this is thin on the ground. The best we have are the regular Health Surveys, studies that measure the prevalence of problem gambling, as determined by a strict set of criteria.

These surveys can at least give us some important information, data that allows us to compare which products are associated with higher levels of addiction. The narrative of 'problem gambling' implies an issue that rests solely with the gambler, but the discrepancy in addiction rates measured by different types of gambling tells us that the problem is connected not just to people but to the types of gambling on offer.

Among those who gamble, as opposed to the general population, the percentage with a problem was measured at 1% in the 2018 survey.[24] Those who play the National Lottery, by a country mile the most popular gambling activity, come in a fraction below that level. Horse racing in a bookmaker's, the kind of activity that gambling companies relied on more heavily before the 2005 Act, was also relatively low, at 2.8%. Not exclusively, but more often than not, the products that have become popular relatively recently, fuelled by industry investment in technology and marketing, are the ones that carry the highest rates. Nearly 13% of people who used machines in a bookmaker's, largely FOBTs, were problem gamblers, while online slots and casino games also showed elevated problem gambling levels, at 8.5%, and betting exchanges such as Betfair showed a rate of nearly 11%. While the fast-growing arena of online sports betting showed a rate of 3.7%, no information was available for sub-categories such as the rapid-fire in-play options that have helped spur the growth in football betting, nor the National Lottery's online instant-win games, which reportedly took £1 billion from gamblers during successive Covid-19 lockdowns.[25] Anecdotal evidence suggests both in-play betting and instant-win games may be significantly more addictive than suggested by the figures for the broader categories in which they sit.

Concerningly, the use of online products also tends to skew younger, which should give us pause for thought about whether those age groups will carry that addiction through into later life, and whether people turning eighteen are entering a gambling market-place whose most popular products are among the most dangerous.

We should also be mindful of the ease with which modern gamblers can now navigate from statistically more benign forms of betting to more high-octane formats. As we saw in Chapter 3, cross-selling, where an operator invites sports bettors to move on to casino products, is rife.

All of this feels ominous, but when we try to use the Health Survey to draw broader conclusions about gambling's place in society, we run into some thorny territory. Members of the gambling industry – not to mention libertarians who resist tighter regulation on an ideological basis – have grown fond of the Health Survey, and that's something that might make cynics a little wary.

One reason the industry likes to cite the Health Survey is that the prevalence of problem gambling in wider society appears – on the face of it, at least – to be not only low but also relatively stable. The rate tends to hover between a range of 0.5% and 0.8% of the general population, according to successive surveys. That's still a lot of people – somewhere between about 300,000 and 500,000 if you extrapolate across the whole of the UK – but it is a small proportion of the population.

Nor does this headline rate appear to be rising. At least one prominent expert believes that the Health Survey is right, that gambling addiction is neither on the increase nor even particularly remarkable by global standards. Dr Mark Griffiths, a psychologist who specialises in behavioural addiction, has been researching problem gambling for more than three decades. 'The actual prevalence of problem gambling has remained pretty static,' he said. 'The data is pretty consistent, the prevalence of problem gambling in this country is comparable to most other places.'

Few people are better placed to make that call than Griffiths. But the way in which the industry relies heavily on this one survey should give rise to some caution. In August 2020, in response to a report by the Social Market Foundation think tank calling for a cap on online spending[26], a spokesperson for the Betting and Gaming Council said, somewhat waspishly: 'We welcome the fact that, in contrast to the siren voices of prohibitionists who claim problem gambling is high and is increasing, this report rightly states that there is no evidence of a rise in problem gambling and that levels have been stable around 0.7% for nearly two decades.'[27]

The BGC's argument goes that, despite the surge in advertising, the VIP schemes, the direct marketing, the daily exposure via foot-ball, the brainhacks and psychological tricks documented in these pages and elsewhere, the proportion of problem gamblers in wider society has remained relatively constant. Surely, if gambling really had conquered Britain – as per the premise of this book – it would be subjugating citizens rather more effectively than that?

It sounds like common sense, but there are abundant reasons to be cautious about how we approach the official statistics on addiction.

## LIES, DAMNED LIES AND STATISTICS

Remember, first of all, that the threshold beyond which gamblers are deemed to have a problem is any score of eight or higher on the PGSI scale. These rates are measured in the annual NHS Digital Health Survey, considered by most interested parties to be the best-available study. But it is not gospel. No study of this nature is perfect and disclaimers in the Health Survey admit as much. The magic number, the rate of problem gambling in wider society, is hotly disputed.

Analysis isn't helped by the way in which NHS data is collected separately by the nations that comprise the United Kingdom. The 2018 Health Survey for England pitched the proportion of problem gamblers at 0.5% of the population.[28] That's around 333,000 people if you were to apply the same rate across the whole of the UK. Factor in those considered to have a less destructive 'moderate-risk' habit on the PGSI scale – a score of between three and seven – and you could add in another 377,000 people.

But there is good reason to believe that the survey may be under-counting. It can only collect data about the people interviewed, who must agree to a visit from someone who works for the National Centre for Social Research (NatCen). Gamblers, NatCen admits in the report, have previously been found to be less easy to contact and more likely to require persuasion to take part, indicating that they may be underrepresented among those who make it to the interview stage.

Nor does NatCen's interview base include people living in institutions. That means it skips over anyone who is among the estimated 320,000 people in the UK who are homeless, or the more than 80,000 who are in prison. These are two cohorts – the survey admits – that are disproportionately likely to be problem gamblers. It also does not include people in psychiatric care – another significant omission, given the volume of evidence that people with mental health issues are significantly more likely than the general public to be problem gamblers. Nor, indeed, does it include the tens of thousands of students living in halls of residence, another deficiency when you consider that the survey estimates the problem gambling rate to be approximately twice as high among people aged between sixteen and twenty-four as it is among the general populace.

It also ignores those not legally allowed to gamble: children below the age of sixteen. According to the latest research from the Gambling Commission, that means it misses about 61,000 problem gamblers between the ages of eleven and sixteen.[29] Some of those children are suffering from serious problems too, judging by the patients treated at the National Problem Gambling Clinic. One teenager plunged his father's business into bankruptcy after stealing £60,000 to fuel a six-year online betting spree. A twelve-year-old used his dad's business card to set up an account and blew £20,000 in one night's online roulette.[30]

Could it be that there is some under-reporting going on as well? The Health Survey acknowledges the tendency for survey respondents to play down the scale of their problem and give 'socially desirable' answers. In other words, not everyone likes to admit in public that they suffer from a gambling disorder.

NatCen tries to get around this problem by ensuring that answers are given anonymously, meaning there should be no reason for respondents to adjust their disclosures out of embarrassment. But our brains don't always operate that way. Someone with a problem may be in denial, not only to others but to themselves. When you fill in a questionnaire at the GP's surgery asking how much you drink or how often you exercise, is it possible that you answer with what you would like the truth to be, rather than what it actually is? I know I do.

Likewise, when the survey asks whether gambling has caused you health problems, including stress or anxiety, might you attribute the cause to some other factor? When asked if you've ever gambled more than you can afford or kept betting to try to win back losses, might you be tempted to forget some of the occasions when you did?

The numbers are based on perception of self, rather than on hard data about, for instance, patterns of play. That's something only the industry has at its disposal. Gambling companies hold a gold mine of data about how people are gambling: the sums, the frequency, the preferred products and times of day. They use it to improve their products and boost revenues and also – if they're being responsible – to intervene when people are losing control. All that juicy data could be used by clinicians to analyse addictive behaviour with greater accuracy than a survey could ever provide. GambleAware knows this. 'In anonymised form, they [data] could be the basis for valuable analysis by the research community,' a report for the charity said in 2018.[31]

For whatever reason, we have yet to see a comprehensive study based on actual play. It's possible that one of the major UK gambling companies is in possession of just such a report that would, at a stroke, dispel concerns about how many of their customers are displaying signs of gambling disorder. If such a thing exists, it is strange in the extreme that – under pressure as they are – they have yet to release it.

In *Vicious Games*, Rebecca Cassidy speaks of the need for governments to force disclosure of information that could be a treasure trove for researchers and clinicians. 'I will continue to attempt to persuade the UK DCMS [. . .] that access to industry data and environments, provided as a condition of licensing, is the only way to ensure that policy makers receive the evidence they need to support their decision-making.'[32] Without this, says Cassidy, much research continues to be 'speculative'.

If the Health Survey is indeed underplaying problem gambling rates, some research indicates that the undershoot might be significant. Alternative methods have produced very different results. In a report that found problem gambling could be costing the UK economy up to £1.2 billion a year, the Institute for Public Policy Research think tank suggested a range of between 0.4% and 1.1%.[33] Meanwhile the SOGS (South Oaks Gambling Screen) survey, which predated PGSI as a measure of problem gambling, typically came out with figures almost twice as high as modern surveys. Researchers in Canada have suggested that this may be because the PGSI problem gambling threshold of eight has been set too high, with a watermark of six or higher likely to be more useful.[34]

In May 2020 pollsters at YouGov released a study performed for GambleAware that sent a tremor through the world of gambling. As many as 2.7% of people in the UK should be classed as problem gamblers on the PGSI measurement, the survey found, or around 1.4 million people.[35] That's more than four times the level suggested by successive NHS Health Surveys. A further 7% of adults, or 3.6 million people, told YouGov that they had been negatively affected by someone else's gambling problem. There is some overlap between the two groups – those who gamble to excess and those affected by someone else doing so. But even factoring this in, we're starting to talk about pretty big numbers. Only 32% of people regularly gamble on any product other than the National Lottery – that's roughly 17 million people. If YouGov's numbers were right, up to 5 million of those people were suffering as a result, an incredibly high degree of negative return for a harmless leisure activity.

We're getting into some real back-of-napkin-calculation territory here, I'll concede. The bombshell YouGov survey that suggested such high numbers was commissioned by GambleAware and the results shocked the charity to the extent that it felt the figures couldn't be right. They were sent to be looked over by Patrick Sturgis, professor of quantitative social science at the London School of Economics's Department of Methodology. Sturgis issued a caveat alongside the figures, saying that they were likely an overestimation due to the way in which the data had been collected.[36] In other words, where the Health Survey may be undercounting, YouGov's findings may be overcounting.

Why? For a start, YouGov carries out its surveys online, meaning it selects from an audience that skews younger and more internet-savvy. Younger people, as every study worth its salt shows, are more likely to be problem gamblers, and habitual internet users are more likely to engage with products such as online roulette or slots, which are associated with higher levels of addiction than going down the bookie's to bet on the horses.

But, crucially, Sturgis said two other things. Firstly, that the YouGov result *could not be ruled out* as an accurate assessment of problem gambling. Secondly, he backed up the notion we've already discussed, that the Health Survey may well have been consistently underestimating the scale of the problem. The true rate of problem gambling, he said, was most likely to fall somewhere between the 0.5% found in the Health Survey and the 2.7% given by YouGov, leaving a margin of error of a cool million people.

If that kind of uncertainty makes us sceptical about the accuracy of problem gambling measurement, we should also reserve judgement on whether the rate is rising or falling. Part of this uncertainty is due to changing methodology; the gambling component of the wider

NHS Digital Health Survey has only been around since 2012, after its predecessor, the British Gambling Prevalence Survey, was scrapped.

Francis Markham, a research fellow at the Australian National University, has looked at forty-five studies done over twenty-five years around the world and found that methodological inconsistency is not unusual. The goalposts keep moving, muddling the picture for researchers and clinicians: 'One of the problems with trying to track the rate over time in the population is the impact that different measurement techniques have on the results you get,' he told me. 'We're just not very good at tracking change over time because we keep changing the methods we use to do it.' Another problem, he said, is that, when you're dealing with relatively low numbers in comparison to the total population, it is nigh-on impossible to be confident about whether small changes denote genuine trends or statistical volatility.

Journalists fall victim to this too. In the past, when the Health Survey has been published, I've been guilty of latching on to an apparent increase – along with other newspapers – and deeming it to be hard evidence of soaring gambling addiction rates. This may have been true but it may also not have been. The numbers are simply too unreliable. I'm happy to acknowledge the times in the past when I, a literature graduate, didn't appreciate that element of statistics.

Low rates within the general population can also give a misleading impression of how dangerous gambling – or individual products – can be to those who use them. 'When you see a number like 0.5% it's easy to say that for most people these products are safe,' says Markham. 'But most people don't gamble very often or at all. What's probably a better measure of how dangerous or safe a particular product is, is the proportion of people who use it frequently who have a gambling problem.'

Take base-jumping, the daredevil sport where you strap a

parachute to your back and hurl yourself off a cliff. Only a tiny percentage of people in wider society are bananas enough to try it, so in the broader population death rates from this activity are incredibly low. The death rate among base-jumpers themselves is rather higher.

Compare that, perhaps, to the product-specific data mentioned earlier in this chapter, which suggested that one in eight FOBT players are addicts, as are one in twelve who play online casino games or slots.

## DO PROBLEM GAMBLING RATES MATTER?

Even if we could be 100% confident that a prevalence survey accurately measured the number of people with a PGSI score of eight or more, we might still want to be wary of affording the statistic too much respect. The truth is, there is far more that the Health Survey doesn't tell us than there is that it does.

For instance, such surveys show whether someone's gambling has passed a certain threshold but they don't offer granular detail because they are based on survey result, not data. If, for instance, the percentage of the population who were problem gamblers stayed the same over ten years, yet that group significantly increased their spending, thus potentially causing much greater financial harm, that wouldn't show up. Similarly, the survey only measures how many people have a PGSI score of eight or above. Little data is available on where they fall on a scale that goes all the way up to twenty-seven, in fact. Imagine, for instance, that in between two surveys the number of problem gamblers stayed the same but that those people were on average suffering much more severely. Say their average score went from eight to twenty-six. That massive increase simply wouldn't be evident in the reported numbers, even though the amount of harm being suffered would plainly be far higher.

We also have no crystal ball that can tell us how the regulatory landscape since the Gambling Act of 2005 might affect these numbers in future – and there is reason to be pessimistic.

As I've mentioned before, a child who was five when the Gambling Act came into force in 2007 has grown into an adult in a country where gambling is a ubiquitous part of the culture. If members of this generation are more likely to be gambling addicts as a result, we are unlikely to see that show up in the figures for several years.

Heather Wardle is one of the foremost experts in gambling behavioural analysis in the UK and has been involved in both the Health Survey and the preceding British Gambling Prevalence Survey. She agrees that the real impact of gambling's cultural saturation may be yet to come. 'There is a cohort of people [. . .] who don't know that gambling wasn't always like this, that it wasn't always on the TV, on your football sponsorship, that there was another way,' she explains. 'I still think we're waiting to see what the trickle-through impact of that is on those who are thirty-five and under.'

Wardle makes another point that may well be the most salient when it comes to our reliance on using prevalence studies as a proxy for Britain's gambling problem: we focus on numbers, on scores that tell us whether someone has a mental health disorder. But you don't have to be identified as having a mental health disorder to have been harmed by it. 'It's just kind of common sense,' she says. 'You have a bad day, you drop an absolute shedload of money that you can't afford, which has knock-on consequences. You might not meet the definition of being a problem gambler. We don't actually have any metrics in Britain of how many people are harmed by gambling.'

A 2021 paper in medical journal *The Lancet* went one step further, saying that prevalence surveys were 'highly problematic and involve misleading indicators of harm, and should not form the basis of policy making'.[37]

Such misgivings are well founded. The Health Survey does not capture the misery of partners like Julie, financially imprisoned and physically assaulted, or Becky, left to bring up two kids while her husband serves a prison sentence. It does not capture the friendships destroyed by an addict's behaviour, nor does it capture the economic effect on those who lend money without knowing where it is going. It does not capture the one-off moment of madness that leads someone to blow their life savings or their mortgage. It does not capture the addicts lost to suicide, nor the grief of those they leave behind.

These are the real-world harms caused by gambling addiction and they do not show up anywhere but in the tales told by those who have experienced it. Until an in-depth study on gambling harm is commissioned, using the same methodology at multiple intervals to measure impacts, we simply don't know.

In 2021 we got something close to a wide-ranging study into harm with a longitudinal element (i.e. measuring change over a significant period of time). Using data from 6.5 million customers of Lloyds Banking Group, researchers from the Universities of Oxford and Warwick analysed the correlation between the amount that people deposited in their gambling accounts and their exposure to harm ranging from financial hardship to unemployment and even death.[38]

What they found was startling. Even at quite low levels of deposits – before factoring in what a gambler might win – they started to see an increase in financial difficulties. The chances of financial harm – such as missed mortgage payments or taking a payday loan – were 'notably stronger' once someone diverted 3.6% of monthly outgoings into gambling deposits. That's equivalent to £91.37 per month for the average household. At that level of spend – more than the average but still relatively modest compared to the highest-spending gamblers – they were one-third more likely to miss a mortgage payment, 22% more likely to use an unplanned overdraft, and 19% more likely to take a payday loan.

Those who devoted £1 in every £10 to gambling – putting them among the top 10% of the industry's highest-spending customers – were twice as likely to miss a mortgage payment as someone who did not bet at all. Analysing customer data over a seven-year period, the researchers identified increased rates of unemployment, disability and 'substantially increased mortality' at the highest levels of gambling.

The study could not say that gambling was causing these outcomes but neither should the lack of a causative effect of a correlation absolve the industry here. Either gambling companies are causing harm, or they are disproportionately profiting from those already suffering it. Both should prompt some soul-searching about what certain parts of the industry have become.

One person who has done some of that soul-searching is Paddy Power founder Stewart Kenny. The Irishman made his fortune from betting and still enjoys a wager. But he has been sickened by the industry he loves now making so much of its money from potentially dangerous products. 'I love betting on politics and soccer matches but I don't see any social benefits in online slot machines,' he said. 'I deeply regret that I didn't see the dangers of the addictive nature of some of the online products till too late. I should have seen the dangers much earlier. If I'm in front of St Peter at the pearly gates, it'll probably be one of the first questions he'll ask me. "How the fuck did you justify that?"'

Kenny's experience goes deeper than most. For many people, what they believe about the depth and breadth of gambling addiction in the UK is likely to emanate as much from their gut feeling as from experience or hard data, scant as it is. We can say with a high degree of confidence that, even at the very lowest estimate, the number of problem gamblers in the UK is above 300,000. If we're minded to believe the YouGov survey's findings, it could be more than four times that many. And if we add in the people whose lives have been negatively affected – the spouses, parents, children, employers and victims of crime – we are probably looking at several million. That means that the person suffering due to gambling addiction is more than a nebulous or abstract concept: it is someone you walked past in the street today, almost certainly someone you know, and quite possibly someone you love.

There is a legitimate school of thought that says that such people will always exist, no matter what anyone tries to do about it; that addiction – in one form or another – is inevitable. There has to be an element of truth in that. But what the stories of addiction and recovery tell us is that, all too often, tragedy occurs needlessly because we, as a society, have let people down. That should prompt us to ask questions about how we are limiting gambling harm and where we might be going wrong.

# 7. THE SAFETY NET: FAILURES IN REGULATION AND TREATMENT

There's nothing magic about regulation.
Too much is bad, too little is bad.

HILLARY CLINTON, IN A SPEECH AT
WALL STREET BANK GOLDMAN SACHS

I'm shocked, shocked, to find that gambling is going on in here.

CAPTAIN LOUIS RENAULT (CLAUDE RAINS), *CASABLANCA* (1942)

Winter was spreading its icy fingers across Britain and the leading lights of the gambling world were increasingly anxious about the threat posed by a 'virulent virus'.

The select group of wealthy and powerful chief executives had gathered at a secret summit convened by Ladbrokes. Top of the agenda was their mounting anxiety that this fearsome disease could wreak havoc on their business empires. The cabal of bosses agreed that they needed to put aside the fierce rivalries that usually saw them fight tooth and nail for every penny spent by Britain's gamblers. Instead they should work together, combining their strength to limit the potential for collective damage.

None of this would be remotely surprising had it occurred in 2021 with Covid-19 rife across the globe. But this was 2013. The sense of unease among these business leaders stemmed not from a global pandemic but from a growing public backlash against the increasingly ubiquitous presence of gambling in British life since 2007. The danger, for the industry barons, was that politicians would cotton on to the shift in social attitudes towards gambling and develop an appetite for a potentially vote-winning crackdown. Income from products such as in-play football betting and FOBTs was booming and the industry could not risk the punchbowl being taken away.

The authors of an internal memo summarising the outcome of the industry conclave urged unity. Without careful strategy, they warned, 'a negative perception will spread like a virulent virus'. Profits were already being constrained, they reported, while a vociferous anti-gambling lobby was dominating the public conversation. They identified 'a large degree of righteous paternalism' that would see the public mood 'swinging away from smoking, heavy drinking, gambling, non-contributors and tax avoiders'. It was time to fight back.

The language of the memo was exactly what you might expect from its authors, both veterans who loved their industry deeply. One was the Ladbrokes chief executive, Richard Glynn. The other, Neil Goulden, had spent fourteen years as chairman of fellow bookmaker Gala Coral. Goulden was also chairman of the Association of British Bookmakers and was now proposing to advise the industry on the way forward via his own private consultancy company.[1]

What was slightly more surprising, given the tone of his rhetoric, was that Goulden was also head of the Responsible Gambling Trust, the leading charity tasked with reducing gambling-related harm in the UK. The trust was responsible for collecting donations from licensed operators, which it used to fund research into gambling harm as well as education and treatment for addicts.

In many respects, it makes sense that someone with in-depth knowledge of an industry should have at least some role in making it safer. Gambling industry veterans, after all, know their customer base intimately, understand the mechanics of various products better than anyone and have spent years observing how the two interact.

It is less clear how the author of a deeply partisan tract that appeared ideologically opposed to regulation, apparently regardless of what it looked like, could play such a key role in making the industry safer. To anyone reading that document, written – don't forget – for the private perusal of gambling bosses, it seemed pretty clear that Goulden had made up his mind: those who sought stricter regulation were the enemies of civil liberties.

This apparent conflict of interest risked having real-world consequences. Goulden and Glynn's paper called for more research to be done, 'which helps to position gambling as an economically valuable and socially responsible leisure pursuit'. In other words, research driven by a desired result and not, therefore, worthy of the name.

Not long before Goulden co-wrote this memo, the Responsible Gambling Trust – under his leadership – had commissioned some research of its own. The work, a study of FOBTs, came amid mounting concern about whether the machines – which made up close to half of bookmakers' high-street revenues – were inherently addictive. The RGT said it had 'put in place a clear structure to protect the independence of the research [. . .] from any industry influence'. A separate board, made up of academics and chaired by a former civil servant, set the research agenda.

Gambling reform campaigner Matt Zarb-Cousin wasn't convinced. The resulting study, he said, appeared to serve the industry's purposes pretty neatly. It focused heavily on examining patterns of play to identify those who might be deemed problem gamblers, which, he argued, placed the onus for staying safe on customers, at the expense of examining whether the machines themselves might be the problem. This line of enquiry was, he reasoned, much less risky or uncomfortable for the industry. Far better to conclude that the danger rested with weak-minded individuals than concede that an industry cash cow was harming people. As the summary of a study by Goldsmiths University pointed out in 2014, 'the idea of "problem gambling" is politically useful . . . It focuses attention on individual gamblers, rather than relationships between the industry, the state, products and policies.'[2]

For all the concerns of the gambling sector luminaries, nobody was talking very much about problem products or a problem industry. They were talking about problem gamblers, problem people, constructing a narrative that leading figures in the industry appeared only too happy to propagate.

Goulden pointed out that any conflicts of interest, such as they were, were 'well known' and allowed him to 'build bridges' between the industry and the people who administer funds for gambling addiction research, education and treatment (RET). He added that industry funding for RET had been falling before his tenure but had doubled during it. 'Collaboration is far better than independent silos,' he said, in an emailed response to me.

That's undoubtedly a legitimate position. But the depth of involvement the industry has had in preventing addiction feels emblematic of a questionable approach to regulation. Instead of putting in place a strict system of enforcement, of crime and punishment, poacher and gamekeeper, the British state relied for years on the conceit that market forces would lead competing operators to do the right thing.

With this ideal scenario in mind, the regulatory regime erected by the Gambling Act 2005 was deeply flawed. It was a system in which poachers and gamekeepers were often one and the same, in which industry executives wielded significant influence over the narrative around gambling-related harm, downplaying their own responsibility, minimising their contribution to cleaning up the collateral damage and demanding unreasonable standards of proof from those who discerned harm in their products.

A paper published in *The Lancet* in 2021 put it neatly. A group of researchers, among them Rebecca Cassidy and Jim Orford, wrote: 'Like the tobacco and alcohol industries, gambling corporations in communication with receptive governments have established a double standard, whereby evidence-based interventions that threaten their business model must meet exceptionally stringent criteria of proof, whereas industry-sponsored so-called responsible-gambling interventions of dubious value – many reminiscent of the Drink Responsibly messaging and similar approaches adopted by the tobacco industry – are accepted without question.'[3]

Goulden and Glynn's memo told a very different tale, a sob story of an industry that was suffering badly at the hands of a puritanical media and the constraints of needless regulation. It didn't correspond to reality. In the year to March 2013, the period during which the memo was written, the UK gambling industry increased the amount it won from punters by 7.5%, from £9 billion to £9.7 billion, well ahead of inflation.

Glynn's own company, Ladbrokes, had experienced a tough year, but not because of puritanical politicians, biased journalists or an overly stringent regulator: rather, Ladbrokes had been on the wrong end of some unfavourable football results, as well as setbacks in building up its online business to cope with growing demand. The company still made an operating profit of £138 million.[4] Such strength had been achieved thanks to some of the phenomena documented in these pages: the growth of in-play football betting, the VIP schemes, the psychological trickery, the money-spinning FOBTs and the powerful marketing and advertising techniques. But all of that relied upon a climate that was not nearly as hostile as Glynn and Goulden claimed.

Indeed, the industry was, if not left to its own devices, at least relatively free to pursue profitability however it saw fit, knowing that any regulatory or political pushback would be much slower-paced than its own innovation. As I documented earlier, advertising – particularly around live sport – proliferated with all but the most meagre of controls. Technology, particularly the smartphone, offered untold new revenue streams, increasing the potential risk to consumers. Yet, astonishingly, companies that preyed on problem gamblers faced precious little jeopardy until relatively recently. The financial penalties they risked for transgressing the conditions of their gambling licences were paltry to the point of being just another cost of doing business.

Moreover, the industry was, over a period of years, allowed to get away with lacklustre efforts to improve player protection, while also paying a pittance to support research, education and treatment related to gambling addiction. All of this has served to keep costs down and profits up, often at the expense of vulnerable people and their loved ones. The more addicts, the more bets. The more bets, the more revenue. How did it come to this?

## A MUZZLED WATCHDOG

The Gambling Commission's headquarters look rather grand from the outside. Victoria Square House served as Birmingham's main post office for more than eighty years, from 1891. It's a fine building in the French Renaissance style, a fittingly solemn location for a watchdog tasked with undoubtedly important work. But the salubrious surroundings disguise the reality of an organisation that has all too often shown itself to be significantly underpowered, not to mention outflanked and outgunned, time and again, by the industry it aims to oversee.

The Commission, created by the Gambling Act of 2005, can wield its regulatory power in all sorts of ways. It can place tighter curbs on dangerous products and force companies to adjust the ways in which they market them to people. It also has significant enforcement powers where it finds that a company has breached the conditions of its licence, such as laxity in money-laundering checks or a failure to intervene when customers show clear signs of problem gambling.

The nuclear option in the Commission's armoury is to either suspend or revoke a company's licence to operate. It's all very well being a multibillion-pound corporation but that's not much use if a regulator takes your licence away. That being the case, the Commission can coerce companies that flout its rules into voluntary settlements, where the firm admits wrongdoing and makes a payment. The money usually goes to fund the Commission's costs and to gambling charities that fund addiction research, education and treatment.

So how has the Commission used its array of weaponry? In the early days of its tenure, the answer was: not very much at all. The regulator's records, which I obtained via a Freedom of Information request, show that from 2007 until September 2013 not a single British gambling company was forced by the Commission into any kind of voluntary settlement relating to the two key areas that would come to be the focus of its regulatory action thereafter: failing to act in a socially responsible way, and preventing money-laundering. Why?

One reason takes us back to the flawed legislation that the Blair-era Labour party designed. The volume of sanctions was so low because much of the worst behaviour was taking place outside the regulator's purview, in overseas gambling centres like Malta and Gibraltar. Until November 2014 online gambling companies didn't actually need a licence from the Gambling Commission to operate or advertise in the UK. This loophole had been left open by the 2005 Gambling Act, a piece of legislation that, remember, predated the invention of the smartphone. Instead, firms based in the European Economic Area, the British Overseas Territory of Gibraltar or 'white-listed' jurisdictions including Alderney, the Isle of Man, and Antigua and Barbuda could take Britons' money but were beholden only to their domestic regulators. Often these regulators were tuppenny-ha'penny operations, beholden to governments that had little incentive to get tough on an industry that had set up shop on their soil, bringing jobs and economic activity. Gibraltar in particular became a huge hub for firms tapping into the UK market, a thriving offshore centre from which companies could launch their charm offensives on British punters. As of 2014, approximately 55% of operators providing online gambling in the UK were based in Gibraltar and regulated there.[5]

In 2014 the Conservative government made a smart legislative change.[6] Now companies were required to have British licences if they wanted to offer products to British punters. The Gambling Commission became responsible for regulating huge swathes of the online industry, which had done pretty much what it wanted until then. It also meant a welcome boost for the Treasury, which had been missing out on hundreds of millions of pounds a year. Operators would now be charged a betting duty at the point of consumption, or rather the point of supply. If you took a bet from a customer in Britain, you'd now have to pay 15% tax on it, regardless of where your servers were based. Government receipts from the various betting and gambling duties jumped from £2.1 billion to nearly £2.7 billion from one year to the next.[7] The regulatory change had also brought into the light how much was actually being spent. In the year to March 2014, online betting and casino companies made £1.1 billion from punters, according to Commission statistics; in the first full year of the new regime, with operators now forced to have a British licence, a more accurate figure of £4 billion emerged. All of that extra cash represented business that had hitherto benefited gambling companies serving British punters but had been conducted outside the eyeline of the regulator. Within online casinos alone, the house take regulated by the Commission went from £27 million to nearly £2.4 billion within a couple of years.[8]

But the offshoring of the British gambling industry had already had an effect that could not be so easily reversed. Dan Waugh of gambling industry consultancy Regulus Partners thinks that one of the biggest mistakes in British gambling regulation was that the requirement to hold a British licence didn't happen much sooner. 'Most of the examples of sharp practice have been uncovered since 2015, which is the point at which the Gambling Commission started regulating the online industry,' he says. 'It's implausible to assume operators suddenly became badly behaved after 2015.' The likelihood, he explains, is that firms had got into bad habits while not under the Gambling Commission's radar, without much fear of repercussion: 'If you're Malta or Gibraltar or the Isle of Man, the gambling industry has significant economic value to you, in terms of the infrastructure, the skilled, well-paid jobs and the taxation. You're seeing massive benefits from it and where harms are occurring, they're pretty much occurring somewhere else.'

By the time of the legislative change, operators had become used to a much more laissez-faire environment with limited scrutiny from the media or politicians. The culture pervaded their businesses and the behaviour exhibited by staff. The aggressive VIP schemes, the rampant bonus offers, the lack of checks as customers frittered away their savings, the sheer disregard for the potential harm that might result from a relentless drive for profit – much of it stemmed from a culture that had been allowed to develop far away, out of sight of the UK authorities who might have identified the dangers sooner and intervened, or been forced to do so by public pressure.

'If you raise a child from birth, you have a chance to impart your values and beliefs,' says Waugh. 'If you take a foster child in, you have someone who already has values and behaviours embedded. The British remote gambling sector was effectively adopted by the Gambling Commission in 2014, having spent its early years and adolescence under a very different regime of parenting.'

Even once the Gambling Commission took on the oversight

of offshore operators in 2014, it was a while before it started to make its presence felt. In 2016–17, a year in which the gambling industry excluding the National Lottery took £10.3 billion, the Commission imposed penalties of just £1.7 million. Amid mounting pressure from the public and politicians, it managed £18.4 million the year after that, followed by £19.6 million, reaching £30 million in 2019–20.[9]

There was still precious little reason for gambling bosses to fear the hot breath of the regulator on their necks: £30 million was about a day's takings for the industry in 2019. In 2018 three directors of Ladbrokes owner Entain (known as GVC at the time) were paid nearly as much – £29 million in salary and bonuses between them.[10]

Nor has there been much reason for companies to fear the ultimate sanction – having their licence revoked or suspended. No major operator has ever suffered that fate in the entire lifetime of the Commission.

The nature of the Gambling Act means that a great deal of this isn't the Commission's fault. Its mandate includes a legal duty to 'aim to permit' gambling – essentially to adopt a precautionary approach to doing anything that would tie the hands of legitimate businesses.[11] One Commission insider suggests that the 'aim to permit' bias has been the source of tension within the organisation, creating friction between two key groups. One is the enforcement division, those tasked with identifying bad behaviour by the industry. They're typically ex-policemen who cleave naturally to the remit of identifying right and wrong. They like to gather evidence and enforce the rules. The other group are the policy chiefs, the people whose job it is to navigate a smooth path between the regulator, politicians and the industry, based on the law as they find it. They are occupied by perhaps more nuanced philosophical conversations about the nature of their role and whether they can or should interfere in the freedom of legitimate businesses to trade. The policy chiefs, of course, are the ones with their hands on the tiller. The aim to permit, says the source, is 'one of the ruling mantras' at the Commission.

What this has meant, in practice, is that only once there is overwhelming evidence that a product is dangerous, or that a company is deploying it in a dangerous way, can the Commission swing into action. As we've seen before, VIP schemes were at the heart of the majority of the Commission's enforcement cases for years but the regulator did not act to rein them in until 2020, and then only due to a crescendo of public pressure. Credit card betting – funding one's wagers with debt – was another obvious driver of financial ruin. Yet that was not stopped until April of the same year, after two years of deliberation.[12] The Gambling Commission had the powers to do these things but did not. With the aim to permit at the heart of its ethos, the Commission was effectively bound by a legal duty to wait until it had cast-iron dossiers of evidence that went beyond the purely anecdotal, or even the glaringly obvious.

The UK is blessed with some of the finest gambling addiction researchers in the world, many of whom have contributed to this book. But in the face of chronic underfunding they have had to battle to make their voices heard. Robust research costs money – money that simply hasn't been there. The result is something of a catch-22. The regulator requires evidence to act but the evidence base is not there, so it cannot. All of this benefits the industry, which has repeatedly referred to the lack of robust research as justification to keep pumping out adverts during football matches, dismissing the case for affordability checks or pushing certain high-octane products. And those companies are hardly about to set aside big bucks to fund research that might see their toys taken away.

That's not to say that the industry doesn't contribute – it does. But the way in which it does so is problematic to say the least. Firms with a UK licence pay a voluntary contribution to research, education and treatment, as part of an agreement that dates back to the early days of the post-2005 regulatory landscape. Until very recently that contribution was set at 0.1% of revenue, often raising less than £10 million a year – peanuts when you consider what it is meant to fund.

The most expensive element funded by these donations is treatment, therapy for the hundreds of thousands of problem gamblers who need it. Then you have education, things like advertising campaigns to raise awareness of gambling-related harm as well as outreach programmes in schools and universities. What's left over for the research part? Not very much.

'The research base has been so slender for so long,' explains my source at the Gambling Commission. He points to examples that most people would instinctively agree seem likely to be dangerous, such as reverse withdrawals. A reverse withdrawal is where a customer wins some money and decides to bank it, but then, in the time it takes for the firm to process the transaction – sometimes as much as a day – changes their mind and ploughs the cash back into more bets rather than, say, Christmas presents for the kids or an evening out with friends. Addiction experts see repeated use of reverse withdrawals as a clear sign that someone has a problem and it's not hard to see why. If you're never prepared to walk away when you've just upset the odds to beat the house, you may not be acting rationally. That's something that a lot of people would feel makes sense instinctively.

'That's fine. But that's not good enough to make regulation,' says my source. 'The Commission and other agencies didn't have sufficient evidence to be able to say that this is harm. There wasn't the proper research available.' The voluntary levy was supposed to fund the sort of research that would help the Commission make these big calls. Instead, he says, even the firms that did contribute to the levy would do so only under duress. 'They'd throw in a few million quid so that the government would never come back and say we need to make the levy statutory. You can't do research based on another year's top-up. That's no way to conduct research funding.'

Faced with a lack of hard evidence, the Commission always found it difficult to act. How could it adopt a strict precautionary approach to gambling products on which it had no evidence due to years of research underfunding?

This brings us to another problem of cold hard cash, namely the funding of the Commission itself. The Gambling Commission's budget varies each year but is typically about £19 million, including its work overseeing the National Lottery. The industry scoops up more than £10 billion from losing punters over the same period – and that's without counting Lottery sales.[13] In other words, about half a day's worth of industry takings could have funded the regulator's entire annual activity. The bet365 boss, Denise Coates, paid herself £466 million in salary and dividends in 2019, a sum that could have funded the regulator's budget nearly twenty-five times over.[14] Gulfs like these are large but perhaps unsurprising. After all, gambling companies are in the business of profit, whereas the regulator is a boring old policeman who is meant to use exactly as much of the taxpayer's hard-earned money as he needs to, and no more.

Tracey Crouch saw that funding gap at first hand when she was the minister for sport in charge of gambling regulation. 'The Gambling Commission doesn't evolve as quickly as the industry and that's in part because it's just not funded well enough,' she said.

The government is responsible for the Commission's budgetary constraints and it has simply not done enough to give the regulator the muscle it needs to bring operators into line. Indeed, in April 2020, just as public concern about gambling-related harm was reaching a crescendo with the amount spent by punters close to an all-time high, the cash-strapped regulator actually began cutting staff.[15] It did so a few short months after the National Audit Office

– the UK body that monitors the effectiveness of state spending – warned that the regulator was fighting with one hand behind its back. The Commission, it found, was constrained by 'inflexible funding' and insufficient evidence about how new products were affecting gamblers. 'The Commission is unlikely to be fully effective in addressing risks and harms to consumers within the current arrangements,' the report concluded. This, in the formal language of the NAO, is fire and brimstone. It wouldn't be long before a high-profile example underlined the point.[16]

In the aftermath of the Football Index collapse, documented in Chapter 5, it emerged that the Gambling Commission had been warned that the Football Index dream would turn into a nightmare more than a year earlier. Yet, constrained by its capacity and its proclivity for erring on the side of inaction, the Commission appeared to do little but sit on its hands for months on end.

What we've seen, for years, is that the regulator has often gravitated towards permissiveness. Even where it wants to act, it can only do so when it has pretty much undeniable proof of harm. Once it does decide to act, it often hasn't had the firepower to do so in a way that actually forces a change in culture.

## THE WATCHDOG BARKS

It would be unfair, though, to suggest that the regulator has been entirely ineffective. A great deal of its work goes on below the surface, the feet of the duck paddling furiously while all appears serene on the surface.

For instance, a large slice of the Commission's time is occupied with vetting the legions of out-and-out crooks and scam artists applying for licences to operate in the UK and turning them down. Its sports betting intelligence unit is constantly trying to prevent corruption in sports betting. The regulator also has responsibility for overseeing the licence to operate the National Lottery, a mammoth task when you consider the sheer size of it – nearly £8 billion a year in takings, thanks to the participation of around 60% of UK adults.[17]

The Commission has also notched up some notable victories that garner less attention than its missteps. A good example of this is the protracted legal battle it fought with pub operator Greene King.[18] The chain wanted the right to offer bingo and high-stakes gambling machines in its pub premises. The plan could have seen gambling integrated into pubs up and down the country, taking the fruit machines already available to people under the influence of alcohol and turbocharging them. Had that proved profitable, you can bet that competitors would have followed suit. The Commission fought that case – fought it hard – and won.

More recently, fifteen years after its creation, the Commission has begun showing that it does have a backbone, even if it hasn't always stiffened it. In 2019, when the government imposed a reduction in stakes on FOBTs, several bookmakers sought to cheat the rules by introducing new games that mimicked the mechanics of the machines, launching them in shops in the same week that the curbs on FOBTs came into force.[19] Betfred's version of this was called Virtual Cycling. It allowed gamblers to place bets on a piece of paper obtained over the counter, showing a graphic similar to a roulette table. The game featured a maximum stake of £500, five times what was possible on the FOBT games that had been banned the previous day. Players bet on when an animated cyclist travelling around a track would be overtaken by virtual competitors, based on numbers corresponding to sections of the track. It was a FOBT, souped up and clad in different clothes. To its credit the Commission made its fury clear,[20] and the companies backed down.

As I've mentioned before, the regulator barred gambling online with credit cards in April 2020, a welcome move, albeit not before time. That same year it set up three working groups to look at how to improve player protection, taking aim at areas of increasing public and political concern. The plan attracted some criticism, not least because the groups were led by industry players who had committed some of the worst transgressions in the areas they were now charged with fixing.[21] Ladbrokes owner Entain was asked to lead a review of VIP schemes, despite being among their most enthusiastic proponents. Playtech and SG Gaming, the architects of countless online slots games and FOBTs, took on responsibility for tackling the dangers of how gambling games were designed. Sky Bet took charge of making advertising safer, drawing on its expertise as the branding partner of Sky Sports, the chief purveyor of gambling ads to the UK's football fans.

The result was a series of new guidelines, some of which I've mentioned earlier in this book. VIP schemes were restricted to those over twenty-five only. All customers entering such schemes would first have to pass thorough checks to prove their spending power and they'd also be subjected to increased safer-gambling checks. On game design, firms were ordered to slow them down and remove options such as auto-play, where players can set the machine to spin on its own, multiple times. Remember 'losses disguised as wins' and the 'illusion of control' from Chapter 3? The Commission addressed those too. No more cheery music when you've actually lost money. No more features giving you the false impression that the slot outcome is anything other than a random-number generator. And on advertising, the working group led by Sky Bet came up with recommendations for online in particular (the sector that isn't quite so valuable to Sky Sports). One of these was the use of technology to prevent, where possible, under-eighteens from seeing gambling content. The industry would also use customer data to ensure paid-for ads were targeted away from vulnerable groups on social media.

To many gambling campaigners, the measures were too little, too late. Exactly where to draw the line with regulation is subjective, and though 'too little' is a matter of taste, it's hard to argue about 'too late'. Many of these restrictions seem like no-brainers now, in the way that smoking in restaurants and on aeroplanes was normal when I was young but is unthinkable – at least to most people – now. Clearly these are measures the Commission could have imposed sooner. Nevertheless, the contrast with the regulator's more supine approach in previous years was striking and – to many observers – welcome, even if overdue. The following year the Commission permanently formalised something it had introduced at the onset of the Covid-19 pandemic: a moratorium on reverse withdrawals. The regulator made the ban permanent in 2021.[22] Some in the industry believe this is likely to prove one of the more effective means of better protecting consumers, because reverse withdrawals are such a common feature of problem gambling activity.

If many of these measures seem like obvious ways of keeping people safe, it's because they are. Campaigners and clinicians had been calling for many of them to be implemented for years. And yet it took until relatively recently for that to happen.

A cynic would conclude that the industry only took part in drawing up these protective measures at the point of the regulator's spear. An even more hard-bitten cynic might wonder at the timing. Both regulator and operators leaped into action shortly before the launch of the government's gambling review, a process that could easily lead to the abolition of the regulator and cause serious damage to the industry's bottom line. I am, like most newspaper journalists, something of a cynic.

Whatever the reasons, progress is surely to be welcomed. If prevention is better than a cure, then blunting the tools that cause harm seems a good way to go. But what about when that harm has already happened? When the debts have piled up or a susceptible mind has been consumed by addiction? Let's start with the money side of things.

Imagine that you are a gambling addict who earns the UK average salary, approximately £31,000 a year, give or take.[23] You log in to your online casino account at midnight and stick £10 on the slots. You lose it and bet £50, then £200, then £250. Pretty soon you're laying down stakes of thousands of pounds at a time. By the time the sun comes up and you emerge, blinking in the light, from your trance-like state, you've lost your life savings. In a desperate bid to get some of it back, you've set up payday loans at usurious rates of interest. In the cold light of day you realise that the monthly bills – utilities, credit card, maybe mortgage – are still due. Financial ruin beckons for you – perhaps also for your family. As you contemplate the full horror of what you've done, there is at least some hope. You may be dimly aware that online casinos are meant to prevent this sort of thing, to check in on people who seem to be losing control. It's a condition of their licence to operate, right?

This is true; operators are meant to intervene if you are showing patterns of play consistent with problem gambling. This can include things like betting through the night, dramatically increasing the size and frequency of your stake, having transactions declined by your bank and requesting reverse withdrawals. When those red flags appear, operators are supposed to check in with you and ensure that you're comfortable with your spending. They're supposed to suggest ways you might cool it a little, perhaps by setting deposit limits or signing up for a self-imposed break. In extreme cases they're supposed to suspend or close your account. All of the above, you're sure, applied to you last night. Yet you didn't hear so much as a whisper of dissent as your spending spiralled out of control. The operator, you realise, must surely be in breach of those licensing conditions. The Gambling Commission will see that and, as long as you show them the evidence, you're bound to be refunded, right? Wrong. Unfortunately for you, that is not how it works.

'We are not an ombudsman,' reads the section on the Gambling Commission's website that makes your blood run cold. 'This means we do not have the powers to resolve gambling complaints or help consumers get their money back.'[24]

That's not to say that the operator who took your money won't get into trouble. As long as you pass on the evidence and the Commission finds that they did breach their licence conditions, they could well be fined, or forced to agree to a 'voluntary' settlement. You won't see a penny of it, though.

When gambling operators pay a fine or settlement, the money typically goes to a charity dedicated to reducing gambling-related harm. If it turns out that they were negligently accepting the proceeds of crime, the victim of that crime should receive restitution.

There is obvious logic to this. Someone who has stolen the money they used to gamble certainly shouldn't get it back if it belonged to someone else. There is also good reason not to restore a disordered gambler's own money to them, at least not directly. The very worst thing you could do for someone in the grip of a gambling addiction is hand them more fuel for the fire.

Brian Chappell, better known to many gamblers by his Twitter handle, Jimmy Justice, has for years run Justice for Punters, a volunteer service to help people who've lost a lot of money from a gambling operator that didn't perform the necessary checks. He's combed through countless documents, including customer-service chats, internal communications and account information that companies must, by law, hand over to customers who request it. Typically, such documents lay out in minute detail the way in which people with gambling disorders have racked up staggering losses over months and months, often without a peep from the online casino that happily took their money.

Having seen so much of this data, Brian came to the conclusion that there could quite easily be an appropriate refund mechanism that would help victims reconstruct their finances while ensuring any money recouped couldn't be used for gambling – for instance by returning it to a responsible third-party trustee such as a relative or a lawyer. 'We soon found out there was nobody interested in that,' he told me. 'Gambling Commission, DCMS, the companies. Nobody gave a jot about these individuals. They had nowhere to turn.'

One place they might think to turn to is the Independent Betting Adjudication Service, an alternative dispute-resolution service set up to arbitrate clashes between customers and betting firms that can't otherwise be resolved. Yet, in IBAS's own words, it does not resolve 'disputes relating to the standard of customer service provided [. . . or] Safer gambling standards maintained by gambling businesses. In other words, we do not consider claims by consumers that they have been allowed to gamble excessively/irresponsibly.'[25]

So what next for the problem gambler now staring financial oblivion in the face? Another logical recourse is the law. Most people who rack up major gambling losses lack the resources to hire lawyers, for obvious reasons, but what if they could scrape together the funds, or convince someone to take on their case in exchange for a commission on any payout? Surely, if a gambling operator has breached the terms of its licence, it should assume legal responsibility for the impact of that breach on a vulnerable customer.

Then again, not necessarily so. The reason for this lies in a landmark legal dispute that pitted a greyhound trainer from Sunderland against the deep-pocketed might of William Hill.[26] The details of the case are convoluted, but I'll do my best to boil it down: Graham Calvert was a compulsive gambler who had a telephone betting account with William Hill, with whom he spent a king's ransom. For the most part, he did pretty well. But even when he was winning Calvert was lucid enough to know that he had a problem, that he needed to stop gambling. On two occasions in 2006 he tried. He sought to take advantage of William Hill's self-exclusion system, which allowed customers to bar themselves voluntarily from placing any more bets.

Despite promising to implement the exclusion, William Hill staff, for whatever reason, did not. Free to keep gambling, Calvert went on to lose nearly £2 million over the course of a few short months. His lawyers argued that bookmakers owed their customers a general duty of care, that they should protect customers from the damage that they or their gambling disorder might do. The judge agreed that Calvert would not have lost the money with William Hill if it had fulfilled its obligation to exclude him from gambling, as it had promised to do. He agreed that William Hill owed Calvert a duty of care. But, crucially, he determined that even then Calvert might simply have ruined himself with another gambling company instead. William Hill's duty of care was limited because ultimately it could not have prevented his losses.

Some law firms, notably Leigh Day, have seen in the ruling an opportunity. The company, known for its campaigning work and class actions, reckons that others might triumph where Calvert failed, provided their circumstances are different. 'We are confident that taking into account the practices of the modern-day gambling industry, the duty of care found to exist in the High Court case of Calvert, can be relied upon, and possibly built upon, to provide redress for the harm caused to disordered gamblers,' the firm says on its website.

It would certainly be fascinating to relitigate a similar case today. Back in 2008, when the judge in Calvert v William Hill made his ruling, it was more reasonable to say that Calvert would have lost the money eventually. That's no longer the case. Safergambling tools have improved significantly, albeit far slower than they should have done, and it could be argued that a customer excluded from one operator ought now to be unable to lose the money with another. In the future, the 'duty of care' argument might be even easier to make. One option gaining traction, even among gambling companies themselves, is a 'single customer view' approach, under which every gambling operator would share details of individual customers, preventing those all-too-common situations where an addict is excluded from one operator, only to set up shop with another. In September 2021, the UK Information Commissioner's Office confirmed that data protection laws should be no hurdle to using such a weapon to protect the vulnerable.

We are not there yet, though. Even in situations where everyone, including the guilty operator, recognises that they have failed to protect a gambling addict from harm, the punter often has little hope of recovering lost funds. Gambling firms make no bones about this. They are quite happy to warn anyone who dares challenge them through the courts that they risk digging themselves into an even deeper financial hole. In plain language, they deter by threat.

In one letter shared with me by a gambler who had been allowed to lose £136,000, the operator was at pains to stress the implications of the Calvert case and others like it: 'The customers lost and were each ordered to pay the gambling operator's (very substantial) legal costs.' The import of 'very substantial' is pretty clear: fight us and you'll be in an even deeper hole than you are now. 'While you may continue to seek compensation from us, there is no cause of action which exists to assist you to recover the money you spent through your account,' they went on. In other words: Go fuck yourself.

As I've mentioned before, there are genuine reasons why a responsible business may not want to hand over large sums of cash to someone liable to blow it all again the next day, fuelling the cycle of addiction. But it's far from clear that a well-meaning desire to prevent the customer suffering a relapse is at the heart of this reluctance to pay out. In the same case mentioned above, after a law firm intervened on behalf of the customer, the company offered him a £30,000 settlement, apparently with no strings attached. It was willing to pay out, just not the full amount. That being the case, it's hard not to conclude that the reluctance to make restitution was about penny-pinching rather than responsible behaviour. The eventual change of heart averted a potentially high-profile legal row too, one that would have taken place against a very different backdrop to Calvert v William Hill and just might have had a different outcome.

There are other ways of keeping people quiet by legal means. I've previously detailed the case of Tony Parente, who stole millions of pounds from clients of the property investment business he worked for, using the proceeds to fund huge bets with Ladbrokes and Paddy Power. One of the key features of the saga was that Ladbrokes made Parente sign a non-disclosure agreement as a condition of it paying a £1 million settlement to some of his victims. The agreement demanded that they say nothing to the Gambling Commission, indicating the level of contempt the company had for the regulator at that time.

The Gambling Commission has since ordered licensed firms to stop using these agreements.[27] The nature of gagging orders is such that it's hard to know whether they have obeyed. But certainly, prior to the regulator's instruction, NDAs were used to keep an untold number of transgressions hidden, allowing companies to strike private deals with wronged parties, rather than see their behaviour examined under the spotlight of public scrutiny. Nobody knows quite how many of these have been signed over the years but a Freedom of Information request I made in October 2020 revealed that the regulator was aware of fifty-seven. In all probability – given that some of these agreements are likely to have hinged on keeping matters secret from the regulator – there will have been many more. These are back-room deals that we will never know about – wronged people paid off for their silence, in all likelihood far less than they actually lost, with no safeguards to ensure the money doesn't go straight back into a football accumulator or a virtual slot machine.

One case in particular underlines how capricious and chaotic the regulatory process can be, from the point of view of someone who has suffered harm.

Darren was twenty-seven when he and his father, George, were involved in a car crash in March 2020. Darren suffered a traumatic brain injury and was placed into an induced coma for nine days. The injuries affected his ability to behave appropriately, including decision-making. Darren became irritable, given to fits of anger and impulsive behaviour. He had bet before but in the weeks and months that followed his accident, with little else to entertain him as he went through rehab and recovery against a backdrop of Covid-19 lockdowns, Darren took things to a whole new level. He took out high-interest payday loans and later dipped into a compensation payout from the accident, using the funds to gamble away tens of thousands of pounds with multiple operators. In January 2021 he took an overdose of medication and was subsequently sectioned under the Mental Health Act and diagnosed with schizoaffective disorder, which provoked psychotic episodes. It was only when George obtained power of attorney that he realised Darren had racked up losses of around £120,000.

During Darren's long recovery, both he and George – armed with power of attorney – made multiple attempts to recoup funds from the gambling companies that had profited from Darren's impaired mental state. George set about sending data subject access requests (DSARs) to the fourteen operators that had won money from Darren. A DSAR entitles someone to view any information held about them by a company, including gambling operators.

The responses he got are evidence of what the regulatory

landscape in the UK essentially means for those on the receiving end of gambling-related harm. With no formal arbitration process available, each company reacted differently. Some did the right thing, returning to George the money that Darren had lost; these included Casumo and Betway, whose response was perhaps dictated as much by circumstance as by desire. The former was, at the time, undergoing a review of its licence by the Gambling Commission, amid concerns about its measures to protect vulnerable people and prevent money-laundering. The latter was still reeling from its record £11.6 million fine for similar transgressions, meted out by the regulator just weeks earlier.

Others took an alternative approach, agreeing to return the money but only with strings attached. William Hill insisted that Darren sign a contract agreeing not to take any legal action and that George withdraw his DSAR. In effect, if he wanted to get the money back for his son, he had to forfeit his right to know how the company had interacted with Darren during his recuperation, and whether it should have known how ill he really was and intervened to staunch his losses. Betfred negotiated directly with Darren several months before he was sectioned; they agreed to repay £5,000 of his £13,500 losses as a 'gesture of goodwill' and have since told George they consider themselves to have done their duty and that there is 'no reason to revisit this matter'. BoyleSports returned some of the money but deducted a portion because they had already paid tax on it. Entain, which owns Ladbrokes and Coral, initially demanded that Darren be subjected to an assessment by their own private mental health provider, a Harley Street outfit called Cognacity. It was only after George said he had been speaking to the media that Entain relented and returned the cash, although I can't say for certain that the spectre of negative publicity affected the decision.

One firm, TonyBet, held out. TonyBet is based in Estonia. It was founded by Lithuanian businessman Antanas Guoga, a former poker player turned entrepreneur who later became a Member of the European Parliament for Lithuania's Labour party. He is better known in gambling circles as Tony G. Tony G is no longer involved in the company, having sold it to Swedish operator Betsson in 2016. The UK outfit was not part of the deal, however, and the company has repeatedly failed to respond to my questions. TonyBet refused to refund George any of the sums that Darren had lost. Not only that, but they would not accept a DSAR from George, despite him providing proof of his power of attorney. Instead they responded to rambling emails from Darren that showed clear evidence of a mental health disorder, demanding proof of ID before they could look into his case. It's clear that, for those who lose large sums of money, there's usually little way of getting redress – and that those avenues that do exist are labyrinthine and intimidating.

The lack of a mechanism for customer redress means responses are inconsistent. One letter to Darren from Betfred underlines this point. 'I have advised you before that there is no legal or regulatory reason to return your funds, this is why you will get different responses from different companies.' This point is crucial: there is no assurance of being able to force companies to do the right thing and restore funds clearly taken from vulnerable people. Those who succeed in doing so tend to be those with the patience or the financial wherewithal to pursue their case relentlessly. Occasionally the threat of a negative story in the press forces companies to act, but operators who do not fear reputational damage – perhaps because they have only a small presence in the UK or are privately owned with no shareholders to worry about – have little incentive to do so.

This is no way for a reputable industry to handle serious matters, yet it goes on to this day. It's a situation that is financially beneficial for major companies and their shareholders, sometimes at the expense of vulnerable people facing financial ruin.

One possible solution has been put forward repeatedly and is gaining momentum. Remember the Gambling Commission's disclaimer saying it's not an ombudsman? Well, an ombudsman is exactly what many campaigners and politicians now want to see.[28] A new body could provide that arbitration between firms and customers who claim they have been wronged. At time of writing, ministers are considering the idea. It would be interesting to see what impact a new organisation dedicated to resolving such disputes would have on behaviour. It might even save families from financial ruin, if addicts' loved ones were able to reclaim funds via an ombudsman's decision. Imagine a world in which a well-funded Gambling Commission relentlessly pursued and fined companies for their failings, while an ombudsman made them return the money to the people who'd actually suffered from the loss of it. That would certainly sharpen the minds of companies that push the boundaries.

But so often gambling addiction isn't really about lost money, at least not solely. Think of Jack Ritchie's parents, who were able to bail him out more than once when he lost control, but who still lost their son to addiction. Think of the recovering addicts in the previous chapter, whose struggles weren't just financial but also rooted in their loss of control, their inability to steer their lives or stop themselves hurting the people they loved.

What about the safety net for those people who do fall victim to gambling addiction and find themselves in desperate need of help?

## THE SAFETY NET

Do you remember the figure I gave in Chapter 6 for the number of people being treated within the National Gambling Treatment Service in 2019–20? It was 9,008. Let's compare this number against that notoriously hard-to-pin-down figure for the number of gambling addicts in the UK – which appears to lie somewhere within the admittedly massive range of 300,000 and 1.4 million. In percentage terms this means that, at most, 3% of addicts are getting help; at the lowest estimate it's a vanishingly tiny 0.6%, fewer than one in every hundred people suffering.

This doesn't tell the whole story. The NGTS does not account for services such as Gamblers Anonymous, which I know has been extremely useful for many addicts. Yet the rate at which gamblers are finding clinical treatment services doesn't look too impressive when you compare it with other social problems. In England there are an estimated 586,780 dependent drinkers.[29] According to Alcohol Change UK, around 18% are receiving treatment – not enough, of course, but a sight better than what we're seeing in the gambling world.

And what happens to the small number who do get help? The good news is that, according to the NGTS, nine out of ten of them leave treatment with an improved PGSI score, indicating diminishing levels of harm being done to themselves and those around them. That's not the full picture, though.

For a start, remember that, while a PGSI score of eight or more indicates problem gambling, the scale goes all the way up to twenty-seven. Many of those who complete treatment, some 40%, see their PGSI score fall, but not below the level at which they can still be classified as problem gamblers. Of those who enter treatment, 24% do not complete it (although this figure improved significantly in 2019–20, down from 35% the year before). A quarter of those who enter treatment are not doing so for the first time, indicating significant relapse rates.[30]

None of this is to disparage the professionals trying to help problem gamblers – they are undoubtedly doing fine work helping addicts understand what is happening to them and navigate a path away from a destructive habit. Cognitive behavioural therapy provided by a clinician tends to be seen as the gold standard for treating serious gambling disorders but there is also value in having other services to hand, such as the array of services administered by the GamCare charity, which can point addicts in the right direction for receiving help, or simply provide a friendly voice to someone reaching a low ebb.

And yet the situation in which we find ourselves, fifteen years after the Gambling Act, feels deeply unsatisfactory.

Looking back at the Budd report, its authors were abundantly clear about what ought to happen alongside the liberalisation of gambling that they recommended. They urged that 'increased funding be made available by the NHS for the treatment of problem gambling; problem gambling be recognised as a health problem by the Department of Health; that Health Authorities develop strategies for dealing with problem gambling'.[31] The reality has differed by several orders of magnitude, and is characterised by a threadbare system full of holes into which gamblers can fall. Addiction has largely been treated not as a public health issue for the NHS to take the lead on, but rather as the unfortunate by-product of an otherwise vital industry, like agricultural waste or minor bank-card fraud. The Department of Health and the NHS have had a limited role in tackling a problem that has clear parallels with substance abuse, as well as severe mental health ramifications. Until 2019 there was just one specialist gambling addiction clinic staffed by NHS experts.[32] Gambling addiction simply didn't feature on the radar of the health services that most people find easiest to access. 'Pretty much every GP I spoke to (four different ones) put me on antidepressants and mood stabilisers,' one gambler told me. 'These obviously didn't help at all as I wasn't depressed. I was an addict.'

Despite the clear health implications of gambling disorder, the arm of government largely responsible for ensuring that the gambling industry cleans up after itself is the Department for Digital, Culture, Media & Sport – a department with minimal expertise in health, not to mention being the chief governmental point of contact for businesses that rely heavily on gambling money, such as broadcasters and sports teams.

The DCMS plays a major role in how the money available for helping addicts is distributed. Although the Gambling Act gave the government the power to impose a mandatory levy on gambling firms to force them to pay for research, education and treatment, successive DCMS ministers have shied away from doing so, despite a growing consensus that has united MPs from across the political divide, addiction experts and the Gambling Commission itself. Instead their preference has been for sticking to the convention of voluntary donations made by an industry that has historically played down the extent of the collateral damage it causes.

Funding for treatment services has been largely routed via GambleAware, which supports a cornucopia of projects, including the National Gambling Helpline, often the most visible entry point to treatment for addicts because it features in companies' responsible-gambling messaging.

The voluntary contribution system has come under fire, for several reasons. First, as my friend at the Gambling Commission alluded to earlier, historically some companies simply refused to pay anything more than a nominal sum that allowed them to say, truthfully, that they were contributing. In May 2019 I wrote that 'the list of companies that gave to GambleAware revealed some firms donated nominal sums such as £1 or £5.'[33] This clearly made a mockery of the idea that the industry could be trusted to redirect profits to good causes. Some companies were simply not bothered; more than that, they were deliberately gaming the system. Partly as a result of this, the money raised by the voluntary system was often not enough: GambleAware was collecting about £10 million annually, rising to more like £15 million in recent years, but Gambling Commission chairman Bill Moyes suggested £70 million was closer to what was required.[34]

There were also legitimate concerns that the industry had too much power over the direction of what funding it did contribute. Not only was GambleAware completely reliant on the industry's continued largesse, but for a long time – until 2018 – its board had included a number of executives from the major firms. It was, said some critics, akin to cigarette company bosses having a role in reducing tobacco-related harm. Even where there was no evidence of impropriety, the whiff of it remained.

In April 2019, then culture secretary Jeremy Wright summoned the bosses of the five largest gambling companies to discuss a topic that was becoming increasingly toxic. I and several other people have submitted Freedom of Information requests in an effort to establish what was said at that meeting – but to no avail. What we do know is that, just twenty-four hours after Wright's summit with gambling bosses, sports minister Mims Davies, Wright's junior with the portfolio responsibility for gambling, insisted that the voluntary system 'does work'.[35] Less than two months later Wright announced that these major industry players had agreed to increase their voluntary contribution from 0.1% of takings to 1% by 2023, to a value of £100 million over the course of the ramp-up.[36]

There is good reason to be sceptical. For one thing, the industry wanted an alarming amount of control over the sums it was donating. One of the attendees of Wright's meeting with the industry was Tory peer Lord Chadlington, a long-time gambling reform campaigner who had proposed a new charity called Action Against Gambling Harm. He wanted the industry to increase its contribution dramatically and to route the money through this new charity. Unlike GambleAware, which had been criticised in the past for its alleged closeness to the very industry whose excesses it was supposed to temper, the new charity would not have the same baggage. This would help dispel, once and for all, the notion that gambling firms were somehow in charge of the purse strings.

Chadlington certainly believed that the industry was willing to divert money away from GambleAware and towards his new body, with its supposedly more ring-fenced, independent approach. Indeed, he went so far as to issue a press release to that effect. It was even signed by the five major gambling companies.[37]

Later that year, though, the firms changed their mind: the money would go to GambleAware, as it always had before. The decision provoked fury among clinicians and researchers. In an open letter to the government, more than forty leading academics and clinicians who specialised in gambling treatment wrote: 'There is considerable concern that the existing system creates significant opportunities for [gambling firms] to influence this agenda. Irrespective of which organisation funds are given to, the [. . .] announcement exemplifies the long-standing weakness of a funding system that allows the gambling industry to regulate the availability and distribution of vital funds to address gambling harms. Increases in funding first promised [. . .] nearly one year ago have yet to materialise and the industry has now demonstrated its willingness and ability to change the direction of funding at short notice.'[38]

In practice, even two years later, in 2021, there had been little uplift in the money received by gambling charities, although the announcement of a £4 million research hub by GambleAware in August 2021 suggested it was starting to trickle through. In any case, the industry had bought itself goodwill from the government and positive publicity in the run-up to the gambling review, without actually having spent very much at all, and certainly less than the £70 million a year that the Gambling Commission had indicated might be appropriate. Nor is there unanimity about the suitability of the service offered by the organisations that do receive the industry's money.

As I've already said, gambling industry messages typically signpost people towards the National Gambling Helpline, run by GamCare, which receives much of the industry's funding. As valuable as the helpline has been to many, in a submission to a House of Lords committee, the Ritchies' charity, Gambling With Lives, raised questions about its efficacy. They pointed out that GamCare's counsellors were only required to have qualifications at NVQ Level 3: 'Being qualified as a mental health nurse does not mean one is qualified to provide. cognitive behavioural therapy (CBT) or other psychosocial interventions, any more than a medical doctor who has worked in paediatrics for ten years is fit to perform heart surgery,' they warned.[39]

Matt Gaskell, consultant psychologist for the NHS Northern Gambling Service, is careful not to be critical of the services provided by GamCare and other services funded via GambleAware. But he thinks the NHS is better suited to being the key focal point for gamblers trying to access treatment and that the specialist clinical knowledge of clinics like his are too often ignored.

'We [NHS gambling clinics] could cope with more people,' he said. 'Everybody is funnelled to the helpline and everyone who does want support will automatically go to a local GamCare provider. That will help a number of people, no doubt, but we have this great opportunity to look at the whole system and how it could be strengthened.'

Gaskell believes that NHS services are best placed to handle what is essentially a health problem. This, he says, would at a stroke remove concerns about the industry's influence on how funds are spent, as well as lead to better outcomes for people seeking treatment.

'Those most qualified, with the best chance of making the most significant impact, are being kept at the very margins. There's a greater role for the NHS to play.'

## A GLIMMER OF LIGHT?

There is genuine cause for optimism. For a start, the NHS is playing an ever-greater role in treating gambling addicts. Where there was just one specialist gambling clinic in 2018, there were three as of summer 2021, with a further fourteen to be rolled out in the coming years. A specialist centre for young people aged thirteen to twenty-five was launched in 2019.[40]

And, as much as technology has presented opportunities for exploitation and transgression of the rules, it is also offering opportunities to help people. Software like Gamban can be installed on computers and phones to prevent addicts from accessing the online casinos and bookmakers that pose a risk.

Those who fear they have a problem can also sign up to GamStop, the industry-wide national self-exclusion scheme. If you've signed up to GamStop after realising you had a problem while betting with William Hill, you are in theory blocked from using Ladbrokes, 888 and bet365 too, for a defined and irreversible period, which is a vast improvement on what came before, namely company-specific schemes that varied in quality and did nothing to prevent you from moving on to the next operator. The site had reached 200,000 registrations as of summer 2021, after a surge in sign-ups during the pandemic.[41]

Tools like Gamban and GamStop are not a watertight defence. They sometimes fail, and if someone is determined to gamble there are so many ways to do so as to render it impossible to prevent. But so many of the horror stories I've heard, of financial ruin and suicide, could have been avoided if there had just been more friction in the number of steps the victim needed to go through before making that first bet of an ill-fated session. Perhaps it would have deferred, rather than prevented, tragedy. Or perhaps it would have delayed things just long enough to allow that person's life to turn in the direction of redemption rather than tragedy.

It should also be said that the industry itself has increasingly woken up to the need to deploy the vast array of technological brainpower at its disposal to recognise and intervene in problem play. At the industry's annual conference and trade show in February 2020, a man from Playtech demonstrated to me an impressive piece of software that uses artificial intelligence to spot when players look to be at risk. All companies have either developed their own systems, or bought them from third parties. In February 2021 Kindred Group – owner of 32Red and Unibet – took the unusual step of opening its books to reveal that 4% of its revenue came from high-risk gamblers showing signs of harm. It pledged to reduce the percentage to zero by 2023, using proprietary technology.[42]

That same year, while there were concerning signs that addicts were playing more intensely during successive Covid-19 lockdowns, there was also nascent evidence that the combination of measures taken by the government, the regulator and the companies themselves were having a positive effect. Gambling Commission figures suggested that the problem gambling rate had fallen from 0.6% to 0.3%.[43] As I've said before, though, we should be wary of statistics like these – but if they are even remotely indicative of the direction of travel, they are to be warmly welcomed.

If things are indeed improving, a lot of that is down to the many good people who work in the gambling industry and genuinely care about protecting people. I interviewed one person who has worked in player protection for the best part of a decade, at a variety of companies. I'll call him Goran because he wishes to remain anonymous. He spoke passionately about developing systems to reduce harm and of intervening even when it cost his employer money and he could have got away with sitting on his hands.

He struck me as honest and I believed him when he cited anecdotes such as these: 'We had one guy who was twenty-one, had an inheritance from his grandma. He deposited £10,000 and wanted to put it on Spain to beat Iceland. He put it on at half-time when Spain were 2–0 up. He was only going to win £500 back. We get real-time transaction monitoring and we could see that. We called him up, asked him where he got the money and why he'd put it on this bet. He explained this was his inheritance. As I was on the phone to him, Spain conceded and he started to panic about the prospect of the bet losing. I agreed that we'd cancel the bet and return the money. They drew 2–2 in the end.'

If the story is true, Goran had saved the customer the pain of losing his inheritance, at the expense of his employer. On another occasion, he told me, he'd monitored a poker player who had sold a company for £150 million. Professional players were following him around the website, taking his money with ease, until Goran phoned him and informed him that he was being made a fool of.

There is a big question mark, though, over how many Gorans there are in the industry and how that varies from online to the high street, from casinos to bingo, from private to stock-market-listed companies, from overseas operators to UK firms.

One of the things that made me believe Goran is that he was up front about the fact that much of the industry wouldn't typically behave as he did. Where companies have improved their player protection systems, he said, the effort has often been motivated by little more than self-interest. Remember the change in the law in 2015, when the Gambling Commission first began to license operators to sell to British punters and the fines suddenly increased? Goran told me that was pivotal. 'Regulatory action and negative publicity is the driver behind it all,' he said. 'If you research people in the industry and look at their profiles, most of them have only started doing anti-money-laundering and responsible-gambling roles since 2015.'

And what of ensuring that they don't hurt people in the pursuit of profit?

'That was a secondary consideration and something that came after the fear of fines.'

It's this last assessment that should make us cautious about believing that progress in protecting the vulnerable is irreversible.

Anyone with an interest in preventing harm should, based on past experience, be wary about what the industry says and does when it presents itself as having turned over a new leaf. Genuine concern for the vulnerable is certainly a factor among individual staff members and executives, but it's hard to conclude that it's behind the industry's relatively recent progress in reducing harm.

One executive, who is cynical about some of his competitors' motives, put it like this: 'I don't accept it's altruism. It's PR and self-preservation to a large extent. It's a giant PR exercise.'

My contention is that what progress we have seen came about as a result of fear – fear of bad publicity, fear of fines from the regulator and, most importantly, fear that the government will finally lose patience and impose draconian measures that make the UK a much harder place to be profitable. But successful businesses don't stay fearful for long. When they face a threat they circle the wagons, take stock and draw up battle plans. It is then that the industry really puts its money, power and connections to work.

# 8. PLAYING POLITICS: FOBTS AND THE LOBBYING GAME

> There is no gambling like politics.
> BENJAMIN DISRAELI, *ENDYMION* (1880)

> There's more politics in the gambling industry than
> there is in parliament.
> TRACEY CROUCH MP

Anyone who has read this far probably has a high tolerance for detailed narrative about a single subject. Most people don't. In the world of print media, a 2,000-word in-depth feature drilling deep into the intricacies of gambling regulation might garner a few thousand online readers at best. The lion's share of those would not make it even halfway through before giving up and clicking on something else. But a punchy 400-word news piece that zeroes in on one or two shocking but easy-to-explain revelations? The sky's the limit with that, even to the extent of effecting changes in policy. These observations aren't meant as a criticism of media consumers, by the way – we're all busy people and we live in a fast-paced age of digital distraction that rewards a short attention span.

News organisations know all of this. They have clever analytical tools that give feedback on how readers are engaging with everything they publish, and they use this information to walk a tightrope between writing about what is important and writing about what people actually want to read, hopefully marrying the two. Clickbait isn't good journalism but neither is a dry, quasi-academic tract.

Occasionally a subject comes along that simply makes what journalists call 'good copy'. It's emotive, rich, developing and the readers don't seem to tire of it. The thematic flashpoint during the period that gave us the Gambling Act of 2005 was the row over supercasinos. They became the focus of moral agonising about Britain's relationship with gambling. It seems almost quaint in the digital age, when every mobile phone offers access to more gambling than could fit in even the most cavernous casino on the Las Vegas Strip.

Yet the supercasino row dominated the agenda in the early years of the century. It diverted attention from the more knotty, detailed bits of gambling regulation that have, in time, proved to be far more important, such as the proper provision of treatment for addicts, the remit of the Gambling Commission, predatory elements of product design and plenty more.

But it makes sense, to me at least, that supercasinos attracted so much attention. Societies engage easily with simple narratives not because our attention spans are short but because such narratives can serve as symbols for something larger and less tangible. Back in the early noughties Britain was about to redefine its relationship with gambling, and supercasinos were simply a lightning rod for societal unease about how the revolution would shake out.

There's a good case for saying that the next era will be defined – in part, anyway – by the prolonged, hard-fought, often vicious battle over FOBTs. On 1 April 2019 the maximum stake on FOBTs was reduced, by law, from £100 to £2, after a political struggle that took several years to play out.[1] It was a curious saga. This one niche little gambling product, totally alien to the vast majority of people, made headline news for months on end and would ultimately trigger a political rebellion that included the resignation of a government minister, as we shall see. But the FOBT row was about more than just one product. It was emblematic of how gambling has been handled in the public sphere. It was a platform for moral outrage, a magnet for lobbyists charging hefty fees and the subject of grubby backstairs political deals. And, yes, it was also a cudgel for journalists to take up, as we sought compelling stories with which to impress editors and interest readers. As with the wider debate on gambling regulation, all of this white noise often drowned out the voices of those who needed to be heard. And there is a case for saying that none of us learned anything from it and that history is already repeating itself.

## WHAT WAS ALL THE FUSS ABOUT?

When I say FOBTs were emblematic of something larger, or a distraction from wider concerns, that isn't to say they were somehow unimportant, or a red herring. But the machines did attract disproportionate media interest, parliamentary speechifying and emotive rhetoric, most notably the tagline 'the crack cocaine of gambling'.

It's a phrase that I, along with many journalists, deployed too often. It is impossible to say for sure where it came from. But in testimony to a Canadian Senate committee in 2005, the president of gambling firm Multigames International, Bill Rutsey, credited Donald Trump with coining it to describe video poker, in an effort to smear a product he saw as competition to his casinos.[2] Whether Rutsey was right about Trump inventing the phrase is debatable, but his supposed involvement was enough to put me off continuing to use a description about which I was already feeling uneasy.

Yet there's no doubt in my mind that FOBTs are very dangerous, more dangerous than almost any other gambling product, and that campaigners had good reason to want them reined in. The statistics speak for themselves. In an article for the *Guardian* in 2017, headlined 'A stupid gamble on evil machines', TV presenter and poker player Victoria Coren Mitchell pointed to figures showing the number of times someone had lost more than £1,000 in a single session on one of these machines.[3] It was 233,071 times in one year, or more than six hundred times every day. I had read the same statistical report but focused instead on a figure that was initially more eye-catching – that gamblers had on at least seven occasions lost more than £10,000 in a day, in sessions that sometimes lasted seven hours or more. Both facts are jaw-dropping, but it was Coren Mitchell who had put her finger on the more pertinent point, one that showed the danger of FOBTs at a national level.

The NHS Digital Health Survey of the previous year, 2016, underlined why so many people were concerned. According to the survey, around 0.9% of people who played the National Lottery were considered problem gamblers. That makes sense; for a lot of people a weekly lottery ticket is their only interaction with gambling. Activities more popular with regular gamblers showed higher rates of problem gambling, unsurprisingly. Bets on horse racing carried a rate of 3.3%, gambling at a casino 6.4% and online slots and casino games higher still, at 8.7%. Machines in a bookmaker's – a category dominated by FOBTs – blew everything else out of the water, at 13.6%. If you threw in those deemed at moderate risk, more than a quarter of FOBT players were found to be in danger from the experience.[4] You can't say that for many products.

Anecdotal experience bore this out. In the course of writing about gambling, I've visited most well-known high-street bookmakers, in different parts of the country. What has always struck me – and seems to vindicate the tone of my reporting – is how almost every time I venture out to visit bookmakers I see people losing their minds on the machines. In late 2017 I was writing a feature about bookmakers 'clustering' shops on high streets in impoverished areas in response to the limit of four FOBTs per shop.[5] I spent time in four bookmakers on Newham High Street that day and witnessed FOBT rage without even having to look for it. In one shop a young man paced back and forth in front of the machine, uttering oaths and gesticulating violently as his numbers repeatedly failed to come up. Later I watched a guy slam his hand into the screen and storm out of the shop. As he marched down the street in fury, I followed him for a while and saw him drive his fist into a shopfront in anguish. I wondered for a moment whether a human being might later find themselves on the receiving end of that anger. On another occasion I was researching a feature in Birmingham. I had heard problem gamblers talk about playing multiple machines at once but I hadn't seen it until then. As I walked up to one of the machines, an agitated-looking man stepped away from the neighbouring machine, blocked my way and gestured for me to find another berth. 'I'm playing that one too,' he said.

This can mean danger for shop staff as well, hard-working people who are often forgotten victims of gambling-related harm. I spoke to a young woman who, as of August 2021, still worked in a bookmaker's in the north-east. I can't say anything about where, or reveal her real name, because I don't want her to get into trouble with her employer, but we'll call her Rhiannon. What struck me most was how inured she was, a girl of barely twenty, to behaviour that many people would find terrifying.

'It's next door to a working men's club. You get people coming in who are under the influence and then they can get a bit upset and angry if they're losing. When I first started, before the FOBT stakes changed, there was an incident on the very first time I'd been left alone [in the shop]. A man picked up a chair and launched it across the room, chucking furniture around. I'd just turned nineteen at the time. I was in total shock and just didn't know what to do. There isn't actually a screen in the shop I work in and the counter is very much jumpable. People have said to me before: "You know, I could easily jump this?"'

Rhiannon said she was past the point of being scared any more. That said, she told me she was thinking of asking not to work the afternoon shifts alone come the winter, when it gets dark early.

If you don't want to take my word or Rhiannon's word for it, you can see what a FOBT frenzy looks like for yourself. Type 'FOBT CCTV' into YouTube and you'll find footage of customers smashing machines with the metal barstools that shops typically provide to keep them comfortable while they play. In 2016 the *Sun* newspaper published a story suggesting such incidents were on the rise. Three years later I used Freedom of Information requests to establish that police callouts to bookies had fallen significantly after the stakes on them were cut to £2.[6]

Before this legislative change, not only were FOBTs dangerous and emotionally provocative for vulnerable addicts but they were also a tool used by criminals to launder dirty money. In an interview with a drug dealer called James in 2013, my colleague Randeep Ramesh explained how it worked: 'Dealers feed their drug money through the machines, losing a little and then cashing out with the vast majority of their stake, James says. They can then collect a printed ticket showing they have gambled that day – meaning that if stopped by police, they can answer questions about why an apparently unemployed young man carries hundreds of pounds in rolled-up cash.'[7]

This is one of the main reasons I am not in any way seeking to downplay the seriousness of the FOBT issue when I say that the debate over their future was, ultimately, a vehicle for something else. FOBTs were a festering boil that needed lancing. But I contend that the FOBT saga – from start to finish – illustrates the nature of attitudes towards gambling policy, as well as the business of politicians, lobbying and regulation more broadly. It should teach us lessons that are in danger of going unlearned.

# LOBBYING AND FRIENDS IN HIGH PLACES

In the thick of the government's years-long deliberation over FOBTs, any outcome seemed possible, from no change whatsoever to the stringent curbs that we ended up with.

As the debate raged, it felt as if I was writing a FOBT-related story every other day, and so, it seemed, was half the British press. It was around then, in early 2017, that I was invited to lunch by Malcolm George, boss of the industry's lobby group, the Association of British Bookmakers. The informal meeting was scheduled for my day off but I didn't have much on, George was a key figure in the industry and – I am a journalist, after all – the lunch was at an extremely upmarket restaurant. George was affable and easy to like. We got through a bottle and a half of wine, which helped grease the wheels of conversation, even though the discussion – on the relative harms of gambling products – was fairly adversarial.

Wining and dining journalists is pretty cheap in the grand scheme of industry lobbying budgets and probably fairly enjoyable on occasion, even when you're dealing with the irritating, holier-than-thou hacks who constantly take moralistic potshots at you when you're just trying to make an honest living. But while putting your case to journalists is important, it's only a small part of the equation. A much larger component is the effort to stack political cards in your favour by employing professionals whose job it is to spend much larger sums of money on the difficult business of changing politicians' minds.

When it came to FOBTs, the competing networks of vested interest were dizzying. On the industry's side you had Malcolm George and the ABB, as well as a phalanx of silver-tongued internal and external public affairs executives working for the major bookmakers themselves. They were already fighting something of a losing battle in the popular media but still had a few tricks up their sleeves. For instance, they had on their side pro-gambling MPs such as Laurence Robertson and Philip Davies, both staunch allies of the bookmaking industry. Both were also frequent recipients of hospitality from bookies, receiving tickets worth thousands of pounds for prestigious dates in the horse racing calendar.[8] There was nothing particularly out of the ordinary about this – companies entertain MPs all the time, particularly MPs who show an interest in their particular line of work. The two men are genuine, avowed fans of horse racing. In Davies's case, though, the largesse went a little further than hospitality: *The Times* revealed in 2016 that, after Davies wrote to Ladbrokes, it had agreed to lift restrictions on his betting account, making it easier for him to operate a potentially lucrative professional gambling strategy.[9] Usually restrictions are placed on punters who show that they can win on a regular basis. Davies was cleared of wrongdoing by a parliamentary watchdog, although, as we shall see, questions about his friendship with Ladbrokes would persist. Whatever the nature of that relationship, Davies did his best on behalf of the gambling industry, sounding the alarm about the effect on jobs that curbing FOBTs would have.

Even after it became clear that the industry had lost the battle on FOBTs, there remained the question of when exactly the stream of cash they guaranteed would be cut off. For bookmakers, who earned close to £1 billion a year from the machines,[10] this was an important question.

Initially, multiple sources in Westminster have told me, the Treasury agreed to make the change in short order, with the cut taking effect in April 2019. Sports minister Tracey Crouch certainly believed that this was the promise she had been given. After spearheading the policy through the parliamentary process, meeting addicts and their families along the way, she knew that any delay could lead to more suffering. There was no time to lose.

There is some debate about what happened next.

In 2018 Crouch told me in an interview that she believed pro-gambling MPs had been instrumental in securing a delay to the policy.[11] '[Culture minister] Jeremy Wright was asked to go and meet Philip Davies, who expressed he didn't like the policy full stop,' she told me. 'For some reason, Jeremy thought there would be a good compromise to bring it in in October. At that point the chancellor shifted and it became a bit of a mess, really, from there. When it became a Treasury announcement, we lost control over the timing. Junior ministers don't get to see the chancellor.'

The passage of time has finessed Crouch's view somewhat. Now she believes that Davies's role in the affair has been overplayed, that the chancellor, Philip Hammond, didn't need any persuading to postpone a policy that risked curbing the Treasury's tax receipts.

Whoever was responsible, Crouch felt that she had been overridden on her own policy, that a promise had been broken, and that addicts would suffer and even take their own lives due to the resulting delay. In one of the more powerful gestures of principle in recent political history, she resigned in protest. MPs on both sides of the House united behind her, demanding that the FOBT stake cut be implemented as soon as possible. It was a rebellion that forced the government to revert to the earlier date after all.[12]

Had she not protested, Crouch believes, the FOBT cut might never have happened at all. The Treasury's scepticism, she says, would only have been heightened by chaos surrounding the UK's Brexit negotiations, which threatened a serious economic hit.

'Philip Hammond was so opposed to it that I think they would have found a reason to not do it. All of my colleagues who were passionate about Brexit would have been distracted by that. So, you know, it would have been really easy to slip through.'

Instead, reform campaigners had scored a notable victory against powerful lobbying interests.

There were reasons to be cynical about the motives of some of those behind the campaign for reform too. The most influential force in the anti-FOBT clan was a group of MPs, composed of lawmakers from all political stripes, called the all-party parliamentary group (APPG) on FOBTs. While the commitment of the group's members to gambling reform is not in question, those who funded it were not without self-interest.

One of the APPG's backers was Bacta, a lobby group for adult gaming centres, the high-street amusement arcades that offer £2-a-spin gambling games. If high-stakes FOBTs were to fall by the wayside, their members stood to pick up some of the custom lost by bookmakers. Another backer was Novomatic, a software company that relied heavily on the kind of lower-stakes machines that would be likely to pick up extra custom if FOBTs were curbed. Also on the list was the Hippodrome Casino, another potential recipient of any custom lost by bookmakers, as well as the pub chain JD Wetherspoon, whose venues are replete with fruit machines.[13]

The bookmakers also cast doubt on the motives of one of the anti-FOBT campaign's most prominent figures – the left-wing political activist Matt Zarb-Cousin, a recovering gambling addict who had spoken movingly of how he had considered suicide and whose motives for wanting a crackdown were obvious. But critics pointed out that his campaigning efforts were backed financially by Derek Webb, a former professional poker player who had made a large amount of money inventing card games for the casino industry. Webb had also donated to Tom Watson, the Labour MP who had emerged as one of the leading anti-FOBT campaigners in parliament. There has, to my knowledge, been no robust evidence presented that Webb had any financial interests in seeing FOBTs curbed. That did not stop the bookmakers from suggesting it, though. In a bad-tempered discussion on television, the ABB's Malcolm George branded Zarb-Cousin casino-funded. It was an error that he would live to regret, after Zarb-Cousin successfully sued him and secured an apology.[14]

I don't contend that any of these various special-interest groups, campaigners and lobbyists were arguing against what they genuinely believed. But at times the turf war going on within the gambling industry seemed to have lost sight of what was important: reducing harm.

'There is a lot of energy expended on different interest groups trying to make a case that one activity versus another is the most harmful thing,' said gambling behavioural analyst Heather Wardle at the time. 'You end up with a polarised debate that misses the complexity of what's causing people harm and what you do about it. I can perfectly understand why different stakeholders do that but it's not particularly helpful. I'd like to see people combine their energies into really thinking about how we help people and stop the horrendous problems they experience.'[15]

So what has changed this time round? The answer is: not a lot, at least not in terms of the dramatis personae. Zarb-Cousin is still campaigning, via his Clean Up Gambling group. He is still receiving funding from Derek Webb, who is also providing financial support to Gambling With Lives and to the APPG on gambling-related harm, chaired by Labour's firebrand parliamentary campaigner on gambling, Carolyn Harris. Webb still has no financial interest in the casino industry, as far as I'm aware. As one person close to him put it: 'He's just very rich and he thinks certain elements of gambling have gone too far.'

Probably the biggest change is that the likes of Zarb-Cousin, Webb, Gambling With Lives and Harris have a tougher enemy on their hands. The gambling industry has got its act together on the lobbying front. The ABB was a blunt instrument, blindly railing against any cut in FOBT stakes until it was too late. It was gaffe-prone and unsophisticated, as evidenced by Malcolm George's old-school wine-and-dine approach to journalists, as well as his clumsy clash with Zarb-Cousin.

Its counterpart for online gambling – the Remote Gambling Association – was largely content to stay out of the matter, with FOBTs a battle for the high-street bookmaking operations to fight.

Neither strategy did the industry any favours, as Paddy Power founder Stewart Kenny points out. 'It was the Trojan horse that destroyed the public image of betting. It was going to happen anyhow with online so readily available but you might not have had such a high-profile campaign.'

Today's lobbying operation is a more sophisticated outfit. In 2018 the industry formed the Betting and Gaming Council, bringing under one roof the lobbying efforts of parts of the industry that had often been at loggerheads. Brigid Simmonds, a veteran lobbyist who had been among those who contributed to the original Gambling Act of 2005, took the role of chairman. Michael Dugher – a former Labour MP with a bulging contacts book of the great and good in politics – was brought in as its chief executive. These were heavyweights steeped in the arduous process of shaping policy at the highest level.

But old habits die hard. The industry may have sharpened up its lobbying game but it still faced the kind of existential threat that makes a wounded animal particularly dangerous. Backed into a corner, its representatives could cut up rough.

Dugher, for instance, hasn't always been as polished in his approach as he might have been, particularly on Twitter. In an online scrap with Zarb-Cousin, fuelled in part by enmity arising from their positions on opposite sides of a civil war within the Labour party, Dugher twice called Zarb-Cousin 'roulette boy'.[16] It was an unforgivable reference to the latter's addiction. In 2020, during a Twitter exchange with Chris Murphy – interviewed elsewhere in this book – Dugher labelled the recovering addict 'deranged'.[17] And in 2021 he took aim at Zarb-Cousin again, suggesting his old foe was a fan of casinos. He later apologised and deleted the tweet, insisting that he had not meant to riff on his opponent's struggles with addiction.[18]

By and large, though, Dugher and the BGC have gone about their business much more intelligently than the ABB did. Kevin Schofield, a veteran journalist, was hired to run the organisation's communications strategy. It wasn't long before the BGC's views began to feature regularly on *PoliticsHome*, a popular news website among MPs and apparatchiks in Westminster, which Schofield had edited until joining the BGC in February 2020. The site had previously hosted articles sympathetic to reform of the gambling industry. But between Schofield's arrival at the BGC and the end of July 2021, a period of less than eighteen months, *PoliticsHome* carried no less than eleven separate features written by the BGC or its staff, helpfully labelled – albeit in pretty small writing – 'partner content'. The site is well read in political circles and Schofield's apparent access to his old employer provided a conduit to the eyes of politicians and advisors who might still be susceptible to having their minds changed. Indeed, Schofield's Westminster pedigree stretched back even further than his time at *PoliticsHome*; he had previously been chief political editor of the *Sun*, arguably the UK's most influential newspaper and a frequent vehicle for anti-regulation news stories.

Where the ABB had been stuffed with industry dinosaurs, the BGC was run by veteran lobbyists, a recent MP with extensive political connections and a journalist with both a hotline to influential former colleagues and an innate understanding of efficient messaging. They make for a formidable grouping and they hit the ground running.

## MARKING YOUR OWN HOMEWORK

Smartly, unlike the ABB, the BGC has made a big show of the industry's voluntary efforts to change. It casts itself not as a lobby group, or a trade organisation, but as a standards body, dedicated to improving the industry's protection of its consumers. Much of this is genuine – there are significant elements of the sector that have realised they need to do a better job of that.

It's harder, though, to judge how many of these improvements have been about self-preservation and how many of them would be happening if the industry were not facing a landmark review of gambling laws. And how many of the industry's concessions, trumpeted by the BGC, have been cosmetic rather than profound?

In the chapter on advertising, I recounted how the industry voluntarily signed up to a whistle-to-whistle ban on advertising during live sports broadcasts, announced in late 2018. The agreement actually predates the formation of the BGC but the lobby group's subsequent presentation of it has been a masterclass in spin.

In reality the ban has been fairly inconsequential. While adverts have ceased, the broadcasts themselves are packed full of gambling imagery. The logos of major brands appear on shirts and pitchside hoardings for ninety minutes of every game, with up to seven hundred of them visible during the period.[19] And in any case, modern gambling brands predominantly target customers via the internet, where adverts have continued unfettered.

The much-vaunted whistle-to-whistle ban is a good example of how the industry has learned and adapted its lobbying strategy since the FOBT debacle, bending with the wind rather than resisting in a way that risks bringing down the whole edifice. In a post-FOBT world, operators know to make concessions they can live with in exchange for good PR and political goodwill.

The industry lobby has also been somewhat tricksy in how it communicates its agenda of raising standards. For instance, the BGC has, on several occasions, loudly proclaimed that the whistle-to-whistle ban has reduced the number of gambling ads seen by children by 97%.[20] This is only true if you add some pretty significant caveats. The seemingly impressive reduction relates to the span of televised football matches, not to the overall number of TV ads seen by children at any other time of day. What's more, it does not include the internet or, for that matter, the radio.

The BGC's memory has been equally selective when it comes to another recent player protection measure, the Gambling Commission's ban on gambling on credit. It's a restriction that seems like a no-brainer . . . Why allow people to use debt to amass yet more debt? That, said the BGC in February 2020, is why the industry stood firmly behind a ban on betting with credit cards. 'We fully and publicly supported' the ban, Michael Dugher told me in a public exchange on Twitter.[21] The BGC may have supported a ban in public but what its members said in private was rather different. According to a Gambling Commission report on the consultation process it ran prior to introducing the measure: 'None of the remote gambling operators who responded supported a ban.'[22]

Somehow the BGC always seems to portray itself as having galloped towards reform like a thoroughbred racehorse, when it later transpires that it was dragged there more like a recalcitrant donkey. That's not to say that there is nothing genuine about its efforts as a standards body. The gambling industry is a disparate one, made up of businesses that have different attitudes towards what constitutes the right degree of player protection. The BGC has managed to unite that industry behind measures such as the whistle-to-whistle advertising ban and improved online protection, increased promotion of deposit limits and improved standards around advertising. In July 2021 the organisation lined up behind calls for a gambling ombudsman too.[23]

All of this is to be commended. And yet there remain nagging questions. How many of these measures are tokenistic rather than genuinely transformational, and why did it take so long for the industry to get serious about its responsibilities? Remember, the industry's 'voluntary' measures often arrive just when there is no alternative. It reminds me, strangely enough, of my cats. When they jump up on the kitchen counter with their dirty little paws, I can gesture and shout at them to get down until I'm blue in the face. It's only when I spring off the sofa and head towards them with menace in my eyes that they actually do it.

What the gambling industry says and does in public is important. But the BGC has more going for it than the consummate deployment of spin. It sits at the centre of a nexus of power and influence that is more sophisticated and influential than predecessor organisations such as the ABB could ever have hoped to be. Its web of connections allows the industry to make representations at the highest level of government, with the content of those meetings often remaining private. Records of ministers' meetings show that BGC staff and DCMS officials met no fewer than seven times between October and December 2020 alone, the months either side of the gambling review being announced.[24]

Perhaps that should come as no surprise, given the importance of the review. It is even less shocking when one considers the revolving door that has been established between British politics and the gambling lobby.

Michael Dugher was a friend of the bookmakers before taking the job at the BGC. As early as 2016, while still an MP, he was blasting the government in the *Sun* newspaper for focusing on FOBTs rather than on scratch cards and the National Lottery, despite the lower addiction rates seen in the latter products.[25] When he resigned as an MP, he walked first into a job with another lobby group, UK Music,[26] and immediately after that into his role with the BGC. He may have left politics but he helped the gambling industry maintain and even improve its track record of making friends in high places.

Dugher happens to be bosom buddies with Tom Watson, the former deputy leader of the Labour party who emerged as one of the key campaigners for gambling reform in the House of Commons. Dugher and Watson are old pals, even godfathers to one another's children.[27] The similarities don't end there. When Watson left parliament he followed a path that will have been very familiar to his close friend. His first port of call as an ex-MP was the chairmanship of UK Music, the body that Dugher had recently left.[28] The other job in his portfolio – a big surprise to many, given Watson's anti-gambling sentiments – was with Flutter Entertainment plc, the giant gambling company that owns Paddy Power and Sky Bet, among other brands.[29] Six years earlier, Watson had described Flutter as 'dirty' and 'money-grabbing' after the company took bets on the trial of former Paralympic athlete Oscar Pistorius, who had murdered his girlfriend, Reeva Steenkamp.[30]

Watson justified the decision to work for the company he had so vehemently criticised as an opportunity to effect change from within.

'I have a long-standing interest in this sector and have consistently called for action to protect those who may be potentially vulnerable to harm,' he said.

'In taking on this role in Flutter, I intend to get under the bonnet of the business – and the industry more widely – to understand how best to further develop and implement industry-leading responsible-gambling policies.

'I strongly believe that working collaboratively with Flutter in this way will allow me to continue to drive positive change.'

Now outside the world of politics, Watson certainly seemed to have developed a better relationship with the gambling industry. He had even adopted some of the rhetorical flourishes adopted by his gambling lobbyist pal. Dugher typically refers to those campaigning for stricter controls on the gambling industry as 'prohibitionists', despite the fact that there are – as far as I know – no mainstream voices calling for gambling to be banned. The description takes on a more insulting tone when one considers that the campaign for reform includes grieving parents such as the Ritchies.

Yet in April 2020, when the BGC persuaded its members to temporarily suspend advertising during the UK's first Covid-19 lockdown, Watson tweeted: 'This marks a real shift in thinking by the gambling industry. Other than prohibitionists, it will be welcomed by all. The hard work of that cross party alliance of MPs is yielding positive results.'[31]

Not only was he praising his old friend but the 'prohibitionist' slur was borrowed from Dugher's lexicon. During the second and third lockdowns, the moratorium on ads that had won his praise was not repeated – a strange decision given that BGC members appeared to have acknowledged the potential risks. Neither Watson nor the BGC mentioned it.

The gambling industry's political connections only grew stronger in the run-up to the government review being launched. Remember the FOBT advocates Philip Davies and Laurence Robertson – and their hospitality from the industry? These are relationships that have only strengthened since then. In November 2020 the trade body began paying pro-gambling Robertson £2,000 for ten hours of work per month, a hefty rate of £200 per hour. It paid him, ostensibly, for advice on sport and safer gambling, although it wasn't clear what expertise Robertson had to offer. When I asked him for comment, Robertson said he would not advocate for the betting industry, nor make submissions to the gambling review on behalf of the cross-party parliamentary group on betting and gaming, of which he is a member.

Maybe he should have held out for more money, though, for his fellow parliamentary gambling advocate Philip Davies was doing rather better. Davies got paid a stunning £50,000 for 124 hours of advice provided to Ladbrokes and Coral owner Entain – about £400 an hour – this time on customer service and safer gambling.[32]

Entain insisted that the role saw Davies provide advice directly to its chief executive, Kenny Alexander. It was purely coincidence that two of Davies's former parliamentary aides occupied senior roles at the company.[33] Entain's head of safer gambling and external affairs, Sophie Dean, had worked for Davies from at least 2013 to 2018, according to parliamentary records and the Shipley MP's website. Meanwhile Entain's chief of corporate affairs, Grainne Hurst, had also worked for Davies as a parliamentary researcher between 2010 and 2012. When she was appointed, Entain said she would help the company 'lead the industry on responsible gambling and develop relationships with the media and external partners'. Just to complete the circle, another of Davies's former aides, Camilla Toogood, works at the BGC. She is its government relations manager.

What's more, Laurence Robertson and Philip Davies were far from alone in enjoying the largesse of the gambling industry. The Euro 2020 football tournament, which actually took place in 2021 due to the pandemic, was an irresistible opportunity for gambling companies to schmooze MPs in the run-up to the government's review of gambling laws.

Firms including Entain and Paddy Power, as well as the Betting and Gaming Council, entertained no fewer than eighteen MPs at the tournament.[34] There were twelve MPs at England's 2–1 semi-final win over Denmark alone. Factoring in tickets to Wimbledon and the races at Ascot, politicians accepted hospitality worth in excess of £93,000 that summer, the last before the conclusion of the government review. Influential invitees from the Conservative benches included two cabinet ministers, Brandon Lewis and Ben Wallace. Labour was represented by party leader Keir Starmer's parliamentary private secretary, Sharon Hodgson, and Mark Tami, an opposition whip. Some lucky recipients even spoke up in parliament on behalf of the industry. On 7 July, the Conservative MP for Blackpool South, Scott Benton, took his seat at Wembley to watch England beat

Denmark in the semi-final of Euro 2020, courtesy of the Ladbrokes Coral owner, Entain – a freebie worth £3,457. Less than four hours earlier, Benton – after declaring his interest of course – had warned parliament that the government gambling review must not be driven by anti-gambling "ideology". All in all, factoring in hospitality and wages for consulting jobs, the industry lavished about £225,000 on 28 lawmakers in the 18 months leading up to the gambling review.[35]

Unlike the VIP gamblers, none of these MPs had to lose large sums of money in order to have hospitality lavished upon them. Also unlike VIP gamblers, all of them would have a voice in, and a vote on, the future of gambling legislation.

But gambling firms have other weapons in their armoury, beyond buttering up MPs. They have also developed weird and wonderful lobbying strategies, often on the very expensive advice of some of the UK's top political and public relations consultants. C/T Group is part of the empire of spin run by Sir Lynton Crosby, the Australian public relations guru who advised Boris Johnson as mayor of London, successfully, and Theresa May as prime minister rather less so.[36] Crosby's outfit won a contract to work with Entain as it geared up for the UK government's 2021 gambling review. Its early work included commissioning a survey gauging public attitudes towards gambling regulation.

It also helped in other ways. In January 2021 Entain set up something called the Players' Panel, a group of its own customers, who wrote short articles highlighting the positive side of gambling and warning against overzealous state intervention in people's lives. That's a perfectly legitimate position, of course. But while Entain did disclose its involvement in the Players' Panel, it didn't always do so with the greatest of enthusiasm. The Players' Panel Facebook page, likely to be a key conduit for its message, didn't mention Entain once. Individual Twitter posts sent out by the group didn't either.[37]

The strategy felt reminiscent of, if not identical to, C/T Group's previous involvement in 'astroturfing' campaigns. Astroturfing is when vested interests create what looks like a grassroots organisation but is in fact a front for, say, corporations, trade bodies or political parties. The grassroots are artificial, hence the astroturf moniker. My *Guardian* colleague Jim Waterson had exposed C/T Group's astroturfing strategy on Facebook, where it had helped orchestrate campaigns shilling for Saudi Arabia's brutal regime, attacking renewable energy and cycle lanes, or promoting Brexit.[38] Entain declined to detail C/T Group's involvement in the Players' Panel and vehemently denied that the group was an astroturfing effort. But it couldn't deny that it had failed to carry out the sort of due diligence that a company should when purporting to be giving a platform to ordinary, innocent folk. One of the panel members had his own Facebook page containing a series of homophobic and racist slurs, as well as expressing support for a group called Stop Immigration Start Repatriation. The lack of rigour involved in setting up the Players' Panel showed that left-field lobbying tactics carried inherent danger.

In this case, the risk was that the campaign would blow up in Entain's face, which it did to some degree. But the danger that should concern ordinary people, rather than corporations, is that increasingly sophisticated lobbying of politicians ends up shoving them from pillar to post, listening to whichever voices shout loudest and are backed by the deepest pockets. We've seen before that, faced with the massed ranks of business interests, politicians can be bamboozled. Yes, we're back to FOBTs – only this time, at the very beginning of their story.

## CRYING WOLF

If ministers want to learn the lessons of the protracted FOBT saga – and avoid having the wool pulled over their eyes – they should also be wary of industry warnings about the law of unintended consequences. At the moment, the spectre that industry lobbyists raise to warn the government off doing anything too draconian is the black market. Rein in legitimate gambling firms too much, they say, and an unregulated industry will spring up to serve the needs of those who want to gamble more than they are allowed to under any new strictures. This industry, they warn, will be run by unscrupulous people who do not care at all about their customers.

There is undoubtedly some truth in the dangers of overeager regulation fuelling the black market. The oft-cited parallel is the Prohibition era in 1920s America, where the ban on alcohol fuelled organised crime and led to unregulated booze that caused serious health issues.

I spoke to one senior industry executive who is broadly supportive of tighter regulation but warns that the black market is more than just a paper tiger: 'Illegal offshore is a proper threat to bear in mind,' he said. 'You've got to be careful and reasonable in what you do. A £2 limit on table games [such as online roulette] would give you a problem with the black market.'

But history suggests that the industry's assessments aren't always as measured as that. When ministers were considering what to do about FOBTs, one of the issues they had to consider was what the impact would be on betting shops. They came to the conclusion that cutting the stake to £2 would cost the industry about £639 million. The estimate, it transpired, had been based in part on a report by accounting and consultancy firm KPMG, commissioned by the gambling industry.[39]

The report prophesied doom, with half of Britain's nearly nine thousand betting shops bound to close, at the loss of twenty thousand jobs, should FOBTs be curbed. These were dire predictions but they came with important caveats. The KPMG research included a disclaimer, namely that estimates of whether customers would respond to FOBT stake reduction by spending money on other betting products – thus mitigating the impact on the industry – had been 'agreed with the industry'. KPMG added that its findings 'should not therefore be regarded as suitable to be used or relied upon by any other person or for any other purpose'.

In other words, the gambling industry had paid for the report and set its terms of reference, and in return had received a crucial piece of evidence that it was using in an effort to convince ministers not to slaughter the fecund FOBT cash cow.

But the government appeared to take the report seriously. Not only was it used in Treasury modelling prior to the decision on FOBTs, but it was still proving influential after the government ultimately decided that the machines were a 'social blight'.

We've seen already that the Treasury, fearful of the impact on its tax take, was minded to postpone the stake-curbing measure until October 2019, to the dismay of sports minister Tracey Crouch, whose dramatic and influential response arguably saved the day. But it's worth noting why the Treasury had started dragging its feet in the first place.

In a select committee session, the chancellor of the Exchequer, Philip Hammond, cited an industry estimate of 15–21,000 job losses as good reason to give bookmakers a grace period before implementing the cut. These were the exact figures cited by KPMG. The industry-funded report, whose own authors had said it essentially could not be relied upon, was still carrying weight with the man in charge of Britain's finances.[40]

The proof has been in the pudding. Figures released by the Gambling Commission in 2020 showed that, rather than 4,500 shops closing, 639 had.[41] Not only was this far less apocalyptic than the industry had predicted, but it was also, at least in part, down to a shift that gambling firms were encouraging towards online betting, where costs are lower and opportunities to bet are thicker and faster.

Even within high-street shops, the spend on FOBTs, which had reached £1.2 billion a year by the time they were reined in, had not disappeared; in fact £400 million of it had shifted to lower-stakes products, which still allowed customers to lose money but limited the extreme cases where thousands of pounds can disappear in a matter of hours.[42] The overall outcome was that gamblers were no longer exposed to a particularly harmful form of play, while the industry had escaped critical damage.

Indeed, some operators even had one last trick up their sleeves to cushion the blow. In April 2020 HM Revenue & Customs lost a legal battle with bookmakers who claimed they had been overcharged VAT on the machines between 2005 and 2013. The cashback was initially estimated at £350 million[43] but it later transpired that William Hill pocketed a £230 million refund, while Entain banked £217.5 million and Betfred picked up £97 million. Bookies' ability to somehow emerge victorious even when they are complaining of defeat should give us cause to harbour significant concerns about how lobbyists are once more at the heart of the battle over the future of gambling in Britain.

The stakes this time are even higher, given the potential for the entire landscape to be altered. And once again we have seen a Big Four accounting firm roped in to produce a report seemingly tailored to the industry's requirements. This time it was PwC, commissioned by Entain, William Hill and The Stars Group – now part of Flutter – to assess the size of the black market in the UK. It found that 200,000 Britons wagered a combined £1.4 billion with black market operators every year.

The *Sun on Sunday* wouldn't normally run a news story about a relatively obscure report on black market gambling operators, but this time it did.[44] Journalist David Wooding warned that 'thousands of teens' were already playing the black market. It is unclear where this claim came from, as it was not in the report that the BGC had commissioned. Nevertheless it lent credence to the warning, which became a key part of the BGC's messaging. That must have pleased BGC communications chief Kevin Schofield, Wooding's erstwhile colleague at Rupert Murdoch's News UK media empire.

With the example of the FOBT jobs report in mind, there were reasons to be sceptical about the BGC's focus on the black market. For a start, the report was completed in August 2019 yet, despite its publicly stated fears about the dangers of the black market, the BGC chose not to publish it until 2020, just as the gambling review was kicking off. It was almost as if the self-described standards body had timed the report's release for lobbying purposes rather than releasing it as soon as possible to aid the fight against illicit gambling sites.

Secondly, there was cause for doubt about the report's findings. The Gambling Commission isn't given to public criticism of licensed operators, but in a letter to the APPG on gambling harm, chief executive Neil McArthur was about as critical of the PwC report as you're ever likely to see from the Commission. It was, he said, 'exaggerated' and 'not consistent with the intelligence picture'.[45] In estimating 27 million visits to black market sites, the report had not distinguished between real website visits by actual punters and automated clicks generated by bots.

Nevertheless the BGC persisted, again via Rupert Murdoch's mouthpiece, this time the *Sun*.[46] Within a month of releasing the original report, it published a follow-up indicating that wagers on the black market had doubled in the space of a year, during the pandemic, to £2.8 billion. That would be equivalent to about 2% of the total value of bets placed in the legitimate sector.

At the same time, bets placed with licensed online operators grew by a far more modest amount – somewhere close to 13%, according to the latest projection available at time of writing, based on Gambling Commission figures.[47] According to the PwC report, locked-down punters were spending only a little bit more money with the well-known licensed operators whose adverts they saw on a daily basis. Yet they were supposedly shovelling twice as much to illicit sites, which offered no guarantee of ever seeing their money again.

Paddy Power co-founder Stewart Kenny, who has as much, if not more, experience of lobbying on behalf of the betting industry than anyone at the BGC, is sceptical. 'We successfully lobbied over a twenty-year period to reduce betting duties [. . .] in Ireland and we always used the threat of the black market as our argument. I'd get my picture taken on the plane to the Isle of Man with a bookie's satchel. We always knew it was a bit of a bogus argument. You're not going to lend your credit card details to black market operators.'

## POLITICAL FUDGE

There are reasons beyond ingrained scepticism to take industry claims and promises with a pinch of salt. In Chapter 1, I mentioned the legal wrangle that ultimately ended in bookmakers agreeing to limit the number of FOBTs to four per shop. According to Richard Caborn, the sports minister at the time, the deal came about via a verbal agreement that seemed expedient then but which, in the fullness of time, proved deeply inadequate.

'The reason you got four in each of these shops was because I got them all round a table and said, "I've no powers [to stop FOBTs] but when I do get them I'll screw you into the ground",' Caborn told me. 'It was a compromise. They knew that if they'd gone wall to wall [with FOBTs], which they could have done, I'd have had no powers to intervene. But I said, "I'm in the process of putting a law onto the statute books and I'll screw you." What I didn't realise was that they'd get round that by setting up more shops.'

This was the clustering phenomenon we saw earlier in this chapter, where operators would open multiple branches on the same street just to fit more FOBTs in. Despite the cost of opening and running bricks-and-mortar premises, it was a strategy that made sense due to the immense profitability of the machines; by 2017 they made up more than half of high-street bookmakers' revenues, bringing in more than £50,000 per year, per machine.[48]

In theory there were mechanisms in place to prevent clustering. The Budd review had recommended giving local authorities the power to determine whether they wanted more betting shops or not. The government adopted this proposal but it was one that came complete with a loophole. Planning regulations bracketed betting shops together with financial institutions such as banks. 'As the internet started taking over banking and building societies consolidated, many of those premises became vacant,' said Jonathan Wolff, who served on the Budd review committee. 'Betting shops were able to just take over those premises without going through local planning. Our idea of local autonomy was irrelevant. There were enough people between the [Budd] report and the law to realise that they needed to make this change to the planning law but it didn't happen. That's my big regret.'

The legacy of this can be seen today, in the disproportionate concentration of gambling venues in the poorest areas. Successive studies have shown that betting shops, amusement arcades and bingo halls tend to open where people have the least disposable income to lose. The latest such study, released by the Standard Life Foundation in 2021, found that 21% of gambling venues were in the top decile of Britain's most deprived areas.[49] The figure for supermarkets was 10%.

Even in cases where local authorities have found ways to put barriers in place against the expansion of bookmakers' networks, cash-strapped councils have often had little incentive to do so. Thriving bookmakers offered a guaranteed flow of business-rates cash from businesses keen to open shop after shop to maximise their FOBT cash, often on high streets where there were already too many vacant lots. This effect only intensified after the global banking crash of 2008 and the government austerity that followed. 'It was either charity shops or betting shops and that's where they saw the revenue stream,' said Richard Caborn. The sports minister had made the mistake of believing that he was negotiating in good faith with a partner that might actually volunteer to take part in a deal that could not be circumnavigated. But gambling companies do not enter into a contract unless they have figured out the probabilities and expect to end up on the winning side.

Something similar was in the air throughout 2020 and 2021. Just as the bookmakers had offered an apparent concession on FOBTs ahead of the 2005 Gambling Act, the modern gambling industry heard the approaching drumbeat of the gambling review and the threat of draconian measures. And once more the industry sought to mark its own homework, to present oven-ready solutions that might appeal to underfunded regulators and politicians who would rather avoid the messy business of passing new laws. Caborn spoke of getting the industry 'around a table' to thrash out a deal on FOBTs that ultimately backfired. As we've seen, former culture secretary Jeremy Wright won a similarly questionable concession from industry bosses regarding funding for addiction treatment in 2019.

The extent to which any industry fights tooth and nail to preserve its own interests should come as no surprise. Gambling firms are by no means alone in working every possible angle they can to bolster their own prosperity. Indeed, the executives who run companies listed on the stock market have a legal obligation, known as 'fiduciary duty', to act in a way that maximises returns for their investors. But it's easy at times to forget just how powerful and connected these vested interests actually are. The prevailing wind in the media over the past five to ten years has turned against gambling companies. Many in the industry complain that they can no longer get a fair hearing in the court of public opinion, that their voices are being drowned out by hysterical prohibitionists. There is an element of truth in that. At the beginning of this chapter I mentioned that the media thrives on simple narratives. Pantomime villains shift papers and nuance tends to get lost. You can lay the blame for that at the door of either journalists or the people who consume news, or perhaps it's a mixture of both.

However, in detailing the frenetic game of lobbying and political influence that the gambling industry engages in, I hope to have shown that what's going on beneath the surface is just as important as the public debate, if not more so. Through their public affairs departments and their external lobbying groups, not to mention the hospitality they offer to MPs at the races or the football, gambling firms have direct access to the corridors of power, as well as informal channels that give them the ear of lawmakers. They employ thousands of people and pay hundreds of millions of pounds in tax and they never tire of reminding ministers of this, often presenting it as benevolence rather than the most basic of contributions that any business must make to the society that allows it to exist.

This confers power and status upon them and also provides the kind of wealth that can be deployed to great effect to influence democracy. A sob story in the *Guardian* or the *Daily Mail* about the suffering of someone with a gambling disorder carries power for a day, maybe a week. But that has limited reach compared to having a politician on the payroll or employing an army of the world's slickest lobbyists to come up with strategies to burnish your image.

When the gambling industry presents itself as hard done by, it's worth remembering the power it wields. It's also paramount that we do not forget quite how the industry has thrived, despite the odds supposedly being stacked against it. Over the past two decades, the

UK's gambling industry has flourished like few others, riding on a sea of punters' money. Some of that money has gone into lobbying; far more has gone into advertising, staff costs and investment in technology. But what about the rest?

# 9. THE HOUSE ALWAYS WINS:
# WHO GOT RICH?

To me, a gambler is someone who plays slot machines. I prefer to
own slot machines. It's a very good business being the house.

DONALD TRUMP, *THE ART OF THE DEAL* (1987)

Between April 2014 and September 2020, gamblers in the UK lost
more than £87 billion to the UK gambling industry.[1] You name
it, they poured their money into it, betting on anything from coin
pushers at seaside amusement arcades to high-roller tables at the
swanky casinos of London's Mayfair.

Company profits, of course, are rather lower. A sizeable chunk
of that £87 billion went out in taxes, including corporation tax and
the levies that the Treasury applies to each bet. Another hefty sum
goes on making the whole operation tick. Gambling firms spend
money on all sorts of things, from property leases and staff salaries
to software development, administrative costs and – from time to
time – regulatory penalties and lawsuits.

Luckily for a select few at the top of the tree, there is plenty of
loot left over when the chips are counted at the end of the day. In
the 2021 edition of the *Sunday Times* Rich List, the most definitive
rundown of Britain's wealthiest people, there are ten entries whose
source of wealth is listed as gambling.[2] These people didn't make
their money by betting on the horses, sidling up to the roulette table
or lumping their wage packet on Harry Kane to score first in a 3–1

win. Indeed, seasoned gamblers would tell you that it simply isn't possible to get rich that way. Even if you were extraordinarily lucky, bookmakers and casinos have the right to refuse service, just like any other business; anyone who gets into the winning habit tends to have their account shut down.

The real winners from gambling made their fortunes another way, by constructing vast cash-generative operations forged from the wagers of millions of punters.

A 2021 paper published in *The Lancet* described gambling as a 'rent-seeking industry that does not create wealth, but rather redistributes it from the deprived and vulnerable, including those affected by gambling-related harms, to the very rich, extracting money from its customers'.[3] Obviously that's a partisan view. Another way to view gambling's big beasts is as a mix of shrewd entrepreneurs and technology whizzes with a knack for seizing opportunities as soon as they arise.

What isn't in question is that they have become multimillionaires – even multibillionaires – in the process. I don't think it's controversial to argue that nobody with several billion pounds to their name can claim every single penny of it was made without, however indirectly, causing suffering to somebody else. That, some political and economic theorists might argue, is the nature of capitalism. But when we chronicle matters such as gambling-related poverty, addiction, family breakdown and suicide, we must also consider who is at the other end of that chain of events. When Jack Ritchie lost so much to gambling addiction that taking his own life seemed the only way out, whose bank accounts were slightly healthier as a result?

This is the world of the gambling fat cats: the entrepreneurs, the wheeler-dealers and the executives who sit at the top of a stream of money that flows inexorably upstream. It is a list that includes old-school bookmakers, technology geniuses, the occasional porn baroness and even Her Majesty's Government. It also includes me and, most likely, you too.

## BRITISH BETTING ROYALTY

### The Coates family

In 2020 bet365 boss Denise Coates paid herself a mountain of money, almost literally. Let's break it down: depending on who you ask, to qualify as a mountain in the UK a body of land must rise to over 2,000 feet above sea level. That's 610 metres if you are, like me, metrically minded. Denise Coates's pay and dividends for the year ending March 2020 amounted to £421 million.[4] If she had stacked that money up in £50 notes, the resulting tower would have been 950 metres high, easily reaching the required height threshold for mountain status.

She needn't have stopped stacking up the bills there, though. This alpine-sized payday was no one-off. It beat her previous record of £323 million from 2019, itself an increase on £265 million in 2018 and £220 million the year before that. In just three years she pocketed more than £1.2 billion, a sum broadly comparable to the annual economic output of a small country.[5]

Given these eye-watering sums, it may come as no surprise to find that Denise and her family are, according to the *Sunday Times*, among the top twenty richest people in Britain. Together with father Peter and brother John, they boast a net worth of nearly £8.5 billion, after an increase of £1 billion in 2020 during a global pandemic.[6] That's more than twice as much as Sir Richard Branson, the Virgin billionaire who owns a transatlantic airline and spends his spare cash exploring space.

Without doubt, bet365 is the definitive success story of online gambling in Britain. The company handled nearly £65 billion worth of bets a year in the year to March 2019. (It has since stopped disclosing this figure.) From those bets, it took £3 billion of revenue (effectively its winnings on the wagers), of which £791 million was operating profit. It hasn't always been this way. What is now a global enterprise with household-name status was, barely two decades ago, a fledgling start-up run out of a Portakabin in the Coateses' native Stoke-on-Trent, Staffordshire.

Denise's father, Peter, the son of a miner, had been a successful local businessman with a string of betting shops to his name. He was a self-made man, a shrewd entrepreneur and much admired in his home town. But it was Denise who harnessed the real jackpot opportunity. She was a graduate in econometrics, the use of statistical methods to analyse economic data. Armed with these analytical skills, Denise recognised the transformational effect that the internet would have on gambling. She bought the bet365.com domain name for $25,000 and borrowed against the company's bricks-and-mortar bookies to fund the development of sports betting technology.[7]

The company left its established but far more lethargic rivals in the dust. While stick-in-the-mud traditionalists such as Ladbrokes and William Hill were slowly building or buying the digital systems they needed, bet365 – with the help of a few internet whizz-kids – was already deploying them at great speed and hoovering up customers. Today bet365, a family business with a relatively short history, takes double the revenue of William Hill, which has a rich betting pedigree stretching back to the early twentieth century.

Some might question how a company that mostly takes casual bets on football from a headquarters in Stoke got to be so big. One explanation may be China. A *Guardian* investigation in 2014 found that punters in China – where, remember, betting is banned in all but a few tightly controlled arenas – had been jailed after apparently placing bets on the bet365 website.[8] The company said it was not breaking any laws but would not confirm whether or not it accepted stakes from customers in the People's Republic.

In accounts filed at Companies House, bet365 has said that offering any disclosure about where in the world it makes its money 'would be severely prejudicial to the interests of the group'.[9] But an online job ad revealed the company was looking for 'Chinese language customer account advisors'. It may, of course, be targeting only Chinese speakers in the UK or elsewhere.

How the Coates family have spent their money is just as note-worthy as how they made it. In 2004, just as the Labour government was putting together the 2005 Gambling Act, Peter Coates gave the Labour party £50,000. The following year, after the Act had gained royal assent, he handed over another £100,000. All in all, Coates has given Labour £225,000 since 2004, according to Electoral Commission records, putting him among the most loyal benefactors of the party that created the conditions for the modern British gambling industry. The flow of money stopped abruptly when Jeremy Corbyn was the party's leader. But Coates Sr may have turned the taps back on, if recent disclosures are anything to go by. He furnished the office of Keir Starmer MP with £25,000, helping the former lawyer claim victory in his bid to become Labour leader.[10]

The more visible outlay has been on football. In 2006 Peter Coates paid £10 million to buy his home town club, Stoke City. The price tag included a £1.7 million purchase and £8.3 million of promised investment. It worked too. Under Coates's ownership, the club finally made it into the Premier League, the world's most lucrative top-flight division. Once they got there, the billionaire put his money where his mouth was. Stoke City were by no means the league's biggest spenders but they punched significantly above their weight. Their record transfer was the £18.3 million paid to Porto for Giannelli Imbula in February 2016. At the end of the 2020–21 season there were three Premier League clubs that had never spent more on a player, despite the transfer fee inflation that has taken place since the Imbula deal.

Of course, this wasn't all just sunk cost; bet365 is the club's parent company and sponsors not only the team shirt but also its home ground, the 30,000-seater bet365 Stadium. This allows the company to supplement what it spends on TV advertising with a guaranteed visual presence on matchday broadcasts and even a mention every time commentators refer to the stadium in passing. As we've already seen, the chance to get your brand in front of literally billions of global football fans is far from a meagre opportunity.

It ought to be pointed out that a lot of the Coateses' money goes to charity and to the taxman.

The Coates family are the UK's biggest taxpayers, contributing £573 million to the state in a year, according to the *Sunday Times Tax List 2021*.[11] This does include payroll and corporation taxes from their bet365 empire, duties that any business pays. However, it is only fair to mention that Denise Coates pays significant taxes on her salary by putting herself on the payroll. She could, for instance, pay tax advisors to find intricate ways to squirrel the money away in tax havens instead. The family also injected £85 million into the Denise Coates Foundation in 2018–19 and committed £9.5 million towards charitable endeavours such as the Douglas Macmillan Hospice and Alzheimer's Research UK.[12] It is not clear whether any of the foundation's money is diverted towards gambling charities or addiction centres but the latest accounts do not detail any such organisations among the many recipients of its money.

The Coateses aren't the only ones to get mega-rich thanks to bet365, by the way. The company's finance director, veteran bookmaker Will Roseff, invested £1 million in the company in 2000. He has a 6.7% stake worth a cool £435 million.[13]

## The Done brothers

The meteoric rise of bet365 may be the definitive success story of British gambling but nobody epitomises the 'rags to riches' narrative better than Mancunian brothers Fred and Peter Done, the founders of Betfred. Their fortune of £1.2 billion[14] may pale in comparison to the £8.5 billion boasted by the Coateses but their ascendancy is, if anything, more impressive.

The brothers were raised in what Peter Done has described as the 'slums of Salford',[15] sleeping four siblings to a room in a modest two-up, two-down home. Both of them left school at fifteen, without any qualifications to speak of, and began working in their father's illegal bookmaking business. They opened their first bookmaker in 1967, funding the start-up costs – according to legend – with a winning wager on England's World Cup victory the year before.[16]

Building their empire into the 1,650-shop network over which they preside today was far from easy. Fred Done once told of being stabbed five times by an angry punter who had lost £50 on a horse ridden by Lester Piggott.[17]

Like Peter Coates, they have not shied away from diverting some of their vast resources into politics. Back in 2007 they donated £10,000 to Labour MP Hazel Blears, who at the time represented their native Salford, but they appear to have drifted to the right with age, or at least to have shifted their spending to those in government. The Dones have been extremely generous donors to the Conservative party over the past few years, giving £375,000 since 2016 via their holding company, Rainy City Investments. Electoral Commission records also show a non-cash donation in 2011 worth £4,680 to the Shipley MP Philip Davies, who, as we've seen, is a frequent and vociferous advocate for the gambling industry.[18]

The pair also have a charitable trust and Fred once donated Betfred's profits from the first day of the Cheltenham Festival to the Royal Manchester Children's Hospital.[19] Another donation, to the

Jessie May children's charity, was also linked to their betting interests; they promised to give £200 for every century break played at the World Snooker Championship, rounded up to £40,000.[20]

These days much of their money comes from services other than gambling. They control the highly profitable Peninsula Business Services, a group housing more than ten companies in everything from employment law to workplace health and human resources. Even this other part of their business empire can't be entirely separated from gambling, though. Peninsula includes Health Assured, a business that provides workplace services such as employee health and well-being programmes. Clients come from both the private and the public sectors, including multiple NHS trusts. The programmes that Health Assured provides include telephone advice on gambling addiction. In other words, the Done brothers get gamblers' money when they bet and their bosses' money when they seek help to stop betting too.[21] In practice, not much of Health Assured's business comes from gambling addiction – apparently only 0.1% of calls (although the company did not say how many calls it receives a year).

Another part of the Done business empire may have a close connection to the problems caused by gambling. Fred Done also invested £150,000 in Angel Advance, a debt management company set up in 2013 and part-owned by other members of the Done family. Angel Advance derives its revenues from advising people struggling with debt. They can pay the company a fee to negotiate reduced repayments with creditors on their behalf. The Angel Advance website even offers helpful 'money saving tips', such as switching to a cheaper supermarket, cutting down on takeaways or letting a spare room to a lodger. When I first reported on the company in January 2020,[22] its budgeting tips did not include stopping gambling. The website did advise customers in difficulty to contact the Samaritans if they were struggling to deal with debt, but while the list of issues they might be facing included job-related stress, alcohol or drug abuse and suicidal thoughts, gambling did not feature. Angel Advance has since updated its website to include a section on gambling, its relationship to debt, and resources on how to quit. The company has also undergone a change of leadership. Its chief executive, Joanne Whittaker, stepped down in 2021 to take up the top job at Betfred.[23]

This aspect of the Dones' business empire has raised questions over the potential conflict of interest in profiting both from gambling and from the provision of services to those seeking treatment for an addiction to it. 'They get paid when you gamble, they get paid when you seek help for it and they get paid when you try to clear your debts,' said Labour MP Carolyn Harris when the Dones' involvement in these businesses emerged.

Like the Coates family, the Dones deserve recognition for charitable endeavours and their contribution to the taxman. They were third in the *Sunday Times* Tax List 2021, contributing £191 million.[24] Again, this included corporation tax and payroll tax from their businesses.

## TECH UPSTARTS

### Teddy Sagi

Sandwiched in between the Dones and the Coateses, in second place among the UK's gambling elite with a fortune of about £3.8 billion, is Teddy Sagi.[25] If you gamble online, the chances are that you've done so using software designed by Playtech, founded by the Israeli entrepreneur in 1999. Most of the UK's major players – William Hill, Ladbrokes and bet365 among them – have used Playtech's software to build their online businesses and Sagi has grown immensely rich as a result.

The course of success hasn't always run smoothly. Sagi was convicted in Israel of bribery and securities fraud in 1996 and jailed for nine months.[26] But the phenomenal growth of Playtech, founded after his release, has helped confine those days to the annals of history. Over the past few years Sagi has burnished his status as a multibillionaire by gradually selling out of Playtech altogether,[27] offloading the remains of his stake for $87 million, one of a series of sales that included a hefty 12% holding in 2016 that netted him £329 million. The *Sunday Times* Rich List estimated his 2021 wealth at £3.8 billion.[28]

He has not been shy about spending the proceeds to splash out on the finer things in life, such as a house on Israel's most expensive road, Galei Tchelet Street.[29] He has also invested in real estate and technology companies, but his most visible venture in the UK is his ownership of the majority of Camden Market in North London, a mecca for tourists seeking cheap clothing and rock and roll memorabilia. Under his ownership it has grown into London's second-largest tourist attraction after Buckingham Palace.[30]

## Mark Scheinberg

Mark Scheinberg is the richest person on the Isle of Man, an offshore centre famed for playing host to companies and trusts seeking to benefit from the degree of secrecy and tax advantage afforded to the Crown dependency.

Scheinberg and his father, Isai, co-founded the PokerStars website in 2001, in the very early days of internet gambling. It rapidly became the world's leading online poker business, acquiring rival Full Tilt Poker in 2012 before eventually being bought out in 2014 by the Canadian stock-market-listed gambling giant Amaya for $4.9 billion.[31] The buyout made Mark Scheinberg a billionaire several times over.

That wealth was not amassed without consequences, at least not for his father. In March 2020 Isai pleaded guilty to running an illegal internet gambling operation after a ten-year battle with US authorities that began when law enforcement bodies launched a nationwide crackdown in 2011.[32] Online poker had been tolerated, despite laws that supposedly prevented it, but eventually the Department of Justice decided enough was enough and Scheinberg Sr – along with three other chief executives – was arrested and charged. He told the court that he knew running an online poker business was illegal in the US but that he'd continued to do so nonetheless. In late 2020 he was sentenced to time already served – meaning no jail time – and paid a $30,000 fine.[33]

## Ruth Parasol

Few gambling entrepreneurs can boast as colourful a career as Ruth Parasol, the co-founder of online poker and casino firm PartyGaming. She is often labelled as an 'internet porn princess' but it was gambling that really made her. Her father, Richard, made a name for himself in California as 'a real hustler', according to a former business rival who spoke to the *Guardian* in 2005, thanks to his network of massage parlours in the Tenderloin red-light district of San Francisco.[34]

Although she qualified as a lawyer, Ruth followed her father into the sex industry, running telephone-sex chatlines that horny callers would dial for relief. The father-daughter team went on to set up some of the earliest 'sex-camming' businesses; at one stage their company IEG owned a warehouse in Seattle where fourteen women, working in shifts, performed for video cameras against a backdrop of one of four themed environments: a bedroom, a health club, a shower and a dungeon. As well as paying to watch them get naked, punters could ring the warehouse on premium-rate phone lines and put their special requests to the women. Parasol eventually left the sex industry and moved into something even more lucrative by setting up PartyGaming. Established with the help of computer whizz Anurag Dikshit, who wrote the site's original software, the business derived the bulk of its income from its phenomenally successful partypoker.com website. Like Scheinberg's PokerStars, the site grew rapidly but also attracted the attention of the US authorities. In 2009 the business paid a $105 million settlement to avoid prosecution.

Ruth Parasol was worth £780 million in 2020, thanks to assets including a global real estate portfolio.[35] She also has a philanthropic streak. Her Gibraltar-based Parasol Foundation Trust works with Cambridge University, the Prince's Trust and the Victoria and Albert Museum, among other organisations, making grants in areas such as education, health and heritage.

PartyGaming floated on the stock market in 2005 with a value of £4.7 billion and subsequently merged with Austrian rival bwin before eventually being subsumed into the FTSE behemoth that is GVC Holdings.

## Martin Moshal

South African Martin Moshal is one of the least visible betting entrepreneurs in the world, certainly when it comes to his connections to the empire he built. For years it was an open secret that Moshal was one of the chief backers behind Betway, the online gambling firm whose UK presence includes the sponsorship of Premier League football team West Ham United, but his involvement did not become public until 2020, after the *Daily Mail* tracked down a spokesman for him in the wake of a story it had written about Betway and its 'grooming' of gambling addicts. The newspaper established that Moshal was the beneficiary of an Isle of Man-based trust that is a shareholder of Betway. The venture capitalist later confirmed that this was the case.[36]

Moshal made much of his fortune from his home in Durban, where he patented a series of technological solutions for the online gambling world and developed them via his company Microgaming. The company has since become one of the industry's leading software players and regularly buys out one of the largest stands at the industry's annual conference and trade show in London, a bustling affair that has occasionally attracted criticism for its tendency to deploy scantily clad models, and even pole-dancers, for the visual delight of the mostly male coterie of executives who attend.[37]

'By the mid-2000s, Microgaming was said to supply more than a third of the online gaming market and clients estimated it was bringing in more than £400 million of revenue annually,' the *Daily Mail* wrote.

Moshal drew on his expertise to set up Betway's online casino and poker platforms and has since amassed a stake in it, although it is not clear to what extent. The website of his philanthropic enterprise, the Moshal Foundation, mentions none of this, saying only that he 'started a software contracting company, which he later sold'.

He and his wife, Ilana, once owned a seven-bedroom mansion in Hampstead now worth £7.8 million.

## FOBT FRONTIERSMEN

Fixed-odds betting terminals are probably the most controversial gambling product of recent years. As detailed earlier in the book, they became a lightning rod for criticism of the gambling industry and even triggered a political rebellion. They made headlines on an almost daily basis at one stage, but far less has been written about some of those who made their money, entirely legally, out of them.

### Stephen Frater

The granddaddy of the FOBT is Stephen Frater, a gambling industry veteran who previously worked for Mecca Bingo and William Hill, where he was head of customer relations. In 1997 he co-founded The Global Draw, the company that first brought internet-based machine gaming to British betting shops. By 2005 the Ealing-based outfit was Britain's fastest-growing private company. Its extraordinary success was detailed in a *Daily Telegraph* feature headlined 'Heroes of Britain's private sector'.[38] 'Sales of its fixed-odds betting terminals increased from £472,000 to £32m in the past four years,' the *Telegraph* gushed. 'In 2003–4 sales at the company grew by more than 300 per cent.'

The following year, Frater cashed in, selling the business for \$183 million.[39] It is not clear what his personal gain on the sale was, but he stayed on and has since gone on to work for the company that bought him out, Scientific Games.

According to a *Daily Mirror* article in 2014, Frater had earned £18 million running The Global Draw as a subsidiary of Scientific Games and owned a £3 million five-bedroom mansion in Essex with an indoor swimming pool.[40]

## Luke Alvarez

Cambridge University philosophy graduate Luke Alvarez entered the world of gambling much later than Frater and was more of a mobile gaming pioneer than a machine man. Having worked in software in the US, he spotted the massive opportunity in digital gambling, online and off.

When he started out in a small Regent Street office, smartphones did not yet exist and mobile gambling was limited to bets taken by text message. As the industry developed, his business, Inspired Gaming, changed with the times.[41] It was bought by Vitruvian Partners in 2010 for £74 million. Alvarez retained leadership of the company and by 2015 it had become a leading player in virtual sports as well as in FOBTs, providing about half of the 34,000 machines dotted around the UK.[42]

FOBTs were yet to attract the level of public opprobrium that eventually saw them all but banned. Inspired was named among the London Stock Exchange Group's '1,000 Companies to Inspire Britain'[43] and George Osborne, chancellor of the Exchequer at the time, had even taken Alvarez along on a 2013 trade mission to China, where the company won a contract to supply the country's state-run lottery.[44]

'Most players are having fun,' Alvarez told the *Daily Telegraph* in 2015. 'By engaging in exciting games that have a bit of volatility, it gives them a buzz. We want people to win money, and to have fun playing.'[45]

In 2016, six years after it was sold for £74 million, a US-based acquisition vehicle bought the business for £200 million.

## A. Lorne Weil

The sales of both The Global Draw and Inspired Gaming have one common denominator: A. Lorne Weil was on the other end of the deal. The American multimillionaire is virtually unknown in the UK but he is the beneficiary of many a spin on FOBT roulette. Weil built the Las Vegas-based gambling technology giant Scientific Games.[46]

Filings with the US Securities and Exchange Commission (SEC) reveal that Weil was paid about $56 million for his final five years as chief executive of Scientific Games, after helping transform the company from a relative minnow with revenues of $48 million into a giant pulling in $1.7 billion annually.[47] The company bought The Global Draw in 2006, and in 2011 it bought Ashton-under-Lyne company Barcrest, a supplier of gaming content to the machines.

Weil left Scientific Games in 2013 but he wasn't finished in the FOBT business. Having built the empire behind thousands of the UK's FOBTs, he used some of the wealth he had amassed in the process to repeat the trick, setting up an acquisition vehicle, roping in some fellow investors and leading the £200 million takeover of Scientific Games's main UK rival, Alvarez's Inspired Gaming. The resulting business, Inspired Entertainment, Inc., has since been eyeing major growth, telling investors in 2017 that it expected to increase operating profits from $34 million in 2015 to $62 million in 2018. It promised to do this by expanding in the UK and further afield, capitalising on gamblers' almost insatiable appetite for the FOBT experience. Such growth meant major returns for Weil, who owned 11.9% of the company.

SEC filings show that his children, through a family trust, also have plenty to gain from his gambling wealth, even though they already enjoy wealth unimaginable to most people who've ploughed money into a FOBT. His son, B. Luke Weil, appeared in the 2003 film *Born Rich: Children of the Insanely Wealthy*, a documentary about the young heirs to family fortunes, which also featured a young Ivanka Trump. In one scene Weil Jr refers to the power that his father's money afforded him at university: 'I can just say: "Fuck you. I'm from New York. My family can buy your family. Piss off." And this is petty, and this is weak, and this is very underhanded, but it's so easy, you know?'


## THE OLD SCHOOL

If there is such a thing as betting royalty, you won't find the tech entrepreneurs among them. They may be wealthy but they are very much the gambling equivalent of 'new money'. They've got the wealth – more of it, in fact – but do they have the pedigree? That's not to say that a history in the British gambling scene makes you an aristocrat. In fact, some of the wealthiest people in British gambling owe their success to rather insalubrious environments. Namely, the greyhound track.


### Victor Chandler

In the world of bookmaking entrepreneurship, the Chandlers are thoroughbreds. William Chandler (1880–1946) began his career as a bookmaker at London's White City greyhound track and went on to own the Walthamstow Stadium track. His son, Victor Chandler Sr, took on the bookmaking business he'd built, and in 1974 Victor Chandler Jr took up the baton in turn.[48]

The younger Victor may have come from the old school but he was possessed of a shrewd understanding of how gambling was developing. He was taking telephone bets on football from Asian clients in the mid-1990s, recognising the allure of English football to foreign bettors decades before it became a global multibillion-pound business. He even set up a company in Antigua and Barbuda to allow wealthy customers to place wagers without paying UK tax on them.[49]

In 1999 he became the first major British bookmaker to go offshore, after obtaining a Gibraltar betting licence, setting the scene for the exodus of companies to tax-light jurisdictions such as Malta and Gibraltar. Known these days as BetVictor, the business has thrived and Victor Chandler was worth an estimated £230 million as of 2018.[50]

## Michael Tabor

Some of Chandler's wealth comes from the 2014 sale of his 55% stake in the family business to one of BetVictor's founding shareholders, Michael Tabor, for an undisclosed sum. Like Chandler, Tabor has greyhound racing in his bones. The glassmaker's son used to spend a couple of days a week at the Hendon Stadium, now Brent Cross Shopping Centre, watching the dogs race.

He became a familiar sight at both greyhound and horse racing tracks, where his bookmaking nous earned him a reputation as a man with a fearsome eye for detail and an unquenchable thirst for gaining an edge. His vaulting ambition saw him fall foul of racing authorities when he was banned for three years in 1970 for paying jockeys for information.[51]

Tabor moved into off-course betting with the purchase of the Arthur Prince bookmaking chain, which he sold in 1995 for £27 million, and enjoyed considerable success in racehorse ownership. He is based in Monte Carlo but also has a £25 million Barbados home, owns a third of the island's Sandy Lane Hotel and has a £14.5 million stake in British pubs group Mitchells & Butlers.

## THE COMPANY MEN

If you can't own a gambling business, the next best thing is to run one. UK financial regulations require stock-market-listed companies to disclose their pay arrangements, which offers an insight into the substantial rewards for the men – because they are almost invariably men – who manage vast swathes of Britain's gambling industry.

### Entain

Formerly known as GVC, Entain is a globe-straddling behemoth that came about through a series of mergers and acquisitions and now includes a diverse portfolio of brands ranging from Ladbrokes and Coral to Foxy Bingo and Party Casino.

Former chief executive Kenny Alexander masterminded the growth of the business from 2007, when it was listed on the junior AIM stock market and valued at just £27 million. By 2021 it was a FTSE giant so supremely confident in its prospects that its board felt able to turn down a bid of £8 billion from US casino firm MGM in January 2021, a decision that was proved right as the company's value continued to soar.[52] Alexander had stepped down by then but he has been handsomely rewarded for steering the company through such phenomenal growth.

Over the last six years of his tenure alone, Alexander took home £71 million in cash and shares, according to the company's annual reports. He held a further £13.3 million in shares at the end of 2019, some from share awards given to him by the company and some purchases from his own pocket.[53] Shareholders have, from time to time, staged pay rebellions at the company's annual meeting, voting against its pay plans.[54] But while the company's generous pay policy has been reined in, it's safe to assume that Alexander made at least £100 million from the company during his tenure.

Alexander is a gambling enthusiast in his private life and doesn't mind who knows it. He told the *Sunday Times* in 2015[55] that he had been indulging since the age of thirteen, admitted to the *Evening Standard* in 2017[56] that he had considered becoming a professional poker player, and confided to the *Daily Telegraph* in 2016 that he bet every day and owned four racehorses.[57] In May 2021 he was fined £1,000 by a court after a late-night escapade in which he stole a takeaway driver's car from outside a kebab shop and went on a drunken joyride.[58] No, I didn't believe it at first either.

## William Hill

If Alexander was well remunerated for turning GVC/Entain from a minnow into a whale, William Hill has been rather less munificent, in part because it hasn't experienced the stellar growth of its rival. Between 2010 and 2019 the three chief executives who served during that period earned £21.3 million between them,[59] roughly the same as what Kenny Alexander made in a single year on three occasions over the same period. It's tough being the boss of William Hill.

## Paddy Power

The company that owns Paddy Power Betfair also pays its bosses rather less handsomely than Entain, at least until recently. Flutter Entertainment CEO Peter Jackson took home just over £2 million in cash and shares in 2019, a slight improvement on the £1.6 million he'd got the previous year, his first in the job. However, 2020 was different. A share-based bonus inflated Jackson's pay to £7.5 million,[60] as a mega-merger with The Stars Group saw Flutter Entertainment become the world's largest online gambling company.

## Playtech

Software firm Playtech paid chief executive Mor Weizer £1.9 million in 2020, taking the total dished out to the company's long-time boss to £21.3 million since 2010. The biggest award was the £4.2 million he received in 2010.[61] The company suffered a revolt against pay from its investors in every one of the three years leading up to 2019, when the remuneration scheme was subject to a rebellion from 64% of voting shareholders, despite the company's claims to have consulted them.[62] In practice, pay revolts like these – and the ones at Entain – do little but cause minor embarrassment and a few awkward conversations with shareholders. Investors can stop a company's future pay plans but can't halt deals that have already been agreed. They tend to opt for symbolic gestures against overly generous pay rather than actually thwarting the bosses of the companies in which they invest their cash.

## 888

Online casino company 888 Holdings has been pretty good to its bosses over the years. Since 2010 they have collected £25 million from the company, including a bumper £8.7 million deal for former boss Itai Frieberger in 2017.[63] That was the same year the company was fined a record £7.8 million by the Gambling Commission over failures to protect vulnerable customers.

## YOU, ME AND HMG

At the beginning of this chapter I calculated that the gambling industry won about £87 billion from British punters between April

2014 and September 2020. By now that figure will most likely have surpassed £100 billion. Over that same period, according to the Office for National Statistics, the industry coughed up about £16 billion in levies on betting.[64] In 2019, the last year for which figures are available, that amounted to £3 billion, or about 0.35% of the government's expenditure of £821 billion that year.

That 0.35% doesn't sound like a great deal but it depends on how you look at it. For instance, it's about 3% of the annual education budget, equivalent to eleven days of schooling. Drill down to the level of individual projects and the £3 billion starts to look larger still. The brand-new Royal Liverpool University Hospital, which has been beset by design flaws, delays and the collapse of Carillion, the government contractor behind it, is set to cost a little over £1 billion. A year of gaming duty could buy you three such hospitals, cost overruns and all. (Although we should not forget about the half a billion pounds in VAT that bookies reclaimed in 2020, as documented in Chapter 8.) The contribution goes beyond what levies raise too. Factoring in benefits such as corporation tax and jobs, accountancy firm EY estimates that the sector contributed £7.7 billion to the economy in 2019 (although it should be said that this was another report commissioned by the Betting and Gaming Council).[65]

To document gambling's contribution to the economy isn't to say that the industry is somehow doing Britain a favour. The UK remains one of the world's most lucrative markets and the firms that do business here do so in full knowledge of the taxation regime. They continue to do so because there is plenty left over once the taxman takes his slice. Nor are they alone in being asked to give a bit back. All businesses are taxed, especially ones that are also acknowledged to cause harm. Duty on alcohol, a well-documented factor in social problems, hit £12 billion in 2019.[66] It's a 'polluter pays' principle that ensures industries – to some extent, at least – clean up after themselves. Those of a more religious persuasion might compare it to an indulgence in Catholicism. You hand over some cash in exchange for reduced punishment for your sins, whether the sanction you're trying to escape is eternal hellfire or tougher regulation.

But money is money. In the *Sunday Times* Tax List 2021, Denise Coates came in first at £573 million, with the Done brothers in third, on £191 million. There would have been more tax-efficient ways for them to have made their money – elaborate tax avoidance schemes, offshore trusts and all sorts of chicanery like that. They chose not to take them. Nobody could deny that the taxman – and by extension the public – is taking a cut. The point I'm driving at is that the money the gambling industry takes from punters is being spent on us. Catch the bus, go to A&E, send your children to school, and you can't escape the fact that, somewhere down the line, some of it was funded by gambling and, by extension, addiction.

I should point out, of course, that the tax benefit is offset – to a degree that is the subject of some dispute – by gambling's social cost. In 2016 the Institute for Public Policy Research estimated that problem gambling cost the public purse £1.2 billion a year.[67] Another think tank, the Social Market Foundation, has estimated that lower spending on gambling would actually boost UK output, with both jobs and tax receipts increasing as money is spent in more productive parts of the economy.[68]

This, of course, is a hypothesis that the gambling industry hotly disputes. Yet, uncertain as the taxpayer's benefit may be, there are more direct ways in which many of us profit from gambling. For instance, the largest shareholder in Entain at time of writing is the giant investment firm Standard Life Aberdeen, recently renamed abrdn, which manages £535 billion on behalf of wealthy individuals but also the pension funds of ordinary people, businesses, local authorities and charities.

The same is true of any stock-market-listed gambling firm,

whether it's William Hill, Flutter Entertainment or 888 Casino. Every one of them counts major investment institutions among its top shareholders. Those institutions see the value of the assets they manage on behalf of clients increase when the value of those stocks goes up, not to mention the benefit of regular dividends. In the final year before the pandemic, when major companies cancelled shareholder payouts to conserve cash and avoid public opprobrium, that quartet of firms paid their shareholders £500 million between them.[69]

For anyone determined to reduce their reliance on gambling for their retirement income, there are options. Increasingly, pension funds have tightened up their environmental, social and governance (ESG) criteria, or offered customers savings products tailored to particular moral or ethical concerns. In 2019 Norway's largest pension fund, KLP, decided, in the words of the *Financial Times*, to 'purge so-called "sin stocks" from its portfolio'. That meant a powerhouse $80 billion fund selling out of any company that derived more than 5% of its revenue from alcohol or gambling.[70] Its clients, the people whose money it manages, would have noticed nothing unless they were particularly keen on ethical investing – or, of course, particularly opposed to it.

These are exceptions rather than the rule. Many investment institutions have abandoned tobacco and, in recent years, fossil fuels. But for the most part, gambling isn't on the purge list and many investment funds have no robust ESG policy to speak of, or simply put money almost indiscriminately into companies listed on the FTSE, whoever they may be.

What this means is that the retirement income of hundreds of thousands of people, probably millions, is in some small way dependent on the health of the gambling sector.

This is a systemic issue. We do not choose to benefit from gambling but nor can we choose not to. We are implicated, we benefit, and that must be factored into any conversation about how much or how little we want to rein in the betting industry. That conversation is happening already.

# 10. NEW FRONTIERS: WHAT'S NEXT?

Gambling is the future on the internet.
You can only look at so many dirty pictures.

SIMON NOBLE, FOUNDER OF THE FIRST ONLINE SPORTSBOOK

Like all seasoned gamblers should do, it's time to take stock and assess our position. Where are we and what comes next?

Everything that has happened in the world of gambling over the past couple of decades has changed our society in ways that we don't yet understand but which are unlikely to be reversed. The genie is out of the bottle. Our minds have been altered by the jazzy advertising campaigns, by the psychological games of cat-and-mouse on which gambling thrives. Our institutions have given over time and effort to the political and regulatory wrangling that has accompanied the changing face of gambling. Football, the national sport, has become almost an afterthought to betting among some sections of society. 'It matters more when there's money on it,' Sky Bet tell us, as if bored by a Premier League that they usually claim is the most exciting entertainment product on the planet. At the extreme end of the spectrum, our friends and families have been scarred by addiction and suicide, or even by bog-standard financial difficulty, the kind that doesn't hit the headlines but closes doors in life, that feeds the stress eating away at our mental health and our relationships. Meanwhile billions upon billions have flowed into the pockets of the gambling industry, its executives, investors and mega-rich entrepreneurs.

But is the world we live in now really so very different from that of 2005, when the modern gambling landscape began to take shape? What change awaits in the next two decades, and the two after that? What's in store for the industry and for gamblers themselves? And what new challenges are emerging as the industry shapeshifts and expands into new areas, both technological and geographical?

Despite the pain visited on so many people and businesses by the Covid-19 pandemic, there's little doubt that the world-leading gambling industry that New Labour's 2005 Gambling Act successfully sought to create has emerged in rude health. Witness, for instance, the stock market value of some of the UK's largest players before the pandemic and after it.

On 1 January 2020, with much of the world still blissfully ignorant of Covid-19, the stock market valued the three major London-listed gambling companies – Entain, William Hill and Flutter – at a combined £14 billion.[1] Between then and mid-August 2021, the FTSE 100 – London's index of leading stocks – fell by 3%. Over that same period the price tag of Entain and Flutter hit a combined £34 billion. Las Vegas casino company Caesars bought William Hill for £2.9 billion, while Entain was the subject of a £16 billion bid from US fantasy sports outfit DraftKings, as of October 2021. The sector has proved a soar-away success among investors, amid a global pandemic. As businesses in sectors such as travel and hospitality battled hurricane-force headwinds, gambling firms sailed through the crisis virtually unscathed, even emboldened and re-energised. One reason for this is that, unlike physical goods, gambling can be delivered to the consumer instantaneously via the internet.

Yes, the industry suffered due to the lengthy coronavirus-enforced closure of the high street, with some 7,700 bookmakers' shops affected. But the financially promising counterpoint to that was a massive shift towards internet betting, where costs are significantly lower. Gamblers bored by lockdown quickly turned to online casino games and virtual slot machines that could be accessed from their sofas. Figures from the Gambling Commission, collated from operators accounting for 80% of the online market, illustrate the increase. Punters lost £325 million online in March 2019, increasing to £432.8 million in the same month of 2020, including the first two weeks of the UK's first lockdown. By April 2021, after a year in which millions of people had spent much of their time at home with little to entertain them, the monthly online take had jumped to £560 million.[2]

A significant chunk of the increase has come from growth in revenue from online slot machines, which carry some of the highest addiction rates of any gambling product. At the start of the pandemic there were 2.6 million active slots players, rising to more than 3.2 million a year later, an extra 600,000 customers. The volume of bets they placed per month rose from just under 4.5 billion to 6 billion. The number of times someone spent more than an hour playing virtual slot machines jumped from 1.9 million per month to 2.6 million.

And, as restrictions on sports such as football, rugby and horse racing began to ease and fixtures resumed, the industry found that the nation's appetite for online wagers had increased. The industry's take from online sports was £160 million the month that the pandemic struck, then £61 million in April 2020 due to the cancellation of fixtures. When sport returned punters lost as much as £320 million in a month – the typically frenetic December period – and were regularly still losing more than £250 million a month throughout 2021.[3]

There are upsides and downsides to this for those interested in minimising gambling-related harm. Those who gamble online can do so more furtively and more feverishly. That's the truth behind those stories of spouses who lost everything without their partner knowing a thing. Yet, in theory at least, it should also be easier for gambling companies to track them, using data intelligently to identify patterns indicating problem play.

From a financial perspective the upsides are plain. The pandemic has accelerated a migration that was already happening, away from expensive bricks-and-mortar stores, with their burdensome costs such as rent and staff, towards the cheaper-to-run, higher-margin digital product. Undoubtedly this means some pain in the short term – change always does. The people most likely to feel that pain aren't gambling investors or bosses but those who work behind the counter. There will be fewer high-street bookmakers by 2023 than there would have been had the pandemic never happened. That's bad news for jobs but it's good news, in the long term, for investors.

There is another, more fundamental, reason why the markets love British gambling companies right now. They are breaking America. Unlike the UK, which consciously set about becoming the global centre of a legitimate, regulated gambling industry, the US took a more prohibitionist approach until very recently. Fans of online poker will remember all too well the events of 'Black Friday', the day in April 2011 when the US Department of Justice seized the web domains of the world's largest online poker companies.[4] Online poker remains illegal in most US states, although illicit sites based offshore have stepped in to fill the gap.

Until fairly recently sports betting was off-limits too. In May 2018 all that changed. The Supreme Court overturned a decades-old ban, giving the green light for the union's fifty states to legalise and regulate it.[5] By mid-April 2021 twenty-two states had already done so and all but three were on the verge or had at least set the process in motion. The rewards on offer for companies that seize the opportunity are huge. Take California, for instance, a state full of people who enjoy the occasional weekend jaunt to the casinos of Las Vegas. The Golden State also has an economy larger than that of the UK. Within years it could easily become one of the world's most lucrative sports betting markets. Now expand that to encompass the rest of the US, a wealthy nation in love with both sport and risk. It's a new gold rush.

In 2021 J.P. Morgan estimated that the US sports betting market would hit $9.2 billion (£6.5 billion) by 2025, nearly three times the size of the UK market.[6] That would be an extraordinary rate of growth in seven years, coming from a standing start.

Armed with fifteen years of experience in a regulated Anglo-Saxon market with plenty of similarities to the US, British industry players have been quick out of the starting blocks. Today all of the major UK gambling firms have sizeable and growing partnerships with US firms. Indeed, some deep-pocketed US businesses have simply opted to buy out their Limey cousins rather than work together. William Hill was scooped up by Las Vegas casino firm Caesars Entertainment. Ladbrokes owner Entain became a target for its US joint venture partner MGM Resorts. Entain rebuffed the corporation's attentions but a second approach was on the cards as of August 2021. Flutter, meanwhile, merged with the US fantasy sports business FanDuel and then merged again, with Canada's The Stars Group, creating a London-listed giant worth more than £25 billion.

Whether the pioneers of the British gambling industry choose to go it alone or accept big bucks from takeover suitors, the future looks incredibly bright as the US opens up: more bets, more losses, more money. Some of the biggest opportunities lie in marrying traditional sports betting with hugely popular fantasy sports websites such as FanDuel and DraftKings. UK football fans might play Fantasy Premier League, a competition that allows you to pick your football team and potentially win cash prizes if the players you choose do well. The likes of FanDuel have taken that and melded it with betting, creating a highly potent sports betting product that pays out financial rewards for success in what is a game partly of skill but also partly of chance. It's a gambling product unlike anything that has so far been available in the UK.

What US regulators and politicians must now reckon with is the inevitable fallout if gambling becomes much more prevalent in the US, yet not enough is done to educate people or prevent harm. For a long time the UK has underperformed in its duty to protect people from danger and to help them when that danger manifests as harm. Whether the US system is ready for what is coming should be a matter of concern in a country whose welfare system historically offers a threadbare safety net to those suffering from poor physical and mental health.

Mouth-watering opportunities lie ahead for gambling firms elsewhere too, including in countries where the state infrastructure may be even less well placed to counter harms. In sub-Saharan Africa, the use of smartphones is much more widespread than many people might expect of a continent that also suffers from so much poverty. In the absence of good national and international analogue communications infrastructure, mobile payments became normal even in rural, impoverished areas long before they caught on in so-called developed countries. This has made internet gambling easily accessible to hundreds of millions of potential new punters living in fast-growing economies where demographics skew towards younger cohorts with an appetite for risk.

While the swelling ranks of middle-class Africans with disposable income means exciting new frontiers for business, poverty remains entrenched in many African countries, while provision of education about gambling is negligible and regulation is either weak in principle or execution. This means that people on the verge of poverty are being exposed to an industry that invites them to take financial risk and is not held accountable if they get hurt.

In 2019 BBC *Africa Eye* released an insightful and at times touching film called 'Gamblers like me: The dark side of sports betting'.

Presented by a hugely personable Ugandan football fan and bettor called Collins Muhinda, the film charted the rise in popularity of sports betting in a country where people – young men in particular – are as mad about football as it's possible to be. Football betting, said Muhinda, was the 'new craze sweeping Africa'. He spoke to youngsters who were easily able to place bets at fifteen without being asked for ID. Some of them slept at Kampala's infamously chaotic bus station and hunted for scraps to live on. Collecting their money at the other end of the chain, explains Ugandan journalist Lydia Namubiru, are companies from all over the world – China, the UK, India, Malta and tax havens like the British Virgin Islands. One of the largest players in Uganda is Betway. The spare change from those destitute bus-stop-dwelling teenagers helps fund its sponsorship deal with West Ham United FC, its pitchside hoardings at numerous other Premier League clubs and the £11.6 million record fine it paid in the UK for failings linked to its treatment of VIP customers. Those funds have also gone towards organisations helping gambling addicts in the UK, but Ugandan addicts, similarly attracted by their love of football, won't see any of it.

The same tricks we've seen in the UK are in evidence here too. So-called 'free' bets, VIP schemes, affiliates who take a cut of the action whether punters win or lose, and virtual sports games that promise faster play than real-life sport. In one of the most troubling sequences of the film, one young man talks of selling his valuables to fund his bets. Another recalls the suicide of a friend, who squandered his tuition fees. Sports betting, said a welfare officer at Mbarara University, lay at the heart of more than half of financial problems experienced by students, in a country that needs its young people to spend their money on higher education if it is to spur development and reduce poverty.

During the making of the documentary, the head of Uganda's gambling regulator was arrested. He and several others were charged with stealing money intended to fund an event educating young men who drive boda bodas, the moped taxis that are a common sight on the streets of Kampala, about gambling harms. Representatives of the Ugandan regulator have not returned requests for comment and I have been unable to establish the outcome of the case. It is possible that he was found not guilty. Nonetheless, the nature of the allegations should raise serious concerns about the standard of governance and regulation in some of the regions where gambling is growing in popularity. Social problems caused by gambling have been reported in other African countries such as Kenya and are likely to present a problem in any economy where people can pick up a smartphone and bet but where the regulatory architecture may not develop at the same pace, against a backdrop of endemic government corruption. Yet markets like these are in the sights of the global industry as it seeks out new ways to boost income and profit: 'There are significant growth opportunities across the globe with around $50bn in gross gaming revenues in over 50 regulated markets in Central & Eastern Europe, Latin America and Africa where we do not currently operate today,' said Entain in its 2020 annual report.[7]

Where regulatory capacity is constrained, we can only take it on trust that local outposts of global gambling companies plan to behave better in those markets than their parent companies have often done in the UK. Even more so when one considers that, even in the UK, standards in the industry have improved only in recent years and only under the spotlight of political scrutiny sparked by public pressure.

From the US to Uganda, new and lucrative frontiers are opening up all the time. An industry that cut its teeth in Britain is repeating the trick, bringing in new punters day after day. Technology offers fresh horizons too. With the rollout of 5G mobile connectivity, opportunities for live in-play betting are set to be turbocharged, to go further and faster than ever before.

The inexorable forward march of technology means there are new activities on which to bet too. Remember those bored aristocrats who bet chunks of their inheritance on the first raindrop to reach the bottom of a gentlemen's-club windowpane? They might have been able to envisage a world in which betting on sporting contests was commonplace, but video games would have blown their minds. Among younger people in particular, eSports competitive video gaming holds increasing appeal, as a spectator sport as much as a participatory pastime. Already gamblers can put money on rapid-thumbed gamers machine-gunning each other to bits in Call of Duty, or going head to head on the football series FIFA. As eSports grow in popularity they are likely to take their place alongside real-world athletic contests as forums for gambling entertainment. Gambling Commission statistics show that UK-licensed operators took just £50,000 from eSports in March 2019. By May 2020 the figure had increased ninety-two-fold, to £4.6 million, as digital events grew in appeal during the UK's first Covid-19 lockdown.[8] Many in the industry believe that eSports betting will eventually snowball, as soon as existing operators – or a savvy new one – figure out how to engage with a generation of gamers who are already big digital spenders.

Some US firms are already working out how to monetise competitive gaming. Companies such as Players' Lounge already allow confident joystick warriors to put their money where their mouth is by betting that they'll beat an opponent at games such as Fortnite and FIFA. Despite the fact that Players' Lounge has no gambling licence, its service is already available to British customers. The Gambling Commission, heavily criticised for its inability to move with the times, doesn't appear to be sure whether a gambling licence is required. Sites like these are representative not just of the rise of eSports but also of another emerging trend: social betting. Just as traditional bookmakers like Ladbrokes focus their marketing on the real-life social side of betting, on football in particular, social media offers the opportunity to tie social interaction and gambling together in a way that normalises the staking of money.

They do so using some of the same techniques that social media sites use to boost engagement. The social betting app BetBull, for instance, designates some of its users as 'influencers' or 'rising tipsters'. You can track their bets and mimic them if you wish. The app displays information about previous wins they've had, although it does not seem to offer information about their losses, which – given that BetBull hasn't gone bust yet – presumably outnumber their wins. The BetBull slogan is: 'A place where we bet together. Never bet alone.' Of course, players are only ever a touch of a button away from the rather less social online casino games.

If products like these present new challenges to regulators, cryptocurrency could turn out to be on another level altogether. Crypto, the best-known example of which is bitcoin, has moved into the mainstream in recent years, with garden-shed speculators piling into the new investment class in their droves. The Gambling Commission does not prohibit operators from accepting cryptocurrencies but it does host a reminder on its website that they offer a degree of anonymity that poses a money-laundering risk. At the moment, household-name operators have largely steered clear, leaving the way open for the likes of Isle of Man-based Sportsbet.io, which has grabbed the attention of British punters via sponsorship deals with football clubs Arsenal, Southampton and Watford.[9] It seems likely that, at some stage in the near future, a major operator will break ranks and delve into a product that, like sports betting, has proved particularly popular with young men who live much of their lives online. It's very hard to imagine the current regulatory system, so outpaced by technological change, being in a state of readiness to spot any unfolding threats posed by cryptocurrency gambling.

Virtual reality is yet another new avenue for gambling firms to explore. Headsets have come on in leaps and bounds in terms of price and quality. Those who enjoy the casino experience but perhaps lack the opportunity or energy can simulate the thrill from their own homes. Similarly, wearable tech and augmented reality could soon allow people to stream sports events through Google Glass and place bets as they do so. There is no information available about how the level of immersion offered by such technology could affect punters' behaviour. In a real-life casino a gambling session might at least be interrupted by the sound of a waiter dropping a glass, a shout from a nearby table or just movement out of the corner of one's eye as people walk by. What incidental distractions will there be in the virtual casino to pull someone out of a potentially dangerous trance? What protections will firms who operate such technologies put in place?

Virtual reality and wearable tech were among the innovations cited in a 2020 article on Casino.com as offering mouth-watering opportunities for the industry and its customers. Others included the so-called 'internet of things', the network of connected devices of which the most prominent example is probably Alexa, Amazon's voice-activated device for the home. The article imagined how future punters might bet. 'You simply say: "I think the striker is going to score in the next two minutes. I want to bet £20." The bet is automatically recorded. Game on.'[10]

These are nascent trends at the moment, partly because so many of the people who enjoy eSports, use VR headsets or understand cryptocurrency aren't old enough or wealthy enough to gamble. In five or ten years these practices may be much more widespread. Many people will have spent their lives watching not football but epic battles of Call of Duty. It seems highly likely that they will want to bet on this activity and that they may wish to do so using digital currencies.

New developments such as these pose significant headaches not just for regulators but also for academics and clinicians. We still have next to no clue about how our brains have been affected by years of constant gambling advertising and the speed of experience offered by in-play betting and other new games. Technological advances offer the opportunity for gambling to become faster, more immersive, less escapable, at the same time as it becomes easier than ever before to live a life of solitude, with our only social interactions manifesting online.

Companies that are quickest to harness and develop new products with mass appeal have much to gain. Just as in-play betting was the making of bet365, or Flutter grew fat thanks in large part to the Betfair betting exchange, some other advances will prove fruitful and become industry norms. It is hard to imagine the regulatory system keeping pace. Those whose job it is to prevent gambling-related harm have been playing catch-up ever since the invention of telephone betting. The precautionary principle at the heart of gambling in the UK largely works in favour of the industry, underpinned by a Blairite philosophy that saw corporate profit as an almost indisputable good in its own right, at the expense of pretty much anything else.

Now, though, Britain finds itself at a crossroads. We have some thinking to do about the place of gambling in our society. And, as one of the most mature gambling markets in the world, it's a process that other countries will be monitoring closely to see what might turn up in their own backyards.

The journey is already underway. As the UK continued to wrestle with the pandemic in 2021, ministers had begun considering the future of gambling regulation, a rethink that came on the back of public disquiet about the way in which the industry had inserted itself into so many aspects of our daily lives. Some industry figures and libertarian commentators see this as the result of puritans (or 'prohibitionists', in the shared lexicon of gambling lobbyists) whipping a credulous public into a righteous frenzy, a vendetta by woke social justice warriors who simply find gambling a bit distasteful. It has been said, more than once, that a paternalistic, primarily middle-class elite is telling ordinary people how to live their lives. An article on sports betting website SBCNews in 2021 referred to the political drive for tougher regulation as 'the parliamentary campaign against gambling'.[11] Ideologues who oppose on principle any form of state interventionism have taken the same stance. The famously contrarian media outlet *Spiked* carried an article by the journalist Brendan O'Neill arguing that gambling is 'a target of moralistic warriors against the vices of the uneducated and unwashed'.[12] As if gambling addiction has ever respected the social class of the people it affects.

Yet the public seems to feel differently. Politicians, the media, mental health experts and campaigners have all met with relatively little pushback when raising fears about gambling's conquest of Britain. Polls consistently show strong support, even from gamblers themselves, for improved safeguards to protect people, for less advertising, and for stricter measures to make sure people aren't frittering their last pennies away.

The gambling review promises to ask and answer these big questions. It spells if not revolution, then certainly evolution of the architecture put in place by Tony Blair's Labour government in 2005. Strangely enough, for those who remember the pre-Blair political paradigm, it is a Conservative government popular with working-class voters that appears to be ready to unpick the free-market ethos of a long-departed Labour party. Swansea East MP Carolyn Harris has led calls from the left for reform but the members of the shadow cabinet responsible for that policy area have said next to nothing. In late 2020 Boris Johnson's government revealed what might be on the menu.[13] Reforms under consideration include a ban on football shirt sponsorship, much stricter afford-ability checks on punters making big bets, and stake limits on online slot machines, similar to those imposed on FOBTs.

The Gambling Commission, it is widely acknowledged, is overdue reform that could include either a significant increase in funding and powers, or even its abolition and replacement. A gambling ombudsman is one parallel solution on the table, to get to grips with the dozens of cases where firms fail their customers and leave them facing financial ruin. There are other, less sexy, options on the table too, such as a the 'single customer view' approach, mentioned in Chapter 7, which would force operators to share data about customers. This, overseen by an independent third party rather than left to the industry to police, offers a significant opportunity to reduce harm. An addict whose account was closed by one firm could no longer switch to another. Operators that fail addicts could not claim the money would have been lost elsewhere.

Undoubtedly all of this will have to be accompanied by a robust plan to tackle the black market. The industry has overhyped that threat, but it has also made legitimate reference to a strong black market presence in countries with tougher regulation, such as Sweden, lending weight to the argument that illicit operators can and will fill the void if reforms are too draconian.

The UK must also address the criminal lack of a safety net for those who do experience harm. Fortunately, gambling is increas-ingly being seen as a public health issue. NHS clinics are springing up around the country, aiming to plug the treatment gap that has endured for so long. Academics are performing groundbreaking work to better understand addiction and inform practitioners seek-ing ways to prevent and treat it. These are important efforts that require greater support from government and companies.

And let's also offer gambling firms credit where credit is due. As I've shown, parts of the industry have begun to take responsibility for the harm they cause, investing in safer-gambling technology and competing to be seen as market leaders in that field. I interact on a daily basis with dozens of gambling professionals who I strongly believe take the matter extremely seriously and believe wholeheartedly that more must be done to protect people. I'm not talking about the sort of sloganeering engaged in by lobby groups that declare 'one problem gambler is too many' while doing everything they can to water down regulatory reform. These are professionals at the coalface of the business who are having difficult conversations with their colleagues about measures that are ultimately revenue-negative. People in the sector with punters' interests at heart are badly served by some of those who run the industry and lobby for it, yet are far less accepting of the need for significant change.

Unsurprisingly, I'm highly sceptical about the extent to which good intentions are actually steering industry behaviour, though. That doesn't even feel like a controversial view; indeed, to anyone with a remotely cynical bone in their body, it should come as no surprise. For the most part, companies – and therefore, to some degree, their employees – respond to financial incentives above all else. As we've seen, directors are bound by what is known as their fiduciary duty to maximise shareholder returns. Although they must abide by regulations designed to protect people instead of profit, that duty of care isn't to their customers or to wider society, but rather to their shareholders. Their overriding incentive is always to boost profit.

It is only thanks to shifting public opinion that this incentive, the profit motive, has gradually come into closer alignment with a drive to ensure people don't ruin their lives gambling. Faced with a groundswell of disapproval and, as a result, an increasingly hostile political climate, firms are fearful of how the bottom line might be affected by a regulatory backlash over which they have no control. By proposing solutions of their own they are taking action to preserve their income for the next twenty years, even if it comes at some cost now. We are witnessing acts of self-preservation, fuelled by a realisation that, if they cannot fight the tiger, they must try to ride it.

We should be wary of letting the industry mark its own homework. We should treat with scepticism public shows of restraint such as the whistle-to-whistle ban on TV advertising during sport. These are cheap gifts bundled up in shiny, eye-catching wrapping paper. In autumn 2021, it was widely reported in the UK press that ministers had made the decision to ban gambling sponsors on football shirts. Interestingly, I had been hearing for some time that the industry was preparing to take this step anyway, recognising the potential to buy goodwill from the public and from politicians with a voluntary move, much like the whistle-to-whistle ban. That isn't to say that such a measure wouldn't be a good idea; it's merely to point out that these are the kind of half-hearted 'solutions' that governments love. They are PR wins that avoid the messy business of legislating and allow big business to offer up a sacrifice that protects other lucrative but less glamorous activities. Give them football shirts and you'll avoid affordability checks.

While we've got our sceptic's hat on, it's worth noting that very little has changed behind the scenes of the drama that plays out on the stages of both traditional and new media. While columnists bluster, campaigners organise and lobbyists spin, the same old vested interests that ultimately hold the reins of power work in the same old ways. We live in a democracy in which our lawmakers brazenly accept £400-an-hour sinecures from the gambling industry while serving in the ruling party reviewing how that industry is regulated. Politicians who once purported to dedicate their lives to public service walk out of office when the going gets tough and pop up the next minute, on six-figure salaries, as grubby lobbyists for an industry that routinely ruins the lives of their former constituents. What does that mean for the prospects of rethinking the relationship between a powerful money-spinning industry and our society?

Amid such rigid power structures, misdirection and hypocrisy can thrive. Paid industry advocates wheel out the spectre of the unscrupulous black market while their paymasters happily do business in countries where gambling isn't legal and no infrastructure exists to support those who are, for whatever reason, unable to enjoy it without damaging themselves and those around them. They boast of new initiatives taken to protect people in the UK while failing to apply them in other jurisdictions if they aren't required to do so. They refuse business to people who show that they can regularly win money but solicit more from those who lose beyond their means.

As the pandemic showed us, the industry's flirtations with altruism can be capricious and are seemingly designed to do little more than curry favour. Operators initially accepted the premise that restraint on advertising during lockdown might be wise, and won plaudits for it. They then abandoned the idea for the second and third lockdowns, when attention was elsewhere, without a word as to why the same principles should no longer apply. We all risk becoming complicit in these hypocrisies, no matter how indirectly. Our pension funds invest in the edifice that many of us criticise. The same media outlets that warn of the dangers of gambling advertising routinely publish the very same ads, often (accidentally) alongside the same article carrying the criticisms. As consumers, we are also implicated. We buy the football shirts that advertise some of the very products whose ubiquity makes us feel uncomfortable. We listen to the podcasts, watch the TV channels, play the computer games that fuel the notion that gambling is second nature, that it is only ever harmless fun, when its dangers are all too apparent.

A generation of people have grown up in a society saturated by gambling, in which hardly an hour passes in which we are not reminded of the opportunity to have a punt. For most people that doesn't present a problem: gambling either holds no appeal for them or is something that they do not struggle to keep below a harmful threshold, like moderate alcohol use. That does not mean that our society is experiencing a tolerable level of damage and it does not mean that enough is being done to protect people. Nor should we forget that we are voyaging into the unknown. Very little evidence exists to tell us what effect gambling's journey into the mainstream since 2007 has had on young minds who've never known anything different.

While there are good reasons to be wary of the industry's self-imposed reforms – and of the efficacy of the ongoing government review – there should be cause for optimism. Big strides have been made in harm reduction, education and treatment. The increasingly high-profile debate around gambling has alerted parents, spouses and friends to the struggles faced by loved ones, where once they might never have twigged what was going on.

Yet huge unanswered questions remain over the effects of what has happened already. We know that online gambling has soared in popularity, that it has made billionaires out of industry entrepreneurs, that gambling and football have never been more closely linked. There's much more we don't know. Think of the footballer with a celebrated career as a tough centre back who gets his head on every ball into the box. The damage, the dementia, comes much later, and the causative links are hard to draw. There is good reason to suspect that something similar and unseen is going on in the minds of young people in a world where gambling imagery is inescapable.

To raise these concerns and to err on the side of caution when it comes to protecting people is not to be anti-gambling, or even paternalistic. Free marketeers lament the nanny state but they never commit fully to the principle. Not even the most hardened libertarian would advocate allowing drug dealers to set up shop outside primary schools.

What this means is that everybody accepts that potentially dangerous products or activities cannot have completely free rein if a society is to be as harmonious, as productive and as comfortable as it can be, for as many people as possible. We draw the lines in different places but most of us accept the idea that some structure, some authority, is needed to protect the vulnerable. It's my belief that, when it comes to gambling at least, we have drawn those lines in the wrong place, or, rather, that the ground underneath those lines has shifted – drastically so.

As 2021 became 2022, politicians were drafting proposals that will govern how the balance will be struck, potentially for decades to come. Gambling logos on football shirts may well go the way of tobacco brands and logic suggests the same would apply to pitchside hoardings. But lawmakers must be careful that football sponsorship doesn't become the super-casino of today, the issue that grabs the headlines while others are neglected.

If advertising is to be a major part of the government's new policy on gambling, it must not be only TV that feels the glare of the spotlight. Online is where both the greatest spend and the most irresponsible behaviour is taking place. It will require intelligent, technology-led solutions to ensure that aggressive marketing of addictive products is targeted away from people likely to succumb, rather than thrown in their faces. Affiliates and the direct marketing of free bets and bonuses should not slip through the net. It already seems as if VIP schemes are not long for this world. That would be a step forward, in my view, but regulators will have to be on their mettle about what incentive mechanisms are put in place in their stead.

Politicians should think hard about integrating affordability checks into online play, ideally at levels that do not affect the vast majority of casual punters. Those who want to place big bets could still do so, with relative ease, on the proviso that they can show that they won't end up selling their family's future out from under them.

That shouldn't be too arduous if the thrill is really worth it. At the very least, there should be no option for customers to set no deposit limits at all. Stake limits for the most high-octane products should not be ruled out. If it's right for FOBTs to be cut from £100 to £2, it's hard to make the logical case for unlimited spending on certain online games that are much the same in their mechanics and their addictiveness.

The regulator should be better funded and could be empowered to crack down much harder on firms that transgress, with bigger fines and licence suspensions that aren't just an empty threat but a reality. New products should be properly tested, either before their release or in a timely manner that means they go through a probation period before receiving final approval.

Mechanisms must be put in place that ensure that people and their families do not face financial ruin because gambling companies didn't do their jobs properly. That could mean a gambling ombudsman, a concept that now seems to have support from within the industry as well as without.

Research, education and treatment ought now to be funded by a mandatory levy, ensuring a regular flow of money into an area that has been underfunded and often appears to be too much at the mercy of gambling operators' whims about where and when to spend. As importantly as anything else, our health system must recognise gambling disorder as an addiction and treat it accordingly. It cannot be right that gambling addicts walk into a GP's surgery and find that their doctor isn't familiar with their problem and doesn't know how to advise them. Despite the welcome growth of specialist gambling clinics, such services are likely to remain too thin on the ground for some time. Understanding of gambling addiction must be embedded much more deeply in our culture, so that we can spot the signs and act accordingly to protect the people we love.

This is not an exhaustive list and I am not presumptuous enough to write a manifesto for the future of gambling regulation. I do, however, think that much of what reformists are now asking for would not threaten gambling companies' right to offer legitimate services to people who want them. They would place hardly any restrictions on the enjoyment of millions of punters.

Some campaigners would say that reforms such as these don't go nearly far enough, that the effects of gambling's explosion into the mainstream are yet to manifest themselves and that only the most punishing of crackdowns will do.

It is likely that, by the time you read this, the government will be finalising its proposals and the tricky back-and-forth process of legislation will be in motion. Given what we know about lobbying and the industry's close connections to many politicians, that democratic horse-trading must be diligently scrutinised.

Whatever the outcome, the genie cannot be put back in the bottle so easily. We may well be headed for an era of tougher regulation, an unwinding of the 2005 legislation that brought us to where we are today. Many will welcome the promise of imminent change, but experience teaches us that new legislation has a half-life. It is usually at its best shortly after coming into effect, deteriorating over time as the industry invents new ways to make money. Once new laws are in place, some degree of behavioural backsliding seems inevitable from a sector that showed relatively little concern for the people it harmed until it faced a societal backlash that posed a genuine existential risk to the industry.

What's more, change does not happen quickly. Like an oil tanker that alters course long after its new coordinates have been plotted, societies take time to adapt. Behaviours have been embedded in our minds, new norms cemented into the cultural edifice.

Gambling's conquest of Britain was far-reaching, brutally efficient and may not yet be complete. Far too many casualties have already been left behind and more will doubtless suffer the same fate. New frontiers lie ahead for the gambling conquistadors too, lucrative markets that may soon be re-enacting the same battles already fought on British soil.

Politicians and, yes, the media, will move on to pastures new. But now is not the time to consider the gambling issue put to bed, in Britain or anywhere else. Indeed, the pace of technological change means the conversation may only just be starting. Now is the time to be vigilant, for the young and the vulnerable, for the friends and families, for Jack Ritchie and for the others just like him.

# ACKNOWLEDGEMENTS

I owe an enormous debt of gratitude to the many people who have helped me write this book and whose experiences have informed my work on the world of gambling and addiction.

The *Guardian*'s erstwhile business editor Julia Finch deserves a big thank you for setting the ball rolling, by sensibly turning down my application to be the newspaper's energy correspondent and letting me loose on gambling instead. Likewise, her former deputy Dan Milmo, who patiently fielded so many of my breathless pitches about new and sometimes convoluted stories about the industry. Also, David Conn, for advising me on how to get the book idea off the ground.

There are many people who campaign for gambling reform, or work in related charities and organisations, who have been generous with their time over the years and who have pointed me in the direction of potential stories. They include Matt Zarb-Cousin, Tony Parente, James Grimes, Brian Chappell, Steve Watts, Danny Cheetham and many more. I apologise if I've left anyone out but I hope that you know who you are.

Academics and clinicians get far less public credit than they deserve for their work. My eternal gratitude to those I have spoken to, or whose work I have drawn on, including Henrietta Bowden-Jones, Matt Gaskell, Heather Wardle, Phil Newall, Rebecca Cassidy, Steve Sharman, Jim Orford and Gerda Reith. In politics, my thanks must go to Carolyn Harris, Tracey Crouch, Iain Duncan Smith and Ronnie Cowan.

I'd like to thank everyone at Faber, in particular my copy editor Silvia Crompton, whose eye for detail is simply astonishing.

Within the gambling industry there are people who have been remarkably open to speaking to me, despite the often critical tone taken by my journalism and our occasional disagreements. Many thanks in particular to Alun Bowden, Dan Waugh, Simon Thomas and Richard Flint.

This book could not have been written without the incredible patience and support shown by my best friend and the love of my life, Franki. Our son Sacha provided the cheeky smiles that powered me on when motivation was lacking. I must not forget to thank Mum and Dad for instilling in me a strong belief in the importance of doing the right thing.

Lastly – and most importantly – I want to thank the many, many people who have been courageous enough to share the often harrowing tales of the battles that they and their loved ones have fought with gambling addiction. Liz and Charles Ritchie feature prominently in this book but there are countless more who have recounted their personal traumas to me with candour and bravery. Not all of those tales have made it into this book but none of them are any the less important. I hope I have done your stories justice. To each and every one of you, thank you from the bottom of my heart.

# NOTES

## Introduction

1 HC Deb, 17 November 2017, vol. 787, col. 347.

2 Simon Bowers, 'Roulette "worsens gambling addiction"', *Guardian.co.uk*, 17 January 2005.

3 Randeep Ramesh, 'High-stakes gambling machines "suck money from poorest communities"', *Guardian.co.uk*, 4 January 2013.

4 Michael Dugher, Twitter post, 20 June 2020, 9.43 a.m., http://twitter.com/michaeldugher.

5 Rob Davies, 'Ladbrokes wooed problem gambler – then paid victims £1m', *Guardian.co.uk*, 17 December 2018.

6 Rob Davies, '"Time to wake up": gambling industry criticised over sexism', *Guardian.co.uk*, 8 February 2018.

## 1. A Brief History of Gaming

1 Reith, G. (1999), *The Age of Chance*. London: Routledge.

2 Atherton, M. (2007), *Gambling*. London: Hodder Paperbacks.

3 Ashton, J. (1898), *A History of Gambling in England*. London: Duckworth.

4 Bartlett, W. B. (2018), *Richard the Lionheart*. London: Amberley Publishing.

5 Unlawful Games Act 1541 (33 Hen 8 c 9).

6 Gaming Act 1664 (16 Cha c 7).

7 Monkcom, S., Bamford, C. & Smith, C. (2001), *Smith and Monkcom's The Law of Betting, Gaming and Lotteries*. London: Butterworths.

8 Ibid.

9 HC Deb, 9 March 1956, vol. 549, col. 2552.

10 The Gaming Act 1845 (8 & 9 Vict, c 109).

11 Gaming Act 1968 (ch.18).

12 Howard Wright, 'He began at the bottom, rose to the top and lifted the whole industry with him', *Racing Post*, 16 October 2011.

13  Cassidy, R. (2020), *Vicious Games: Capitalism and Gambling*. London: Pluto Books.

14  'Brown scraps betting duty', *BBC.co.uk*, 7 March 2001.

15  David Hencke, 'New betting tax pays off for Brown', *Guardian.co.uk*, 14 January 2005.

16  Gambling (Licensing and Advertising) Act 2014 (ch.17).

17  Martin Hickman, 'Jackpot! Bookies avoid £1bn tax', *Independent.co.uk*, 1 February 2013.

18  Waugh, D. (2016), 'Budd Revisited – Gambling in Great Britain 15 Years On'. *UNLV Gaming Research & Review Journal*, *20*(2).

19  Budd, A., Bishop, D., Bose, M., Dean, P., Gray, J., Hoddinott, J., Marks, P., Nathan, S., Weekes, A. & Wolfe, J. (2001), 'Gambling Review Report'. Her Majesty's Stationery Office: London, UK.

20  Tim Shipman, 'Report reveals blight of supercasinos', *MailOnline*, 1 September 2006.

21  Melissa Kite, 'Opponents of new gambling law are snobs, says Tessa Jowell', *Telegraph.co.uk*, 24 October 2004.

22  Waugh, D. (2016), 'Budd Revisited – Gambling in Great Britain 15 Years On'. *UNLV Gaming Research & Review Journal*, *20*(2).

23  Budd, A., Bishop, D., Bose, M., Dean, P., Gray, J., Hoddinott, J., Marks, P., Nathan, S., Weekes, A. & Wolfe, J. (2001), 'Gambling Review Report'. Her Majesty's Stationery Office: London, UK.

24  Waugh, D. (2016), 'Budd Revisited – Gambling in Great Britain 15 Years On'. *UNLV Gaming Research & Review Journal*, *20*(2).

## 2. Advertising: Hook, Line and Sinker

1  Tom Payne, 'Gamblers paid to keep betting', *MailOnline*, 17 February 2019.

2  Ofcom, 'Trends in gambling advertising', November 2013.

3  Roy Greenslade, 'Ladbrokes ads banned for "irresponsible attitude towards gambling"', *Guardian.co.uk*, 17 September 2014.

4  Mark Sweney, 'Paddy Power advert featuring Ryan Giggs's brother banned', *Guardian.co.uk*, 8 May 2019.

5  John Glenday, 'Number is up for "socially irresponsible" Paddy Power ad', *The Drum*, 29 November 2017.

6  Pamela Duncan, Rob Davies & Mark Sweney, 'Children "bombarded" with betting adverts during World Cup', *Guardian.co.uk*, 15 July 2018.

7 Rob Davies, 'State should restrict gambling ads seen by children, industry says', *Guardian.co.uk*, 10 August 2018.

8 Rob Davies & Mark Sweney, 'UK betting firms back live sports advertising ban', *Guardian.co.uk*, 6 December 2018.

9 Betting and Gaming Council, '"Whistle to whistle" ban a huge success', 21 August 2020.

10 Stephen van Rooyen, 'The inconvenient truth about gambling adverts', *TheTimes.co.uk*, 10 December 2018.

11 Gambling Commission statistics.

12 Mark Sweney, 'Ofcom: young people watch a third less TV on sets as they move online', *Guardian.co.uk*, 7 July 2017.

13 Rob Davies, 'Rise in gambling ad spend fuels fears over impact on children', *Guardian.co.uk,* 24 November 2018.

14 Mark Sweney & Rob Davies, 'UK betting firms to stop advertising on TV and radio during lockdown', *Guardian.co.uk*, 27 April 2020.

15 Carole Cadwalladr & Emma Graham-Harrison, 'Revealed: 50 million Facebook profiles harvested for Cambridge Analytica in major data breach', *Guardian.co.uk*, 17 March 2018.

16 Ginnis S. & Kitson H. (2020), 'The impact of gambling marketing and advertising on children, young people and vulnerable adults'. London: Ipsos MORI.

17 Rob Davies, 'Google to let YouTube users opt out of gambling and alcohol ads', *Guardian.co.uk*, 10 December 2020.

18 KBV Research, *Global In-app Advertising Market*, September 2019.

19 Sam Bradley, 'ASA bans William Hill ad served in Mario Kart app for targeting kids', *The Drum*, 18 September 2018.

20 Mark Sweney & Rob Davies, '*I'm a Celebrity . . .* app maker forced to pull gambling adverts', *Guardian.co.uk*, 6 February 2019.

21 Tom Witherow, 'Gambling addicts who search for help via iPhones get bombarded with adverts for betting firms instead', *MailOnline*, 31 March 2020.

22 Milly Glaister, 'Google lifts paid search gambling ban', *Campaignlive.co.uk*, 16 October 2008.

23 Kantar Media, 'Digital Advertising Intelligence Solution', August 2018.

24 Rob Davies, 'Online casino advert banned for targeting problem gamblers', *Guardian.co.uk*, 9 October 2019.

25 Ben Chapman, 'Gambling addicts searching on Google for help bombarded with ads for online casinos', *Independent.co.uk*, 3 January 2020.

26 Mattha Busby, 'Revealed: tipsters deliberately recommend losing bets to punters', *Guardian.co.uk*, 1 September 2017.

27 Ofcom, 'Audio on demand: the rise of podcasts', 30 September 2019.

28 Mattha Busby, 'Revealed: how gambling industry targets poor people and ex-gamblers', *Guardian.co.uk*, 31 August 2017.

29 Adam Satariano, 'What a gambling app knows about you', *NYTimes.com*, 24 March 2021.

30 Orford, J. (2020), *The Gambling Establishment*. Abingdon: Routledge.

31 Banks, J. (2014), *Online Gambling and Crime: Causes, Controls and Controversies*. Farnham, Surrey: Ashgate.

32 Ibid.

33 Newall, Philip W. S., et al. (2019), 'Testing a Gambling Warning Label's Effect on Behavior', *PsyArXiv*.

34 Alistair Magowan, 'Gambling adverts will "drown out" new warnings against betting – campaigners', *BBC.co.uk*, 21 February 2019.

35 Rob Davies, 'Gambling firms' social messages are "thinly veiled" adverts, say MPs', *Guardian.co.uk*, 10 Mary 2020.

36 MacGregor et al. (2020), 'The effect of marketing and advertising on children, young people and vulnerable people'. NatCen Social Research.

37 Ibid.

38 Bougettaya et al. (2020), 'The relationship between gambling advertising and gambling attitudes, intentions and behaviours: a critical and meta-analytic review'. *Current Opinion in Behavioral Sciences*.

39 Rob Davies, 'Majority of public support total ban on UK gambling adverts, poll finds', *Guardian.co.uk*, 16 June 2021.

## 3. Brainhacks, Dark Nudges and Gambling by Stealth

1 Schüll, N. (2012), *Addiction by Design*. Princeton University Press.

2 Dostoevsky, F. (1887), *The Gambler*.

3 Newall et al. (2019), 'Live-odds gambling advertising and consumer protection'. *PLoS ONE*.

4 Thaler, R. H. & Sunstein, C. R. (2008), *Nudge: Improving Decisions About Health, Wealth, and Happiness*. Yale University Press.

5 The Behavioural Insights Team (2021), 'Applying behavioural insights to design better safer gambling tools'. GambleAware.

6 Henslin, J. (1967), 'Craps and magic'. *American Journal of Sociology*.

7   Langer, E. J. (1975), 'The illusion of control'. *Journal of Personality and Social Psychology.*

8   Schüll, N. (2012), *Addiction by Design.* Princeton University Press.

9   Newall et al. (2020), 'Request-a-bet sports betting products indicate patterns of bettor preference and bookmaker profits'. *Journal of Behavioral Addictions.*

10  Harrigan et al. (2014), 'Games of chance or masters of illusion: multiline slots design may promote cognitive distortions'. *International Gambling Studies.*

11  Livingstone et al. (2008), 'The relevance and role of gaming machine games and game features on the play of problem gamblers'. Independent Gambling Authority of South Australia.

12  Dixon et al. (2013), 'Losses disguised as wins in modern multi-line video slot machines'. *Addiction.*

13  Rob Davies, 'Gambling firms in Great Britain ordered to slow down online slot machines', *Guardian.co.uk*, 2 February 2021.

14  Sharman et al. (2015), 'Dual effects of "losses disguised as wins" and near-misses in a slot machine game'. *International Gambling Studies.*

15  Gambling Commission statistics.

16  National Gambling Treatment Service statistics.

17  Schüll, N. (2012), *Addiction by Design.* Princeton University Press.

18  Rob Davies, 'Gambling firms in Great Britain ordered to slow down online slot machines', *Guardian.co.uk*, 2 February 2021.

19  Rob Davies, 'Gambling-style apps offered on Facebook without age checks', *Guardian.co.uk*, 27 December 2017.

20  Gambling Commission, 'Young people and gambling', December 2017.

21  Alex Hern, 'Video games are unlocking child gambling. This has to be reined in', *Guardian.co.uk*, 28 December 2017.

22  Mattha Busby, 'Loot boxes increasingly common in video games despite addiction concerns', *Guardian.co.uk*, 22 November 2019.

23  Zendle et al. (2019), 'Paying for loot boxes is linked to problem gambling, regardless of specific features such as cash-out and pay-to-win'. *Computers in Human Behavior.*

24  Rob Davies, 'Video game firms face prosecution over gambling by children', *Guardian.co.uk*, 22 July 2019.

25  Wardle, H. (2021), *Games Without Frontiers.* London: Palgrave.

## 4. VIPs: Vulnerable Impressionable Punters

1 Rob Davies, 'Record £11.6m UK gambling fine meted out to Betway', *Guardian.co.uk*, 20 March 2020.

2 Rob Davies, 'Gala Coral pays out £880,000 over gambler who stole to feed habit', *Guardian.co.uk*, 27 April 2016.

3 Katie Morley, 'William Hill made my brain-damaged mother a VIP and she gambled away £88,000', *Telegraph.co.uk*, 3 April 2020.

4 Rob Davies, 'Online casinos ignored my obvious signs of addiction, says gambler', *Guardian.co.uk*, 22 April 2019.

5 Rob Davies, 'MansionBet allowed VIP gambler to use redundancy payout to keep betting', *Guardian.co.uk*, 19 April 2020.

6 Tom Witherow, 'Tragic gambler who was "groomed" with a bonus', *MailOnline*, 27 May 2020.

7 Tom Payne, 'Gamblers paid to keep betting', *MailOnline*, 17 February 2019.

8 Rob Davies, '"It keeps you coming back": the rise of VIP gambling schemes', *Guardian.co.uk*, 2 January 2020.

9 Rob Davies, 'Gambling firms criticised for "enticing" loss-making customers', *Guardian.co.uk*, 10 November 2019.

10 Rob Davies, 'Betting firms won £1.3m in stolen money from gambling addict', *Guardian.co.uk*, 14 June 2021.

11 Rob Davies, 'Ladbrokes wooed problem gambler – then paid victims £1m', *Guardian.co.uk*, 17 December 2018.

12 Tom Witherow, 'Bookie "plied fraudster with cash bonuses": Flutter accused of allowing punter to bet £282k of stolen funds', *MailOnline*, 27 April 2021.

13 Dhir v Flutter Entertainment Plc (Rev 2) [2021] EWHC 1510 (QB) (04 June 2021).

14 Select Committee on the Social and Economic Impact of the Gambling Industry, 4 February 2020.

15 Select Committee on the Social and Economic Impact of the Gambling Industry. *Gambling Harm – Time for Action* (HL2019–21 79).

16 Rob Davies, 'Ladbrokes wooed problem gambler – then paid victims £1m', *Guardian.co.uk*, 17 December 2018.

17 Rob Davies, 'Report shows betting industry's reliance on problem gamblers', *Guardian.co.uk*, 2 January 2020.

18 Betting and Gaming Council, 'BGC welcomes new rules on VIP schemes', 30 September 2020.

## 5. The Gamblification of Football

1 HC Deb, 9 January 2020, vol. 669.

2 Eleanor Hayward, Jason Groves and Tom Witherow, 'Boris Johnson leads calls for football bosses to scrap a deal selling FA Cup rights to gambling giants such as Bet365 which lets fans watch live matches if they place a bet', *MailOnline.co.uk*, 9 January 2020.

3 Djohari et al. (2020), 'The visibility of gambling sponsorship in football-related products marketed directly to children'. *Soccer and Society*.

4 'Grobbelaar loses match-fix damages appeal', *Guardian.co.uk*, 18 January 2001.

5 Statista.

6 Cassidy, R. & Ovenden, N. (2017), 'Frequency, duration and medium of advertisements for gambling and other risky products in commercial and public service broadcasts of English Premier League football'.

7 Rob Davies, 'Gambling Commission fines Sun Bets firm over "piegate" incident', *Guardian.co.uk*, 13 April 2018.

8 'Huddersfield fined £50,000 by FA for kit sponsorship stunt', *Guardian.co.uk*, 5 September 2019.

9 Mattha Busby & Rob Davies, 'Church criticises Wayne Rooney over Derby gambling tie-up', 9 August 2019.

10 Winlink Marketing Ltd v The Liverpool Football Club & Athletic Grounds Ltd [2020] EWHC 2271 (Comm) (14 September 2020).

11 Derek McGovern, 'Nottingham Forest could cost bookie Victor Chandler', *Mirror.co.uk*, 4 February 2012.

12 Simon Goodley, 'Revealed: how bet365 profits from Chinese punters who risk jail for gambling online', *Guardian.co.uk*, 3 October 2014.

13 Joey D'Urso, 'How Premier League shirt sponsors "facilitate illegal gambling"', *The Athletic*, 3 February 2021.

14 Rob Davies & Barney Ronay, 'Gazprom v Abu Dhabi: an alternative guide to the Champions League ties', *Guardian.co.uk*, 15 February 2019.

15 Andy Hunter, 'Daniel Sturridge cannot play football until June as betting ban is extended', *Guardian.co.uk*, 2 March 2020.

16 David Hytner, 'Kieran Trippier banned for 10 weeks for breaching FA's betting rules', *Guardian.co.uk*, 23 December 2020.

17 John McCarthy, 'How ads fund football piracy – and how to counter it', *The Drum*, 7 October 2020.

18 Martha Kelner, 'FA announces end to all sponsorship deals with betting companies', *Guardian.co.uk*, 22 June 2017.

19 David Conn, 'New Premier League chief says betting shirt sponsors and VAR here to stay', *Guardian.co.uk*, 4 February 2020.

20 Rob Davies, 'Sky Bet criticised for featuring gambling addict Paul Merson in adverts', *Guardian.co.uk*, 29 March 2019.

21 Rob Davies, 'Gambling logos feature 700 times in football match, says C4 documentary', *Guardian.co.uk*, 5 June 2021.

22 Gambling Commission statistics.

23 McGee, D. (2020), 'On the normalisation of online sports gambling among young adult men in the UK: a public health perspective'. *Public Health*.

24 Josie Clarke, 'Ladbrokes ad banned for showing socially irresponsible gambling behaviour', *Independent.co.uk*, 7 July 2021.

25 Djohari, N. & Weston, G. (2019), 'Recall and awareness of gambling advertising and sponsorship in sport in the UK: A study of young people and adults'. *Harm Reduction Journal*.

26 Rob Davies, 'Third of UK football fans put off buying kit if it has betting sponsor', *Guardian.co.uk*, 11 October 2020.

27 Greg Wood, 'Football Index collapse: MPs and peers urge Johnson to hold public inquiry', *Guardian.co.uk*, 14 April 2021.

28 Select Committee on the Social and Economic Impact of the Gambling Industry, *Gambling Harm – Time for Action* (HL2019–21 79).

## 6. Addiction, 'Affected Others' and Suicide

1 Select Committee on the Social and Economic Impact of the Gambling Industry, *Gambling Harm – Time for Action* (HL2019–21 79).

2 Williams, R. & Wood, R. (2016), 'What proportion of gambling revenue is derived from problem gamblers?' Alberta Gambling Research Institute's 15th Annual Conference.

3 American Psychiatric Association (2013), *Diagnostic and Statistical Manual of Mental Disorders* (5th ed.). Arlington, Virginia.

4 National Gambling Treatment Service statistics.

5 Rob Davies, 'Ladbrokes under investigation over gambler's payday loans claim', *Guardian.co.uk*, 29 September 2017.

6 National Gambling Treatment Service statistics.

7 Rob Davies, 'Bookmakers "helped gambling addict squander injury compensation"', *Guardian.co.uk*, 19 August 2020.

8 National Gambling Treatment Service statistics.

9  Banks et al. (2019), 'Prevalence of gambling disorder among prisoners: a systematic review'. *International Journal of Offender Therapy and Comparative Criminology*.

10  Tom Witherow, 'Betting firm Betway lets gambler, 30, with severe addiction blow £370,000 he stole from his cake business employer', *MailOnline*, 21 November 2019.

11  *BBC.co.uk*, 'Norfolk finance director and gambling addict stole £1m from firm', 2 January 2019.

12  Rob Davies, 'Betting firms won £1.3m in stolen money from gambling addict', *Guardian.co.uk*, 14 June 2021.

13  Rob Davies, 'Gamblers "lost more than £10,000" on fixed-odds betting terminals', *Guardian.co.uk*, 14 March 2017.

14  Schüll, N. (2012), *Addiction by Design*. Princeton University Press.

15  NHS Digital Health Survey 2016.

16  National Gambling Treatment Service statistics.

17  GamStop statistics.

18  Rob Davies, 'UK gambling addiction much worse than thought, says survey', *Guardian.co.uk*, 19 May 2020.

19  National Gambling Treatment Service statistics.

20  Goodwin et al. (2019), 'A typical problem gambler affects six others'. *International Gambling Studies*.

21  Wardle et al. (2019), 'Problem gambling, suicidal thoughts, suicide attempts and non-suicidal self-harm'. GambleAware.

22  Håkansson, A. & Karlsson, A. (2020), 'Suicide attempt in patients with gambling disorder – associations with comorbidity including substance use disorders'. *Frontiers in Psychiatry*.

23  Jamie Grierson, '"He haemorrhaged money": the bereaved parents taking on the gambling industry', *Guardian.co.uk*, 15 July 2016.

24  NHS Digital Health Survey 2018.

25  Mason Boycott-Owen, 'Lottery made over £1bn from "addictive" online games during lockdown', *Telegraph.co.uk*, 18 July 2021.

26  Social Market Foundation, 'Gambling review and reform: towards a new regulatory framework', August 2020.

27  Daniel O'Boyle, 'BGC blasts SMF's "arbitrary and random" deposit cap proposal', *iGaming Business*, 5 August 2020.

28  NHS Digital Health Survey 2018.

29  Gambling Commission, 'Young People and Gambling 2020'.

30  Dan Warburton, 'Gambling addict kids losing up to £100,000 treated at first NHS clinic for children', *Mirror.co.uk*, 24 October 2020.

31  Forrest, D. & McHale, I. (2018), 'Gambling and Problem Gambling Among Young Adolescents in Great Britain'. *Journal of Gambling Studies*.

32  Cassidy, R. (2020). *Vicious Games: Capitalism and Gambling*. London: Pluto Books.

33  Rob Davies, 'Problem gambling costs UK up to £1.2bn a year, says report', *Guardian.co.uk*, 13 December 2016.

34  Williams, R. (2017), 'Best practices in assessing problem gambling and gambling-related harm'. 11th SNSUS Conference.

35  GambleAware press release, May 2020.

36  Sturgis, P. (2020), 'An assessment of the accuracy of survey estimates of the prevalence of problem gambling in the United Kingdom'. GambleAware.

37  Van Schalkwyk et al. (2021), 'A public health approach to gambling regulation'. *The Lancet*.

38  Muggleton et al. (2021), 'The association between gambling and financial, social and health outcomes in big financial data'. *Nature Human Behaviour*.

## 7. The Safety Net: Failures in Regulation and Treatment

1  Randeep Ramesh, 'Gambling charity chair lobbied for bookmakers, documents show', *Guardian.co.uk*, 6 January 2016.

2  Cassidy et al. (2014), *The Goldsmiths Report*. Fair Game: Producing Gambling Research.

3  Van Schalkwyk et al. (2021), 'A public health approach to gambling regulation'. *The Lancet*.

4  Ladbrokes Annual Report and Accounts 2013.

5  Gibraltar Betting & Gaming Association Ltd v The Secretary of State for Culture, Media & Sport the Gambling Commission & Ors [2014] EWHC 3236 (Admin) (10 October 2014).

6  Gambling (Licensing and Advertising) Act 2014 (c.17).

7  HM Revenue & Customs statistics.

8  Gambling Commission statistics.

9  Ibid.

10  GVC Annual Report and Accounts 2018.

11  Gambling Act 2005 (c.19).

12  Rupert Neate & Rob Davies, 'Gambling Commission considers ban on credit card betting', *Guardian.co.uk*, 26 March 2018.

13  Gambling Commission statistics.

14  bet365 Group Annual Report and Accounts 2019/20.

15  Rob Davies, 'Gambling watchdog's plan to cut staff astonishes campaigners', *Guardian.co.uk*, 5 April 2020.

16  National Audit Office (2020), 'Gambling regulation: problem gambling and protecting vulnerable people'.

17  Camelot UK Lotteries Annual Report and Accounts 2019/20.

18  Greene King Brewing And Retailing Ltd & Anor v The Gambling Commission (Rev 1) [2017] EWCA Civ 372 (25 May 2017).

19  Rob Davies, 'Bookmakers accused of bypassing FOBT rules with roulette-style games', *Guardian.co.uk*, 1 April 2019.

20  Rob Davies, 'Paddy Power and Betfred may face watchdog sanctions', *Guardian.co.uk*, 2 April 2019.

21  Rob Davies, 'Gambling watchdog under fire over betting firms' role in addiction taskforce', *Guardian.co.uk*, 24 January 2020.

22  Gambling Commission press release, 2 February 2021.

23  Office for National Statistics, 'Employee earnings in the UK 2020'.

24  Gambling Commission website.

25  IBAS website.

26  Calvert v William Hill Credit Ltd [2008] EWCA Civ 1427 (16 December 2008).

27  Julia Kollewe, 'Gambling regulator warns firms over use of gagging orders', *Guardian.co.uk*, 31 January 2019.

28  Rob Davies, 'Labour proposes a new ombudsman for gambling industry', *Guardian.co.uk*, 18 June 2019.

29  Alcohol Change UK website.

30  National Gambling Treatment Service statistics, 2019/20.

31  Budd, A., Bishop, D., Bose, M., Dean, P., Gray, J., Hoddinott, J., Marks, P., Nathan, S., Weekes, A. & Wolfe, J. (2001), 'Gambling Review Report'. Her Majesty's Stationery Office: London, UK.

32  Amelia Gentleman, 'Inside the NHS's only specialist gambling clinic', *Guardian.co.uk*, 6 June 2016.

33  Rob Davies, 'Gambling industry fails to meet charity donation target', *Guardian.co.uk*, 3 May 2019.

34  Speech by Gambling Commission chair Bill Moyes, 25 April 2019.

35  Rob Davies, 'Government under fire for failing to back mandatory betting levy', *Guardian.co.uk*, 25 April 2019.

36 Betting and Gaming Council, 'Largest BGC members pledge £100m for treatment services', 15 June 2020.

37 Alice Hancock, 'Gambling addiction body warns on UK's outdated law', Guardian.co.uk, 9 December 2019.

38 Rob Davies, 'UK betting firms' move to redirect problem gambling funds raises concerns', *Guardian.co.uk*, 24 June 2020.

39 Select Committee on the Social and Economic Impact of the Gambling Industry (HL), 25 February 2020.

40 Sarah Marsh, 'NHS to open first gambling clinic for children', *Guardian.co.uk*, 24 June 2019.

41 Rob Davies, 'Number of gamblers trying to block themselves online surges', *Guardian.co.uk*, 5 April 2021.

42 Dan Roan, 'Problem gamblers generate 4% of Kindred revenue', *BBC.co.uk*, 8 February 2021.

43 Gambling Commission statistics.

## 8. Playing Politics: FOBTs and the Lobbying Game

1 Rob Davies, 'Bookmakers prepare for store closures as FOBT stake is cut', *Guardian.co.uk*, 30 March 2019.

2 Senate of Canada, Standing Committee on Legal and Constitutional Affairs, February 2005.

3 Victoria Coren Mitchell, 'A stupid gamble on evil machines', *Guardian.co.uk*, 20 August 2017.

4 NHS Digital Health Survey 2016.

5 Rob Davies, 'High stakes battle on the high street: Newham's fight against FOBTs', *Guardian.co.uk*, 3 November 2017.

6 Rob Davies, 'Curbs on FOBT stakes fuel fewer police callouts to bookmakers', *Guardian.co.uk*, 14 June 2020.

7 Randeep Ramesh, 'The gambling machines helping drug dealers "turn dirty money clean"', *Guardian.co.uk*, 8 November 2013.

8 Rob Davies, 'Gambling firms charmed MPs ahead of betting review in 2016', *Guardian.co.uk*, 1 January 2017.

9 Andrew Ellson, 'Pro-gambling MP faces an inquiry over betting account', *TheTimes.co.uk*, 21 March 2016.

10 Gambling Commission statistics.

11 Rob Davies, 'Killing machines: Tracey Crouch on why she resigned as minister over FOBTs', *Guardian.co.uk*, 17 November 2018.

12  Rob Davies, 'Government makes U-turn over delay to £2 FOBT maximum stake', *Guardian.co.uk*, 14 November 2018.

13  APPG on gambling-related harm, income and expenditure statement 2017/18.

14  Zarb-Cousin v Association of British Bookmakers & Anor [2018] EWHC 2240 (QB) (19 July 2018).

15  Rob Davies, 'Betting turf war is torpedoing efforts to help problem gamblers', *Guardian.co.uk*, 21 February 2017.

16  Michael Dugher, Twitter post, 18 July 2017, 10.50 p.m., http://twitter.com/michaeldugher.

17  Michael Dugher, Twitter post, 25 April 2020, 11.44 a.m., http://twitter.com/michaeldugher.

18  Mason Boycott-Owen, 'Gambling industry chief accused of mocking recovering addict on Twitter', *Telegraph.co.uk*, 5 February 2021.

19  Rob Davies, 'Gambling logos feature 700 times in football match, says C4 documentary', 5 June 2021.

20  Betting and Gaming Council, Twitter post, 25 October 2020, 9.20 a.m., http://twitter.com/betgamecouncil.

21  Michael Dugher, Twitter post, 26 February 2020, 7.38 a.m., http://twitter.com/michaeldugher.

22  Gambling Commission, 'Changes to licence conditions and codes of practice on the use of credit cards for gambling (consultation response)', 14 January 2020.

23  Dominic Walsh & Charlie Parker, 'Betting and Gaming Council calls for gambling ombudsman', *Guardian.co.uk*, 5 July 2021.

24  Department for Digital, Culture, Media & Sport, Ministerial meetings, 1 October to 31 December 2020.

25  Steve Hawkes, 'Theresa May blasted for "beating up" on bookies and told to "widen gambling review" to include scratchcards and National Lottery', *TheSun.co.uk*, 28 December 2016.

26  UK Music website, 'UK Music appoints Michael Dugher as new chief executive', 27 April 2017.

27  George Eaton, 'What does Tom Watson want?', *NewStatesman.com*, 18 September 2019.

28  UK Music website, 'UK Music appoints Tom Watson as new UK Music chair', 30 March 2020.

29  Rob Davies, 'Tom Watson takes job as adviser to Paddy Power and Betfair', *Guardian.co.uk*, 17 September 2020.

30 Rob Davies, 'Tom Watson's remarks calling Paddy Power "dirty" emerge as he takes job', *Guardian.co.uk*, 18 September 2020.

31 Tom Watson, Twitter post, 27 April 2020, 3.06 p.m., http://twitter.com/ tom_watson.

32 Rob Davies & Richard Partington, 'Two Tory MPs take gambling jobs before review of betting laws', *Guardian.co.uk*, 11 November 2020.

33 Rob Davies, 'Tory MP's ex-aides work at betting firm that paid him £50,000', *Guardian.co.uk*, 12 November 2020.

34 Rob Davies, Almost £225,000 in wages and freebies taken from gambling industry by 28 MPs, *Guardian.co.uk*, 15 November 2021.

35 HC Deb, 22 July 2021, vol. 699, col. 1242.

36 Rowena Mason & Anushka Asthana, 'Tories paid Crosby's firm millions for advising May's election campaign', *Guardian.co.uk*, 8 August 2017.

37 Rob Davies, 'Betting firm accused over "astroturfing" with customer lobby group', *Guardian.co.uk*, 16 February 2021.

38 Jim Waterson, 'Facebook Brexit ads secretly run by staff of Lynton Crosby firm', *Guardian.co.uk*, 3 April 2019.

39 Andrew Ellson, 'Gambling research "funded by bookies"', *TheTimes.co.uk*, 20 January 2018.

40 Rob Davies, 'Government's FOBT decision influenced by "discredited" report', *Guardian.co.uk*, 12 November 2018.

41 Gambling Commission statistics.

42 Ibid.

43 Rob Davies, 'William Hill and GVC expected to claim back £350m in FOBT tax', *Guardian.co.uk*, 20 May 2020.

44 David Wooding, 'Thousands of teens lured into blowing £1.4billion on black market online gambling, shocking report reveals', *TheSun.co.uk*, 20 December 2020.

45 Rob Davies, 'UK gambling firms accused of exaggerating scale of black market betting', *Guardian.co.uk*, 18 January 2021.

46 Harry Cole, 'British punters bet £2.8bn on black market bookies last year – twice as much as two years ago', *TheSun.co.uk*, 4 February 2021.

47 Gambling Commission statistics.

48 Ibid.

49 Evans, J. & Cross, K. (2021), 'The Geography of Gambling Premises in Britain'. University of Bristol.

### 9. The House Always Wins: Who Got Rich?

1 Gambling Commission statistics.

2 *Sunday Times* Rich List 2021.

3 Van Schalkwyk et al. (2021), 'A public health approach to gambling regulation'. *The Lancet*.

4 bet365 Group Annual Report and Accounts 2019/20.

5 Rob Davies, 'Bet365 boss's £421m pay for 2020 takes earnings over £1bn in four years', *Guardian.co.uk*, 31 March 2021.

6 *Sunday Times* Rich List 2021.

7 Rob Davies, 'Meet Denise Coates, the best paid woman in the world', *Guardian.co.uk*, 24 November 2018.

8 Rob Davies, 'Revealed: how bet365 profits from Chinese punters who risk jail for gambling online', *Guardian.co.uk*, 3 October 2014.

9 bet365 Group Annual Report and Accounts 2019/20.

10 Electoral Commission records.

11 *Sunday Times* Tax List 2021.

12 Charity Commission records, Denise Coates Foundation.

13 *Sunday Times* Rich List 2021.

14 Ibid.

15 Lucy Roue, 'From "Salford's slums" to billionaire businessman – how Peter Done beat the odds', *ManchesterEveningNews.co.uk*, 16 December 2018.

16 Graham Rock, 'Gambling a-gogo', *Guardian.co.uk*, 29 April 2001.

17 Josh Layton, 'Betfred owner Fred Done was stabbed five times and needed 32 stitches – but wouldn't change experience', *Mirror.co.uk*, 25 November 2013.

18 Electoral Commission records.

19 Neal Keeling, 'Fred Done donates more than £1m to children's hospital in memory of his wife', *ManchesterEveningsNews.co.uk*, 15 March 2019.

20 JessieMay.org.uk, 2 May 2021.

21 Rob Davies, 'Betfred owners make millions from company treating gambling addicts', *Guardian.co.uk*, 16 January 2020.

22 Rob Davies, 'Betfred owner linked to firm that advises people struggling with high debt', *Guardian.co.uk*, 18 January 2020.

23 Bill Barber, 'Fred Done appoints Joanne Whittaker as new Betfred chief executive', *RacingPost.com*, 10 March 2021.

24 *Sunday Times* Tax List 2021.

25 *Sunday Times* Rich List 2021.

26 Roger Blitz, 'Playtech founder cashes in after creating multiple millionaires', *FT.com*, 6 March 2014.

27 Ben Martin, 'Playtech founder sells stake in the gambling software company', *Reuters.com*, 23 November 2018.

28 *Sunday Times* Rich List 2021.

29 Chaim Levinson, 'Flouting the Law, Wealthy Residents Take Over Israeli City's Sea Cliff', *Haaretz.com*, 25 August 2020.

30 Patrick Graham & Jemima Kelly, 'Playtech seeks deal with online trading platform AvaTrade', *Reuters.com*, 14 May 2015.

31 Nathan Vardi, 'Amaya Gaming In Deal To Buy PokerStars For $4.9 Billion', *Forbes.com*, 12 June 2014.

32 US Department of Justice website, 'PokerStars Founder Pleads Guilty', 25 March 2020.

33 Jerome Garcia, 'Isai Scheinberg Sentenced with "Time Served" and $30,000 Fine, *GamblingNews.com*, 24 September 2020.

34 Ian Cobain, 'Revealed: poker game partners and certain winners in £4.8bn net float', *Guardian.co.uk*, 16 June 2005.

35 *Sunday Times* Rich List 2020.

36 Mario Ledwith & Tom Witherow, 'Millionaire South African philanthropist, 49, is revealed as secretive backer of under-fire bookmaker Betway amid outrage over its "grooming" of gambling addicts', *MailOnline.co.uk*, 31 January 2020.

37 Rob Davies, 'MP attacks "archaic" use of scantily-clad models at gambling trade show', *Guardian.co.uk*, 4 February 2020.

38 Sylvia Pfeifer, 'Heroes of Britain's private sector', *Telegraph.co.uk*, 15 May 2005.

39 Amy Yee, 'Scientific Games looks to extend in Europe', *FT.com*, 7 May 2006.

40 Nigel Nelson, 'Inventors of the "crack cocaine of gambling" sold their creation for £100million', *Mirror.co.uk*, 26 January 2014.

41 Luke Alvarez, 'Rage against the machines is ill-founded', *TheTimes.co.uk*, 6 February 2014.

42 Nick Dorman, 'George Osborne on trade mission with tycoon who makes machines labelled "crack cocaine of gambling"', *Mirror.co.uk*, 12 January 2014.

43 Richard Browning, 'Revealed: The UK's 1,000 most exciting and inspirational companies', *MailOnline.co.uk*, 13 December 2013.

44 Nick Dorman, 'George Osborne on trade mission with tycoon who makes machines labelled "crack cocaine of gambling"', *Mirror.co.uk*, 12 January 2014.

45  Elizabeth Anderson, 'Gamble pays off for Inspired Gaming group', *Telegraph.co.uk*, 14 January 2015.

46  Rob Davies, 'The multimillionaires making a packet out of Britain's gamblers', *Guardian.co.uk*, 10 October 2017.

47  SEC.gov filings.

48  David Cook, 'What has the Chandler family brought to the gaming industry?', *GamblingInsider.com*, 24 May 2016.

49  Paul Gallagher, 'Meet the pioneers who are making millions from online gambling', *Independent.co.uk*, 17 February 2013.

50  *Sunday Times* Rich List 2018.

51  Julian Muscat, 'Life's a gamble', *TheOwnerBreeder.com*, 2 July 2012.

52  Rob Davies & Jasper Jolly, 'Ladbrokes owner's shares leap after it rejects £8.1bn MGM bid', *Guardian.co.uk*, 4 January 2021.

53  Entain Annual Reports and Accounts.

54  Alice Hancock, 'Investors revolt against executive pay at Ladbrokes owner GVC', *FT.com*, 5 June 2019.

55  Daniel Dunkley, 'I've been betting since I was 13, but Bwin must be my best punt', *TheTimes.co.uk*, 13 September 2015.

56  Russell Lynch, 'Kenny Alexander: The poker-playing GVC boss itching to get chips in middle when takeover cards are dealt', *Standard.co.uk*, 7 April 2017.

57  Ben Martin, 'The odds are on FTSE 250 place for GVC chief', *Telegraph.co.uk*, 17 January 2016.

58  Gordon Currie, 'Former betting tycoon, 52, is fined £1,000 for stealing takeaway driver's car from outside kebab shop and going on drunken joyride', *MailOnline.co.uk*, 22 May 2021.

59  William Hill Annual Reports.

60  Flutter Entertainment Annual Reports.

61  Playtech Annual Reports.

62  Joanna Partridge, 'Shareholders urged to vote out Playtech chair over gender imbalance', *Guardian.co.uk*, 17 May 2021.

63  888 Holdings Annual Reports.

64  Office for National Statistics.

65  Betting and Gaming Council, 'Report reveals huge jobs and tax contribution made by betting shops, casinos and online gaming', 29 March 2021.

66  Office for National Statistics.

67 Rob Davies, 'Problem gambling costs UK up to £1.2bn a year, says report', *Guardian.co.uk*, 13 December 2016.

68 Social Market Foundation, 'Reducing problem gambling would mean more jobs and tax revenue', 10 March 2021.

69 Annual Reports and Accounts for Entain, William Hill, Flutter Entertainment and 888 Holdings, 2019.

70 Madison Darbyshire, 'Norway's biggest pension fund cracks down on "sin stocks"', *FT.com*, 28 May 2019.

### 10. New Frontiers: What's Next?

1 Yahoo Finance.

2 Gambling Commission statistics.

3 Ibid.

4 Martin Harris, 'Black Friday: Reliving Poker's Darkest Day Five Years Later', *PokerNews.com*, 12 April 2016.

5 Rob Davies, 'Britain's bookmakers jockey for position in US betting watershed', *Guardian.co.uk*, 29 April 2018.

6 Robert Simmons, 'J.P. Morgan: US sports betting market could hit $9.2bn by 2025', *EGRglobal.com*, 16 February 2021.

7 Entain Annual Report and Accounts 2020.

8 Gambling Commission statistics.

9 Charlie Walker, 'Arsenal criticised over gambling promotion on the club's Twitter feed next to a Junior Gunners post as tough new rules are drawn up to protect kids from betting offers – but regulations only cover UK gaming companies', *MailOnline.co.uk*, 18 February 2021.

10 Sofia Brooks, 'Bet to the future', *Casino.com*, 4 May 2020.

11 Ted Menmuir, 'Winning post: Parliament debates state control on gambling and football', *SBCNews.co.uk*, 17 May 2021.

12 Brendan O'Neill, 'Corbynistas don't want to liberate the poor – they want to control them', *Spiked-Online.com*, 6 July 2017.

13 Rob Davies, '"Reformer's shopping list": gambling laws review starts next week', *Guardian.co.uk*, 4 December 2020.

# INDEX

147–9, 241, 246, 329; transgressions (examples) 128–34

Virgin Games 74

virtual reality (VR) and wearable tech 333

virtual sports betting 15, 329 *see also* eSports betting

voluntary settlements 237, 253–6 *see also* recovery of money to (problem) gamblers

Wallace, Ben 287

Wardle, Heather 26, 123, 279

Waterson, Jim 289

Watson, Richard 129

Watson, Tom 42–3, 57, 278, 284–6

Waugh, Dan 42, 239

wealth, individual, through gambling-related business 299–301; company executives 316–18; company owners 301–16

Webb, Derek 278, 279

Weil, A. Lorne 313–14

Weil, B. Luke 314

Weizer, Mor 318

Werkman, Anthony 129

whistle-to-whistle bans on TV advertising 58–61, 158, 282–3, 338

White Bullet (anti-piracy specialist) 179

white-label firms 174

White's (gentlemen's club) 27–8

Whittaker, Joanne 307

William Hill (bookmakers): advertising 58–61, 70, 73, 81, 87; bought by Caesars 324, 327; commissions PwC report on black market 292; executives' earnings 316; founds telephone or postal service (1934) 29; opens first betting shop (1966) 30; recovery of money to gamblers 250–1, 252, 255; requested bets 105; sports betting app 72; stock market value 324; VAT refund 292; VIP scheme 130, 142; bought by Nomura (1997) 30–1 *see also* Bowcock, Philip

Windsor, Barbara 56

Winlink Marketing 167–8

Winner.co.uk (online casino) 133–4

Winstone, Ray 51–2, 86

Witherow, Tom 133

Wolff, Jonathan 36–7, 295

women gamblers: addiction 205–7; advertising targeting 56

World Cup, TV advertising during 53, 56–7, 97

Worrall, Phil 135, 197–8, 200

Wright, Jeremy 261, 277, 296

YouGov surveys 222–3

young adults: in Africa 329; gambling brand exposure and awareness 88; gambling clinic 264; gambling culture in football 183–4; under-representation in Health Surveys 220; social media advertising to 69, 71–2 *see also* children and adolescents

YouTube 71, 79–80, 175

Zarb-Cousin, Matt 233–4, 278, 279, 280–1

Zendle, David 121, 122

'the zone,' experience during gambling 202–4, 207, 333